Wildlife Detective

A retired police inspector, **Alan Stewart** specialised in poaching cases in the 1960s and 70s. Most of his service with Tayside Police from 1980 to 1993 was in CID in Perth and Drugs Branch at Force HQ. He was appointed Force Wildlife Liaison Officer in 1993. He lives in Perthshire with his wife Jan, two dogs and twenty domestic ducks. Alan Stewart is featured as one of BBC Scotland's Wildlife Detectives.

Wildlife Detective

a life fighting wildlife crime

ALAN STEWART

ARGYLL PUBLISHING

This paperback edition 2008

Argyll Publishing
Glendaruel
Argyll PA22 3AE
Scotland
www.argyllpublishing.com

British Library Cataloguing-in-Publication Data.
A catalogue record for this book is available from the British Library.

ISBN 978 1 906134 25 9

Printed and bound in the UK by
CPI Mackays, Chatham ME5 8TD

To Jan, my wife, whose patience has been tested for over forty years by my absence from home, either for long hours of policing or to indulge my wildlife-related hobbies. This is exemplified in a note left by a young French student for her successor on a holiday exchange with us a number of years ago, 'In this house lives a policeman. You will never see him!'

Acknowledgments

There are many friends who have given help in one form of another during my compilation of this book. They are too numerous to mention individually but nevertheless I value their contribution enormously. There are also many of my colleagues, within Tayside Police and other organisations, who feature as characters in the book, sometimes identified and sometimes not. If they are not identified by name they may recognise the part that they played. I enjoyed all of these investigations – some of them even adventures – and I cannot stress enough how much I valued their comradeship.

However there are two people whose help and encouragement I must acknowledge by name. First is Sean Bradley of Thirsty Books/ Argyll Publishing, my son-in-law and editor, whose coercion and encouragement resulted in my putting pen to paper in the first place. Second is Sheriff Kevin Drummond QC, *inter alia* – in legal terminology – a cartoonist and whose artistry (and foreword) graces this book but who is foremost a respected sheriff in the Borders Courts. When I told Kevin I was writing a book his comment was, 'What on earth took you so long?'

Contents

PART III MODERN TIMES

Foreword

The latter end of the twentieth century and the early years of the twenty first have arguably seen more interest and activity on environmental and wildlife matters than any other time in our modern history. The wildlife corner of the legal world was formerly a quiet one and law enforcement in this particular field was largely dependent upon the hobbies and, sometimes, the personal connections of local country police officers. To some extent that remains the case but specialised wildlife police officers are an emerging part of all of our police forces. The concept of the 'wildlife crime officer' is germinating in the early years of the twenty first century.

In political and legal terms the main area of interest in this field, from about the late 1960s, was limited to firearms law where growing restrictions on firearms ownership and use were seen to be impacting on field sports and target sporting shooting. This is not the time or the place for a discussion on legislative developments since that time but, since at least the passing of the Wildlife and Countryside Act 1981, rural, environmental and animal welfare issues have become a growing and active part of the political landscape.

My own professional entry into this area of law was principally through my involvement in target shooting sports. As an advocate who was himself active in competitive target shooting I had become known to solicitors who had clients with countryside interests. Many of the people with whom I was involved in target shooting were also involved in game shooting and my familiarity with Firearms legislation made me an obvious target (forgive the pun) for discussion on problems. Firearms cases in particular and wildlife crime issues in general became a growing part of my practice.

In the late 1970s and early 80s relations between what could broadly be described as the shooting community and the police could scarcely have been described as co-operative and the sporting shooting organisations such as BASC and BFSS were being called upon more and more by their members for support particularly in firearms licensing disputes with the police. Hostilities which first emerged from licensing issues were also beginning to spill over into other areas of wildlife law.

For reasons which don't matter here I eventually became one of the original appointees to the Firearms Consultative Committee at the Home Office which was established by the Firearms (Amendment) Act 1988. That Committee brought police and sporting shooting interests together in a single working group in the hope of producing sensible and effective firearms policy and legislation.

I had first become aware of the name of Alan Stewart in the early 80s through my professional work at the Scottish Bar in what I fondly referred to as my 'green wellie practice'. At that time Alan's was simply a name which was occasionally and casually mentioned in the course of cases in which I would be instructed or at conferences and meetings which I attended addressing firearms licensing issues. My recollection as I write now in 2007 is that those references to Alan were seldom, if ever, in the context of a policeman out to make a name for himself as a crusader (as some were perceived) but rather, in the climate of the time, as a police officer who actually knew something about countryside matters. Tayside Police, of which Alan was a member, were at the time beginning to make a name for themselves in 'green wellie' circles.

It was in that broad context that I eventually met Alan and I suspect that it would be fair to say that in the early days of our acquaintance we might possibly each have viewed the other as belonging to the 'other side' of the broad countryside debate. For my part, it did not take long for that perception to change, because I recognised in Alan a policeman with an inherent sense of fairness and a fundamental understanding of the balance which requires to be struck in accommodating the conflicting interests at work in rural issues. Some of these issues such as game shooting, foxhunting and others can produce deeply held emotional responses in participants and opponents, sometimes with unfortunate results.

In this account of his service as a police officer and latterly as a civilian with Tayside Police Alan Stewart visits a number of those areas of dispute from the standpoint of a serving police officer. It is a series of anecdotes, experiences and observations which, in my opinion, are a unique record of some of the conflicts which have emerged in the development of wildlife law and practice spanning the latter end of the twentieth century and the beginning of the twenty first.

At the same time as I was reading Alan's book I was also reading Jose Ortega y Gasset's *Meditations on Hunting*. (The word 'hunting' is used in its European sense of 'pursuit of a quarry' as opposed to the English usage of hunting with dogs.) Ortega was one of Spain's leading philosophers of the twentieth century and was a Doctor *honoris causa* of Glasgow University. He published this series of essays in 1942 and in them he analyses the philosophy which underlies man's predatory instinct: as part of that analysis he finds that. . .

> [hunting] involves a complete code of ethics of the most distinguished design; the hunter who accepts the sporting code of ethics keeps his commandments in the greatest solitude, with no witnesses or audience other than the sharp peaks of the mountain, the roaming cloud. . . and the passing animal. In this way hunting resembles the monastic rule and the military order.

In other words, says Ortega, fieldsports could be said to have what could be described as a common law or set of universal moral principles which exist independently of any statutory framework.

Later Ortega says, 'the fisherman who poisons the mountain brook to annihilate suddenly, all at once, the trout swimming in it, *ipso facto* ceases to be a hunter.'

The obvious point being made is that not every method of catching the prey comes within that code of ethics and indeed some methods exclude the perpetrator from the honourable category of being a 'hunter'. It is the pursuit of the poisoner by a guardian of the code of ethics which lies at the heart of this book.

T.A.K.Drummond QC
March 2007

Introduction

I have just taken a telephone call from a man who wanted to remain anonymous. He told me that a particular individual within a housing estate in Perth is trapping finches in the wild to launder into the lucrative trade in captive songbirds. As it happens I am already aware of this man and his doubtful activities but just don't have quite enough evidence to apply for a warrant to search his premises. The information gleaned from the telephone conversation confirms my suspicions and gives me a much clearer picture of my target, the finch trapper. I now know the manner in which he is operating, where his net is hidden under the stairs of his house, and how he transports his illegally captured wild bullfinches, goldfinches, siskins and greenfinches to a contact in England. The fact that my partially public-spirited informant will not give me his name and address frustratingly takes me no closer to obtaining a search warrant. Nowadays all intelligence is assessed on a nationally agreed system, the first part of the assessment being the evaluation of the source of the intelligence. Since the caller wishes to remain anonymous I cannot gauge the reliability of what he has just told me and so cannot rely on his additional information to get the desperately-needed search warrant.

It is February 2007 and I reflect on how much policing has changed since I started as a police cadet in1964. This information would easily have been enough to obtain a search warrant at that time, and for many years after, but times change. Sometimes changes are for the better, sometimes not. Frustration in policing unfortunately has an omnipresence in 2007 and this is especially true in enforcing wildlife crime. Is it because the police have not yet properly adapted to enforcing wildlife law in the twenty first century? Has the balance swung too far in favour of a suspect or a person accused of and charged with a crime? Or is the procurator fiscal's service understaffed and overworked? Judge for yourself from this account of the wildlife crime investigations in which I have been involved over forty years.

•

A Policeman's Lot is not a Happy One, says the song. I would suggest that the words of the song are not strictly true. Extremely Interesting but Tempered with an Ever-Increasing Degree of Frustration is probably more accurate. But this infinitely more apt description does not scan as well!

Yes there have been days, weeks or longer spells during the past four decades when my enthusiasm or interest waned, but for the vast majority of the time I thoroughly enjoyed myself. On most days I looked forward to going to work and on days where we were about to undertake a pre-planned operation I couldn't get there quickly enough. There were never two days the same and a surprise – not all pleasant – lay round every corner. I must admit I got a real buzz out of achieving a good result from either a quick solution to a tricky situation or from painstakingly gathering evidence over weeks or even months to put a good case together. Apart from a short spell in the 1980s when I wished that I had been a vet (though my limited education would have precluded this) I had no wish to earn a crust from anything other than the profession of which I was one small cog in a big wheel.

I joined Perth and Kinross Constabulary as a police cadet in 1964, and worked in Perth, mainly carrying out office duties of different sorts though occasionally getting out and about under the supervision of a police constable. It was in this role that I learned to type, which has been a tremendous benefit over the years as pencils gave way to biros, which graduated to typewriters, then word processors and eventually computers, which, rightly or wrongly, are the life-blood of modern policing. On 15 May 1966 I was old enough to become a police constable – at a mere eighteen and a half years old – and I joined the big league! I spent a further couple of weeks working in Perth, then, before my posting to work at Dunblane, I was off for an eight week initial training course at the Scottish Police College at Tulliallan Castle, the first of two very intensive training courses that every police officer has to undertake.

The training at the Scottish Police College included at that time dealing with poaching incidents, though this has now been dropped as a core subject at the college and is taught in-force. Virtually the only legislation relevant to wildlife crime at that time was the Protection of Birds Act 1954. I was aware of this legislation simply because I had the interest to look for it. I knew that the police had the responsibility to enforce it but it never appeared in the college curriculum. It was therefore not surprising that most police officers in my earlier years went through their service with little thought for the crimes committed against birds, animals or plants.

My background was in the countryside, with a fascination in anything that grew there, lived there or took place there. At an early age I could identify most animals and birds, knew the crops that were growing in every field, and even had a boring knowledge of varieties of barley and wheat, breeds of sheep, cattle and hens, and even the names for most parts of the harness used by working Clydesdale horses. Worse still, as a boy I could identify some of the more common ailments farm livestock were subject to, such as calcium or magnesium deficiency and orf in sheep, and ringworm, mastitis or grass sickness.

It was little wonder that during the whole of my policing career, despite my enjoyment of general policing, the satisfaction of the more elite criminal investigation work and the drama and excitement of drug squad work, I was never happier than when I was allocated a call that had something to do with animals.

The book is principally about wildlife crime and the force-wide investigative responsibility which I acceded to later in my police career. It is unsurprising that dealing effectively with the wide spectrum of wildlife crime is a specialist role so the early part of the book must deal with how I gained some knowledge and experience of dealing with poachers in the more formative years of my police service. This experience would stand me in good stead later on, even though neither I nor anyone else at that time had ever heard of – or considered the responsibilities of – a wildlife crime officer.

Alan Stewart
February 2007

PART I

Old Times

'Y'cannae search me without a warrant.'

Chapter 1

Home-Made Scones and Dynamite

In Dunblane the new police recruit experiences the kindness of farmers' wives in the kitchen, the persistence of game poachers and an explosively novel recipe for taking salmon.

When I started in May 1966 as a raw Constable No 48 of Perth and Kinross Constabulary, stationed at Dunblane, my interest in agriculture was immediately spotted by the sergeant, Angus Morrison. It may have been nothing more perceptive on his part than seeing me from time to time chewing on a stem of grass or noticing the rings round my legs where the hair had been worn away by the regular use of wellies – what Billy Connolly once called *the rings of no confidence*. The sergeant must have appreciated my rare skills and announced in his lovely Hebridean accent that I was 'chust the man for the stock books'.

I couldn't believe my luck at getting this plum job. Farmers by law have always had to keep records of the livestock they buy and sell and to enter details, such as ear tag numbers, in their stock book. It was the responsibility of the police to check these stock books bi-annually to ensure that entries were being made judiciously, and to sign the stock book after the last entry to show that the entries were accurate. Since the Dunblane beat had a huge number of farms, I spent many days driving round the area visiting the farmers.

Farmers don't work a mere forty hours a week like most of us, and their day often starts before many others are up and about and continues well past the time that we have our feet up and are watching television, or in those days, listening to the wireless. Naturally they will allocate most of their energy to jobs that are going to generate income. Anything but filling in bloody stock books!

This administrative recalcitrance often worked to my benefit.

When I located the farmer in the steading, out in the fields or very occasionally in the house, the response often was, 'Come away in, I've just a couple of entries to put in the book and that'll be it up to date'. Once inside the farmer would summon his wife and the instruction was usually, 'Maggie (or Jeannie or Lizzie) gie the bobby a cup o' tea and some scones while I get the stock book.' Two cups of tea and several home-made scones later the farmer would emerge from his hiding place into the kitchen and proudly present a stock book with the last two or three pages all written in the same ink and clearly done as a 'job lot', despite the wide variety of dates on which the cattle were bought or sold.

Nowadays, since the BSE and foot and mouth outbreaks, the buying and selling of livestock is controlled much more tightly and all cattle now have an individual 'passport' that can prove origin and parentage. The checking of stock movements has, rightly, long since passed from the police and is now with Local Authority Animal Health Inspectors.

Much of our work at Dunblane related to road traffic offences, which we detected in huge numbers from our daily patrols of the A9. The availability and emphasis on traffic work influenced many of the officers to later follow a career in the Traffic Department, an aspect of policing that really didn't appeal to me. I was much more interested in general policing as my appetite hadn't yet been whetted to follow a career in dealing with crime. In the two and half years I worked at Dunblane I only remember one house being broken into and co-incidentally part of the evidence in solving this was a flower, a tiny forget-me-not, that we noticed in the suspect's hair, having stuck there when he crawled under a hedge to gain access to the garden. This tiny piece of evidence enabled us to put enough pressure on the suspect to get him to admit that he had crawled through the hedge. Having made this admission it was inevitable that he would eventually tell the whole truth and in police terminology, he 'put his hands up' to breaking into the house. It was an incident that maybe pointed towards my future career path – dealing with crime and dealing with wildlife.

My first salmon poaching case greatly influenced my career, virtually making me a specialist in dealing with poaching cases overnight. The circumstances turned out to be unique in my forty years of policing; I have still not heard of another police officer having a similar case. It was sparked from the most basic of good policing practice, observation, inquisitiveness, evaluation and most importantly of being aware of crime trends. This is how it came about.

Each police force had its own weekly bulletin, which gave details of some of the more serious crimes committed, criminals arrested, criminals wanted for interview or criminals travelling into other force areas to commit crime. Times have changed for the better and all of this information is now available to the bobby on the beat at the touch of a computer key. It can all be accessed virtually in 'real time' without the need to wait for a week for a bulletin. In any event I read in the Stirling and Clackmannan Police bulletin that two of their salmon poachers, both from the village of Fallin, were travelling each weekend to the River Deveron near Turriff to take salmon from the river. Their names and addresses were given, as was the fact that they were using a grey Mini van with the registered number WAG 844.

That weekend in October I was day shift and out on patrol on the A9 in a Jaguar police patrol car. I had with me a police woman with just weeks under her belt as a police officer and, as I had just started in May, our combined police experience was little more that six months. Much of the patrol consisted of parking somewhere with a view of the passing traffic and looking for something of criminal or road traffic interest that we could get our teeth into. We were nearing the end of our shift on the Sunday afternoon when a grey Mini van approached travelling in the direction of Stirling. As the police car driver I had the better view as it was approaching from my offside and I saw that there were two men in the van. While every other driver with a clear conscience has a look at a police car as they pass, these men stared straight ahead. Pretend we don't see the cops and with a bit of luck they may not have seen us. Even without bearing the number plate WAG 844 this would have been a vehicle to have a closer look at, but with this number plate its fate was sealed.

The men had 43 salmon in the back of the van and told us that, as regular salmon anglers, they had just had one of the best fishing weekends of their lives. Conditions had just been right for worm fishing and the fish had been snapping at the worm almost as soon as it had been cast into the pool. Fishermen are experts at tall tales and it got better. They said they had caught so many fish they didn't know what they were going to do with them all and would we like a couple! Our response was that we would like more than a couple: we wanted them all. We also wanted the two people that were in charge of them who we were arresting for unlawful possession of salmon.

Fish poaching has now been consolidated into one piece of legislation, the Salmon and Freshwater Fisheries (Consolidation) (Scotland) Act 2003, but at that time it was covered by the Salmon and Freshwater Fisheries (Protection) (Scotland) Act 1951. Unlawful possession of salmon or sea trout is always the best starting point for an investigation, and other charges can be added if and when more information becomes available. Once the men were charged and safely in a police cell we would begin the search for more evidence as to how the fish had been taken. It was also interesting that the men had £300 each in their possession. This was a lot of money in 1966 and I had a strong suspicion that they had sold a number of the fish they had caught and the 43 we had were only what was left.

Police can never be experts in everything that they deal with and, depending on the particular investigation, experts in other fields are regularly called in to assist before a case goes to court. This is nowhere more relevant than in the field of wildlife crime, which of course includes poaching. In this particular case I called in water bailiffs from the Forth District Salmon Fisheries Board. Their examination of the fish showed that each one of the 43 had a mark in its mouth consistent with having been caught by a hook, but all of us were convinced they could not have caught so many salmon legally. We were sure the salmon had been taken by the use of Cymag. This is the trade name for sodium cyanide, a white powder which gives off hydrogen cyanide gas when exposed to moisture. If a quantity of Cymag is thrown into a river at a fast flowing part upstream of a pool holding salmon, the salmon will effectively be suffocated, will thrash about on the surface, and once dead can be easily scooped out of the river as they float downstream. If we had to place bets on the way the fish were taken, this is where the smart money would have been placed.

On the Monday morning the men were due to appear from custody at Perth Sheriff Court. (Dunblane had its own sheriff court but it only operated on a Wednesday). An arrangement would be made with the procurator fiscal to leave their case till the last of the morning's cases. In the meantime, at 8.30 am, I was waiting at the doors of the Freshwater Fisheries Laboratory at Faskally, Pitlochry, with a random sample of six of the salmon in the boot of the police car. This laboratory has some of the leading Scottish experts on matters relating to freshwater fish, and their evidence is essential in proving that salmon have been taken by Cymag.

The fisheries experts got to work on the salmon and before long they had a result. If I had placed a bet on Cymag my money would have gone down the drain. My first salmon poaching case and it was a method of taking fish almost unknown in Scotland: they had been taken by explosives. All of the blood vessels, including the capillaries, had been ruptured by the detonation of some sort of explosive in the pool. I was flabbergasted but this evidence was sufficient for another two charges to be added: those of taking the fish by proscribed methods, which included the use of explosives, noxious substances or electrical devices, and the fact that two or more persons had been acting together in this activity.

The two accused pleaded not guilty and later faced trial at Dunblane Sheriff Court. I don't know whether or not the sheriff, Sheriff Prain, had a particular interest in salmon poaching cases but the trial lasted till well after 6 pm, something I have not heard of since. They were both found guilty and were fined £30 each, with the alternative of 30 days imprisonment. Despite the fine being at the lower end of the scale, neither paid the fine and I got the satisfaction several months after the trial of arresting them both for a second time and taking them to Perth Prison.

There were two important lessons from that case. The first was to appreciate the lengths to which criminals committing crime sometimes go to cover their tracks, even to the extent of marking the mouth of each of the fish with a hook so that they looked as if they really had been caught legally. The other was never to make assumptions before the full facts have been established.

Since this incident in 1966 I have seen the effect of explosives during specialist training courses designed for that purpose. In one of the demonstrations some explosive was set off in a pond. The resulting waterspout went nearly 50 feet into the air and when I saw it I thought back to the River Deveron and how effective a tool explosives would be to an unscrupulous salmon poacher.

As for Cymag, it was taken off the market in late 2004. Its legitimate use in the gassing of rats and rabbits had come to an end, probably because of the real risk to the health of those using it. Its effects are of course fatal, though if caught early enough the drug amyl nitrate can sometimes ameliorate its effects. Its effects were demonstrated in an incident in 2005 when a gamekeeper found several part-filled Cymag tins left behind by his predecessor. For whatever reason he decided to put all the powder into one tin, and in so doing was badly affected by the toxic hydrogen cyanide fumes. An ambulance was called and, as is the case with fatal or potentially fatal accidents at a workplace, the police were informed. For my part, as wildlife crime officer, I arranged for experts from the Scottish Agricultural Science Agency (SASA) in Edinburgh to collect and make safe the Cymag. Meantime I phoned one of the previous manufacturers of the substance, Zeneca, a company based in Grangemouth. I spoke to a woman there, explained the incident that had just taken place, that a man was seriously ill from the effects of Cymag and was being taken to Ninewells Hospital in Dundee, and was there any further information she could give on Cymag that might be of assistance to the hospital. She said she would need to speak with someone else first and could I hang on. I hung on. She came back to the telephone after a few minutes, and I must confess I was more than a little stunned by what she had to say. Very politely and in a matter of fact manner she said, 'I have to ask you first of all if the man was prescribed the Cymag by his doctor'.

The explosives case was the only salmon poaching case that I dealt with in my two years at Dunblane, but I gained an excellent grounding in dealing with poachers who shot pheasants from the roadside. It is an offence under the Game (Scotland) Act 1832 to be on land during the daytime in unlawful search or pursuit of game. This Act, like most of the game legislation, is extremely old and was enacted in times when feudal landlords reigned supreme and the protection of 'their' game was extremely important. The power under the Game (Scotland) Act 1832 to arrest poachers is given to the landowner and his servants or employees, with no specific powers being given to the police. Several of the offences require simply the evidence of one credible eyewitness and, until shortly after I joined the police, could be prosecuted in court under a private prosecution taken by the factor of the estate.

The powers delegated to the landowner remain, as does the single witness evidence, though I have never known a case to be taken on the evidence of only one person. Even though there still are some old pieces of legislation – and some newer Acts, such as in the Wildlife and Countryside Act 1981 – where a single witness to the taking or destruction of wild birds' eggs is sufficient for a conviction, my own preference is to stick by the principles in Scots Law where the main facts of a case should have corroboration from some source or other.

In Dunblane we never had a problem with the lack of evidence in offences under the Game (Scotland) Act, nor did we have to make special patrols to catch game poachers. Gamekeepers on the estates in the area were extremely efficient at catching poachers, especially on the nearby Keir Estate on the borders of Perthshire with Stirlingshire. This was a huge estate covering many thousands of acres and with a very intensive pheasant rearing capability. Consequently there were hundreds of pheasants by the sides of all the country roads round the estate, a temptation to poachers and easy targets from the car window with an air rifle or .22 rifle. To demonstrate the number of pheasants in the area, on shooting days bags of 300 or 400 pheasants were commonplace. Thankfully this would not happen today, when most of those involved in game shooting are more respectful both of their quarry and of public opinion. Most people who shoot any game species nowadays are not looking for huge bags. Pheasant shooters would much rather have 150 well presented birds in the bag at the end of the day, in other words birds that had flown high and fast and had been testing shots. This is far preferred to the slaughter – since that's what it used to be in many cases – of clouds of low pheasants, some still semi-tame, being driven over the guns. Even in grouse shooting there are many guns that prefer a walked-up day to a driven day. Walking-up grouse over pointers is just as testing for a shooter though bags are much smaller. In addition all of those participating – not just the gamekeepers – get exercise by having to walk rather than be driven to a shooting butt.

In my Dunblane days, however, it was a regular event each Autumn and Winter for two or three Land Rovers to draw up at the front of the police station and to see a couple of poachers, usually from Stirling, Alloa or Glasgow, being marched in to the office by three or four burly keepers. The keepers would leave the poachers in our charge, return to their Land Rovers, and bring in their next load. This would consist of a number of rifles and a variety of game shot by the poachers from their car window. Though the game was mostly pheasants, I have dealt with cases that included grey partridges, mallard ducks, black game, rabbits and hares. I quickly learned that the person involved does not need to be on the land with a weapon; it is sufficient for him to be shooting *onto* the land from the road, or, in some cases, to send his dog onto the land to course a hare, while he remained on the road. The accused persons in these cases would be charged and released, and their weapons and the game they had taken would be kept as productions, with the game being put in the freezer until the case came to court.

There seemed a never ending stream of kamikaze poachers who wanted to drive out of the conurbations to the west of Dunblane, have a few pot shots in Perthshire at roadside wildlife, meet some of the local gamekeepers for a chat, have tea with the local constabulary, and conclude their nice day in the country with an appearance at Dunblane Sheriff Court. There they would unhappily part with what was usually about £5 for their troubles, to be paid up at 10/- per week. There were seldom reports of roadside poachers where they were not either traced by the keepers or the police. The outcome was so inevitable that I could never understand why they kept coming.

As a change from policing traffic offences, crime and disorder (drugs hadn't really arrived yet) I was hooked on dealing with poachers, and a bigger variety was to follow when I was transferred to Perth in the autumn of 1968.

Chapter 2

Strangers in the Night

Now working in Perth, the bobby's beat is extended to include the banks of the River Tay which allows for the catching of a lone poacher and a first class informant to boot.

Clearly the policing of a town the size of Perth was substantially different to the very rural policing of Dunblane and its surrounding villages. Nevertheless the fact that one of Scotland's best salmon rivers, the River Tay, runs through Perth, and some of the Tay's tributaries are adjacent to Perth, was a major advantage to me in dealing, as an adjunct to general policing, with poaching offences. Again, my first salmon poaching case shaped the way forward and influenced to an inordinate extent the success that was to follow.

With my country childhood, darkness never held any fear for me. I know many adults who would never dream of walking alone in the darkness. I have even known one or two police officers who hated the dark, one regularly walking down the centre of the road in dark streets on night shift lest he be attacked by some apparition or other vile creature of the night lurking in a dark close. At least the distance between the centre of the road and the mouth of the close gave him some advance warning of the terrors that in his imagination might follow.

My nocturnal rambles one night not long after I had arrived in Perth took me up the side of River Tay on the North Inch, a large municipal park. I had been bored walking through the town centre on the second half of the night shift and decided to extend my beat. It was early October and a fairly dark night with just enough moon by which to navigate the narrow and partly overgrown path that runs beside the river once the manicured parkland has been left behind. It takes roughly twenty minutes for the eyes to become accustomed to the darkness and that was just about the point at which I saw a single figure with a fishing rod beside the river not ten yards upstream from me. As a trout fisher myself I was immediately aware that my riverbank partner was not playing by the rules. When he cast out into the river there was a loud splash. Though I could not see whatever lure he was landing in the water, I knew it to be much heavier than a hook with a bunch of wriggling worms or a small minnow or spoon. He was reeling in the lure using a really violent jerking motion and it was then that I realised that rather than trying to entice a salmon to have a fatal bite, he was trying to make contact with any salmon resting in or passing through the pool so that the treble hook on the end of his line sunk into the body of the fish.

I watched silently, intrigued by this method of fishing that I was aware of but had never seen, and fascinated that I had chanced upon a poacher that I was almost close enough to grab. I then realised that he was right beside the river while I was on the path maybe four of five feet higher. I knew that if he turned round I would be silhouetted against what light there was in the sky and that he would easily see me. I had no time to take remedial action and lie down flat on the ground. I was also too close to him to radio for assistance since unless he had his ears stuffed with cotton wool he would have heard me. The inevitable happened in that he turned round to ensure his line didn't get snagged as he made a further cast. . . and he saw me. Repetition and familiarity with what he was doing probably committed him to continue the cast, which was what he did, and the lure landed with another splash somewhere towards the centre of the Tay. Instead of throwing down his rod and running he began to reel in as if his right arm had been supercharged, but he was too late; I had taken the few steps required to be beside him.

Readers may think that this is a foolhardy thing to do, to jump down beside a person whose nature and motives are completely unknown. At this part of the River Tay the water is deep and the current is very strong and in a year yet to come I recovered the body of a person who drowned at this very spot and was washed up on a shingle bank in the middle of the river about 400 yards downstream.

Danger is not always foreseen, and even if it is, it is not always given due consideration by police officers. They will sometimes assess the possible risks and take action to minimise them but this is by no means the norm. In any case, risks are hard to predict with surprises often part of the equation. A couple of decades later when I was in the Drug Squad and working from Police Headquarters at Dundee I was part of an operation to take out a drug dealer in the Douglas area of Dundee. Several drug users who had called at the target's house had been arrested after they had made their purchase and had left the house and there were only two of our squad left, another detective sergeant and me, to secure the house where the dealing was taking place and to arrest the dealer.

The major drawback was the presence of a German shepherd dog in the house which intelligence indicated that the dealer kept in a cupboard. The incessant barking every time someone called at the dealer's door confirmed that the dog was there, and we had worked out a strategy involving the use of our batons if we were attacked by the beast. We gained entry to the house without much fuss – a bonus since there were only two of us – and I was relieved to see that the dog was securely locked behind a strong mesh frame in a cupboard in the hallway. I then burst into the living room of the house to be met by the biggest rottweiller I have ever seen. I learned later that this was a particularly unpredictable dog and I can only think that it got a bigger fright than I did. I said at the start that I was never happier than when dealing with animals. I should probably exclude large and dangerous dogs from that statement.

Getting back to my predicament at the side of the River Tay, with water that swirled past with the menace of magnetised black oil threatening to drag me from the safety of the bank, and the evil salmon poacher who was colluding with the river to commit me to death by drowning, the reality was nothing of the kind. The poacher, apparently unaware of the law of corroboration in Scotland, handed me his rod and all but said, 'It's a fair cop guv' or whatever the Perthshire version of this cockney phrase is. I examined the rod, so far as I could in the dark, and saw that the 'lure' was a large treble hook near the end of the line, finishing with a chunk of lead. Little wonder there was a splash when it hit the water. I could also feel that the line was extremely thick for legal salmon fishing but would be ideal for heaving a salmon out of the river just as quickly as it could be pulled ashore. With a combination of my relative inexperience (less than three year's service), relief that I was still on *terra firma*, and just a degree of sympathy for a lone poacher, I told him that he was getting a warning on this occasion and that he should quit while he was ahead.

After this riverbank encounter and completely by chance, I happened to meet the poacher, who I shall call Mr X, on a regular basis. From my subsequent conversations with him it became clear that he had no intention of giving up poaching. I knew by that time he also had an eye for a fast buck, sailed close to the wind in some of his dealings, and indeed sometimes fell overboard and finished up in the cells. It must have become equally clear to him that I had no intention of giving up trying to catch poachers and that I would be a substantial threat to his pastime, one which also turned out to be part of his livelihood. Mr X then started to give me information about other poachers and indeed about other types of crime. I'm sure his reasoning was that if he set me on the trail of other poachers that left the way clear for him. Since I could only be in one place at a time, and since he knew where I was likely to be as he had given me the information that would take me there, he would be elsewhere poaching salmon in relative safety. It was an unwritten arrangement that benefited both of us. In biological terms it could be described as symbiosis. In terms of informants he was a gem and I never regretted our first meeting on that dark October night.

•

Not all prowls in the darkness resulted in complete success. One night shift in early November when things were quiet in the city and I was on a mobile patrol, we dumped the police car about midnight and had a walk along the narrow path that follows the River Almond, a tributary of the Tay, up towards the village of Almondbank. The Almond is a great river for a very late run of fish. While most other rivers locally had good Spring runs of salmon plus their main runs of salmon somewhere between August and October, the Almond was usually much later, with runs even up till mid December. Why this is I have no idea. The strange fact is that no matter when salmon come into a river – and that can be in any month of the year – they all spawn at roughly the same time, usually the beginning of winter. There are strong views that it is the first real frosts that trigger spawning, and because of global warming their spawning time is becoming even later, lasting now in some cases into January.

Different rivers open for fishing at slightly different times of the year. The Tay is the earliest river, with the salmon season opening on 15 January. Even salmon coming into the river at that time may have to wait in the river to spawn nearly a year later. Most of my river lore over the years has come from either water bailiffs or salmon poachers. Though I don't agree with what they do, I have a grudging respect for the knowledge salmon poachers have of their quarry and, in order to line their pockets, of how to separate it in large numbers from its natural environment. There is nothing surer than if there are salmon in reasonable numbers in the river the poachers will be there. If there are none, they don't waste their time looking.

On this particular night there was no moon and it was pitch dark. Once we had left the car and entered the darkness I wondered about the value of looking for poachers when visibility was virtually zero, but since it was a still night with not the slightest puff of wind we decided to go for it. It was a lovely walk up the riverbank, and the senses of smell and hearing were heightened. The first smell to reach my nostrils was that of dying Himalayan balsam, a pernicious weed that we have inherited in Britain in the same way as other foreign interlopers such as Japanese knotweed, grey squirrels, mink, ruddy duck, American signal crayfish and many more. It is a lovely looking plant, with a mass of pink flowers on top of tall stems in the summer but the fact remains it shouldn't be in Scotland and river banks would be much less crowded, but alas less colourful, without it. The second smell was the pungent odour of the oozing, oily mud that covered the marshier parts we had to squelch through. The squelching was unfortunate. We wanted to hear and not be heard but in the absence of special police-issue hovercraft boots the odds were even on both sides.

Once the marshy area had been safely, if noisily, negotiated we were back on the path. Every ten or twenty yards we stopped to listen, hoping to hear the plop of a lead weight and treble hook into the river in its quest for the flank of *salmo salar*, but nothing could be heard except for the *kee-wick, kee-wick* of a tawny owl somewhere overhead.

Progress was slow, with every forward step being placed quietly on the ground and every sense straining for some signal that could be interpreted. The path was little over eighteen inches wide; I was leading and my colleague, PC Peter Murray, was following. Humans only have five senses but a sixth sense seemed to come into play in the next few steps. I neither heard nor saw anyone ahead of me but I just knew someone was there. I stopped abruptly and Peter almost bumped into me. I waited for the sound or the faint outline of someone coming towards me. There was silence. I waited for a period that seemed interminable but was probably only thirty seconds, then switched on my torch, fully expecting to see a figure or a number of figures standing facing me on the path. There was nothing. No stationary figures, no scurrying figures. Nothing. Until I lowered the beam of my torch. There on the path not ten feet from me was a bag that held eight salmon.

I was amazed that two groups could meet and almost collide in complete darkness, yet each group was sufficiently aware of their surroundings and the importance of all their senses that each somehow knew of the other's presence. I'd love to know who had been carrying the bag of salmon but I suppose we had the last laugh. I took the eight salmon to the Tay District Salmon Fisheries Board Superintendent, Garry Gibb, who on hearing how we had come by them said he had no more space in his freezer for salmon and I should divide them up amongst the shift. Salmon steaks all round!

•

In the months following the riverside encounter with Mr X, he began to come up with the goods. He started to feed me information that regularly led to the capture of poachers, the recovery of various stolen items, and to the apprehending of several of the criminals who had been involved in purloining the goods in the first place.

In early September of the following year, after a long dry summer, the water level on the Tay was fairly low and there was a build up of salmon in a large and very deep pool at the lower harbour. This pool was known locally as the Friarton Hole. Because of the tagging of some of the salmon, it was learned that many of the fish during times of low water ran up the river a few miles at night, but if there was insufficient fresh water coming down the river, they returned to their holding pool. The Friarton Hole was such a pool. It would be at least thirty, if not forty, feet deep and I am sure in a dry season would hold many hundreds of salmon. I often sat in the police car at a vantage point overlooking this pool and watched in awe at the sight of salmon leaping in the pool almost continuously, sometimes three or four at a time, venting their frustration at being stuck in the lower reaches of the river, females full of roe and males full of milt, and not being able to gain access to their spawning grounds in the tributaries that flowed into the mighty Tay and to the burns that in turn flowed in to these lesser rivers.

The deepest part of the Friarton Hole was at the side furthest from the city and the riverbank there was part of Moncrieffe Island. Moncrieffe Island is not a tiny patch of marooned land; it is large enough to hold a substantial number of allotments and to host an 18-hole golf course. The main part of the Tay flows round the front – or west – side of the island, while there is a far smaller yet still significant flow of water round the back.

The island can be accessed by a narrow gangway running alongside the railway line on the railway bridge leading from Tay Street in Perth across to the Perth to Dundee road. Half way across there is a set of iron steps leading from the railway bridge down to the north end of the island. There was, and still is, a regular trudge of gardeners who clang across this wrought iron gangway, carrying heavy loads of tools, fertilisers and picnic baskets on the outward journey, and laden with fresh carrots, potatoes and other allotment produce on their return. The island could also be accessed for a very short time at low tide, when the river at the back of the island was shallow enough to cross, or in times of drought, completely dry. It was difficult for us to access the island via the railway bridge steps as anyone crossing the railway bridge was high off the ground and naturally silhouetted against the sodium lights of Perth. We had tried several times in the past but it was clear that the poachers had a lookout and mostly they had disappeared by the time we walked from the steps up the quarter mile of path through the trees to reach their favourite poaching spot.

I met Mr X one September day and asked what was happening in the world of salmon poaching. I knew that salmon poaching was taking place regularly at that time on Moncrieffe Island. I had also no doubt that Mr X was one of the leading lights in this practice. He told me that one of the wilier and more successful poachers – for ease I'll call him Wyllie – had taken a good bag of salmon the night before, but that he was too wary of the risks of being stopped by the police during the night to bring the fish off the island then. He had come to the conclusion, probably rightly, that he was less at risk in the hustle and bustle of the middle of the day when police attention was in the main diverted elsewhere. My informant said that about 10.00 am this poacher would go back on to Moncrieffe Island and bring off his fish at a time when at least half of the officers policing Perth were having their meal break.

I and another officer, PC Stewart Rhind, missed our meal break that day and sat in an unmarked police car watching the steps leading up from Tay Street to the railway line over the Tay and its footpath leading to Moncrieffe Island. Just after 10.00 am we recognised the figure of Wyllie making his way up the steps and across towards the island. He was lost to our view as he neared the steps leading down to the island but I had walked up to the prime poaching spots often enough to know that the return journey would take him about forty minutes. I had also learned from Mr X that he would use the phone box on Tay Street at the bottom of the steps leading from the railway bridge to make contact with a friendly taxi driver who obviously was getting a fare sufficiently in excess of the standard rate to block off his olfactory senses against the pervasive smell of a bagful of salmon.

At 10.50 am a figure appeared on the railway bridge heading towards the town. He was bent almost double under the weight of a heavy bag on his back and for a fleeting moment I almost felt sorry for him. He was staggering inexorably towards capture and a fine.

Once the poacher had entered the phone box, dumping his bag outside, the rest was easy. Only three sides of most public phone boxes are glass and it required little skill to sneak up on his blind side. His night's work of ten salmon, all bearing the tell tale sign of a double hook mark somewhere on the body, some of them with the flesh ripped by his enthusiasm to land them, had come to nothing.

•

Phone boxes appeared to be Wyllie's nemeses, and I was to meet him more than a decade later, when I was a detective constable, at another telephone box. A car had been broken into and a number of items had been stolen. Though there was probably no great financial value on the items stolen, two engagement rings had been amongst the booty. The vehicle owner had just lost his wife and the rings were of great sentimental value to him, so he put an advert in the local newspaper stating that he would give a reward of £100 for information leading to the recovery of the rings. Some days later the owner of the car had received a telephone call from the thief and an arrangement was made that they would meet and a swap would be made: two rings for £100. The car owner was not to call the police otherwise he would never see the rings again.

Thankfully the gentleman had the sense to contact the police and I was allocated the enquiry. The meet was to take place at 8.00 pm in South Street in Perth just down – that is towards the River Tay – from the main Post Office. I took up a position in one of the bank of public telephone boxes outside the Post Office, while my colleague, DC John Mackay, remained in a vehicle well out of sight but ready to move in to assist when the time was right.

Right on cue at 8.00 pm, I saw a well known face walking down South Street on the opposite side of the road from where I was and from where the victim was awaiting the meet that would recover his precious engagement rings. It was, of course, my poaching friend from the encounter in the telephone box in Tay Street, Wyllie. I radioed John Mackay and told him that I had a suspect in view. Wyllie then walked up South Street, still on the opposite side of the road, checking vehicles and looking up at windows for any sign of watching police officers. He then came walking down my side of the road, but by that time I had the telephone handset to my ear and was watching his reflection in the small mirror in the phone box. He passed without a glance at the phone box and approached the victim's car, which obviously didn't have to be described to him since it wasn't long since he had broken into it to obtain some of the goods which he was now going to sell back to the distraught owner. I saw the passenger's window being rolled down, as it was nearest to the pavement, and an exchange taking place. There were clearly no pleasantries and Wyllie walked off from the car seconds later, heading back along South Street towards me. The variation on the telephone box theme was that the last time he had been inside the phone box and was caught by someone outside. This time he was outside the phone box and neatly grabbed, as he was passing the phone box, by someone inside.

It gave me great satisfaction that the engagement rings were returned to the owner. I suspect that Wyllie was dealt with by way of a fine. Due to the sheer number of cases police officers deal with, they are not always aware of the penalty imposed on every person that they charge or arrest unless it's a case in which they have a particular interest or if it goes to trial, in which case the reporting police officer is normally still in court to hear the verdict and the sentence.

•

Though weighted treble hooks with which to rake and hook the flanks of the salmon were the favourite tools of the poachers on the River Tay around Perth, some of the more entrepreneurial poachers were a step higher on the ladder and owned a gill net and a dinghy. The gill net is made of very fine nylon with the squares just the right size to allow a salmon to get its head through, then trap it behind the gills, as the name of the net suggests. The nets are almost invisible in the water and extremely effective in landing a good catch of salmon in a relatively short time. The net has floats on the top edge to keep that edge near the surface. It has lead weights on the bottom and one end is attached to the river bank while the rest of the net is paid out from the dinghy as the poacher rows out towards the centre of the river. As they swim up from the sea, salmon prefer the deeper parts of the river with strong currents, parts well known to the poachers.

Mr X, to my knowledge, didn't have a gill net, which is perhaps why he gave me the next piece of information. He was well acquainted with fresh runs of salmon up the River Tay and naturally wanted a good share of the fish for himself. Logically if he could knock out some of the competition his odds of a bigger bagful of salmon would increase. Nets were a threat to him and this would be to my advantage. On this occasion there was a good Spring run of fish, always lovely firm bars of silver commanding a far better price than the fish running at the back end of the year which were starting to discolour and become soft due to the length of time they had been in the river. Mr X told me that if I waited behind a particular shed in the Council refuse dump I would be rewarded around midnight with a salmon poacher heading homewards, his netting operation finished until the next night. This poacher was also well known to me and since he had a forename associated with Christmas festivities I'll call him Santa.

That night I borrowed a police cadet, Willie Semple, and went to the ambush point in plenty of time for the rendezvous with Santa. The night was quite clear and would also have been quite still had it not been for the plethora of rats scurrying round our feet, their squeaks and squeals breaking the silence. I never realised that there would have been so many rats on the Council dump, but I suppose with the variety of interesting food available to them it was the ideal place for rodents to take up residence. On most of these rural excursions in pursuit of criminals of one sort of another there is something pleasant to watch, to listen to or to smell. Not this time, and I was hoping that Santa might be running ahead of schedule.

Shortly before midnight we became aware of a figure emerging from the shadows probably about 100 metres distant. As the figure came closer we could hear the puffs and grunts as he came up the hill, which augured well for a recovery of a decent number of salmon. He stopped and I wondered if he had seen us but I could see that he had just put two bags on the ground to regain his breath, and he was soon underway to a rendezvous of which he was still unaware. He came round the corner of the shed where we had staged our ambush and the trap was sprung.

Santa was arrested for unlawful possession of salmon and instruments that could be used or had been used in the unlawful taking of salmon or sea trout. One bag contained a dinghy and a gill net, still with salmon scales sticking to it, while the other bag contained eight fresh-run salmon of a very even size, somewhere about 10 to 12 pounds. Strangely none of the contents were wrapped in Christmas paper. Santa was gutted at being caught. He was a really elusive salmon poacher, mostly working on his own or with another very efficient salmon poacher whose activities I'll come to shortly. He was desperate not to lose his dinghy and net and offered us the bag of salmon for ourselves if we would just let him walk off. He promised faithfully that he would tell no-one about the 'deal'.

I have always been one for 'deals' provided they benefit the public interest but the offer of this deal was corrupt and in the long term would only be to the benefit of Santa. So it was no deal. Santa was fined and continued poaching, though whether with a net I know not. Had he managed to sell on his night's catch to some unscrupulous hotelier or fish merchant he would have been about £300 better off. I doubt if his fine would have matched this figure.

•

I have often wondered about the long-term effect on the nerves of criminals being caught by police officers who just step out of the darkness and arrest them. One minute they're walking along pleased with their night's work and the next minute it all goes horribly wrong. Will their next nocturnal adventure be so full of confidence or will they tread more warily, stopping, listening and looking every few minutes and avoiding likely ambush points?

Santa had a friend that I briefly referred to earlier. He didn't have a sleigh but had a motor bike. Since he's a friend of Santa I'll call him Rudolph. Rudolph annoyed me intensely for two reasons; he was a particularly unpleasant criminal, and though I had caught him for other types of crime I could never catch him for salmon poaching. Mr X and some other sources kept me updated on Rudolph's progress. I knew that he also had a gill net and that he kept his poaching gear and his salmon in a particular relative's shed. Though I sneaked a look in this shed from time to time it was always empty, but I knew I was on the right track as it stank of salmon.

My information was that Rudolph was selling his salmon to a fishmonger and game dealer in Edinburgh. I visited the shop with the Tay District Salmon Fisheries Board superintendent Garry Gibb but though there were plenty of salmon in the shop with the tell-tale marks of having being netted there were none that I could link back to Rudolph. I also found in the shop about twenty or thirty copy receipts bearing Rudolph's signature so I knew how often he was making the trip to Edinburgh and how much he was making from salmon poaching, which if taken over a year was considerably more than my salary.

I and others set up a regular watch on the M90 on the outskirts of Perth for Rudolph's motorbike. My information from Mr X was that Rudolph was making the trip about midday but even though we varied the time of our observations two hours either side of noon we never did catch him. He remained a thorn in my side for years after as one of only two regular salmon poachers that I never managed to bring to book. Being a fair-minded sort of chap, I was working on the reasonable premise that all the poachers should get their turn of being caught.

CHAPTER 3

Dealing in Deer

Deer poachers from Fort William visit Perth to sell their ill-gotten wares and the Moncrieffe Island poachers get a visit from the law.

In the 1970s and 1980s one of my main hobbies was game shooting, especially rabbits and wood pigeons. This brought me into regular contact with the main game dealer in the Perth area, Tom Band, who, along with his two sons, Bruce and Neil, were friends as well as businessmen to whom I sold some of my game. Probably the main source of revenue of this game dealer's business was the buying and selling of deer. To abide by the law, venison dealers must keep records of the deer they buy. These records include the name and address of the person selling the deer, the estate or farm on which the deer were shot, and the registration number of the vehicle transporting the deer to the game dealer's premises. These records are checked annually by what was then the Red Deer Commission, now the Deer Commission for Scotland, and are open to inspection by a police constable at any time. I have known some game dealers that have been sloppy in their record-keeping but this particular one was fastidious with his records, and also had a very good nose for a deer poacher.

I received a call at home one day from Tom Band, who told me that he had just had two men in with eight red deer stags. They gave their names and addresses and told him that they had shot the deer on Inverailort Estate in Glenfinnan in Inverness-shire. This rang alarm bells with Tom as he bought red deer from all over Scotland, including from Inverailort Estate. The deer were always picked up by him at the estate, never delivered to Perth, so something was wrong. He noted the registered number of their van for his records and told the men that he would need to go the bank for money to pay them as there was not enough in the till. The men were undaunted, replying that they would be back the next day with more deer and would be happy to get paid then.

I obtained the registered number of the vehicle for checking against the Police National Computer. None of the names given for the venison dealer's register matched the registered keeper. I then came on duty early and made contact with the police at Fort William. The registered keeper of the vehicle came from Caol, a village near Fort William, and was known to the local police as a deer poacher. I asked them to look out for the vehicle, which would be well on its way back home, and to detain the two occupants for me under Section 2 of the Criminal Justice (Scotland) Act 1980, which gave power to the police to detain a person suspected of having committed an offence for a period up to six hours (provided that the offence was punishable by imprisonment) and to interview the person during that period as often as was necessary. It also gave the police time to make enquiry and obtain the evidence necessary to be able to arrest, then charge, the suspect. If sufficient evidence, either from enquiries or from the interview of the suspect, could not be obtained before the expiry of the six hours the suspect had to be released and could not be detained on these same grounds again. Section 2 of the Criminal Justice (Scotland) Act 1980 has since been replaced by Section 14 of the Criminal Procedure (Scotland) Act 1995 but the powers and effects are the same.

In the meantime I called at the game dealer's premises and took possession of the deer as productions in the case. I had earlier asked Tom to have a look at the deer to try to establish by which calibre of rifle they had been shot. They had been shot with a high calibre rifle suitable for shooting red deer but three of them had been poorly shot, one having been shot twice and one having been shot three times. Tom could tell me that compared to deer submitted previously from Inverailort Estate, both the standard of shooting and the standard of handling the deer was poor and he was convinced they had neither been shot nor butchered by Inverailort stalkers.

I then made contact with the estate by telephone and they were able to tell me that by chance they had found the grallochs – the head, legs and innards – of eight stags that morning. They were freshly killed, near the roadside, and most likely had been shot the previous night either from the road or close by. In the meantime Fort William police had done their stuff, and had stopped the vehicle just before it reached Caol. The men's van was covered in the blood and the hair from deer they had dropped off at Perth, samples of which were taken by the Fort William officers for any comparisons I might want to have carried out.

Along with a colleague, PC Jim Findlay, I headed for Fort William to interview the two detainees. When we arrived I learned that one had been convicted twice for deer poaching offences, and the other had one previous conviction for deer poaching. One was a particularly dour sort but his fellow conspirator in cervine slaughter was a bit more forthcoming so I started with him. No-one ever admits to an offence right away and an interview always begins with bluff, double-bluff and complete denial, then advances to skirting around the truth, finishing with a partial admission. He at first denied having been in Perth that day, which was to my advantage as I could prove that he had. He then said that he had just 'gone for the run' and had no idea what was in the back of the van. It was unlikely that any sheriff would believe that story. As I anticipated, he then relented further and stated the whole thing was the idea of his co-accused and he had just strung along. Ten minutes of interview later and he admitted that they both had gone out in Glenfinnan the night before and had shot the deer from the roadside, using a rifle that they had borrowed as neither of them, because of their convictions, could obtain a firearm certificate. I had to make do with that as I could see that no amount of persuasion was going to get me any further. The rifle may have been borrowed or it may also have been an unlicensed weapon that they had cached away somewhere safe to carry out their deer poaching. Anyway he had told me more than sufficient to enable him to be charged.

The second person was a different character altogether, and was very reluctant to say anything. He started off with the familiar 'No comment' but it's amazing how soon people tire of repeating this, especially if the interviewer goes back to easy questions to answer that really don't add evidence to the case. Questions about the ownership of the van. How long he had owned it. Was a Ford Transit a reliable van? Most police forces used them. Could that be a recommendation for the ordinary punter to buy one? This got him out of the boring 'No comment' routine and we were on our way to some form of truth. Even though he was obstinate and morose, this chap had a grain of decency about him, admitting he was the ringleader and that the poaching had been his idea. He admitted that it was he who had shot the deer, but when I asked him where this had taken place I had pushed my luck too far and he realised he had told me far too much already. End of interview.

I charged each of the men with taking deer without lawful authority; being two or more persons acting together to commit this offence, in other words gang poaching; taking them during the hours of darkness; and unlawful possession of eight red deer. We took the men back to Perth and they appeared from custody at Perth Sheriff Court the next morning. The dour fellow was jailed for nine months as it was he who had the most convictions, while his apprentice was jailed for six months. The deer were forfeited by the court and the two accused were told they were very lucky not to be losing their van. It is interesting that they and so many others pled guilty at their first court appearance. This was pretty much the norm in the seventies and even into the very early eighties but such early pleas are almost unheard of nowadays. Could this be because there is less money to be made by defence lawyers with an early plea or are my suspicions unjust?

•

A week or two had passed without our shift having caught a salmon poacher on Moncrieffe Island so I made contact with Mr X. He assured me business was brisk and a good number of salmon were being caught but the lookout situation had improved. No fishing (or foul-hooking to use the more precise but less romantic term) was taking place without a lookout being posted down near the steps leading from the railway bridge. The lookout had a whistle and a blast on this would warn his associates in crime if danger in the form of either police officers or water bailiffs were approaching. It was to be the turn of Mr

X to be the lookout the following night so I asked him how we could get on to the island without being seen. His reply was that we could access by the back of the island about two in the morning as this would be the lowest point of the tide and we should be able to walk across the gravel. The River Tay is still tidal at this point and indeed it is a further mile upstream, over twenty miles from the sea, before the effects of the tide are lost. I asked if coming on to the island at this point would compromise him but he was confident that it wouldn't. As the lookout, he could not be expected to see both the steps and the back of the island from the vantage point used and all the poachers were aware of this.

The following night my colleague, PC Graham Jack, and I made a successful crossing to the island without so much as wetting our boots. We made our way up through the trees, many of which are limes and poplars. I'm not sure which of these trees it is but one of them in Autumn gives off the loveliest scent, which somehow reminds me of the smell given off when sucking the make of sweets called Oddfellows. On this August night this was a delightful smell, blending into the smells coming off the allotments as we passed by the boundary fence, spoiled momentarily by some over-ripe brassicas, then back into the aroma of freshly cut grass as we reached King James VI Golf Course.

Making use of the cover given by bunkers and small groups of trees on the golf course we made our way slowly across the island towards the Friarton Hole. The last fifty or so yards before we reached the tree-lined river bank was bereft of any cover so that was a crawling job; we didn't want to be caught out at the last hurdle. Once we reached the cover of the trees and bushes again we were close to the riverbank and it would just be a case of locating the first poacher. Trees and bushes are never easy to navigate quietly since the ground roundabout is usually strewn with dead branches and every step was taken with great care lest we stood on a branch. A branch snapping in the absolute silence of Moncrieffe Island in the middle of the night would be as if a gunshot had gone off; a starting pistol that would encourage every poacher off his starting blocks with the acceleration of an Olympic runner.

At last we spied our quarry. A figure with a fishing rod in his hand silhouetted against the shimmering silver of the river, reminiscent somehow of a garden gnome. He was reeling in when we first saw him, with the savage jerking motions with which we were both now familiar. No contact with the flank of a salmon that time so he cast again into the depths of the Friarton Hole. His concentration on attempts to foul-hook a fish allowed us to close the gap by a few yards so that we were less than six paces behind him. Our timing was out by a few seconds and he turned to cast again but this time saw us. He had maybe thought about this moment for years and rehearsed his exit strategy in his mind innumerable times. In little more time than it takes to blink, the rod was thrown into the river and he was off along the banking like a bat out of Hell. Chasing him was pointless since, when he had turned, we had gained an advantage as well: we had recognised him. I'll call him Spud since that bears a certain resemblance to his name. He disappeared out of sight along the path and no doubt, like the Pied Piper, he had amassed a considerable following of other poachers by the time he reached the steps up to the railway bridge.

Our next job was to recover the fishing rod and the illegal lead weight and treble hook that made it so different from the tackle employed by a sporting angler. Our traverse across the island had taken almost two hours, and the first chinks of daylight could be seen emerging from Kinnoull Hill and further down the Tay to the east. Graham and I utilised our time until there was sufficient daylight to see the sunken rod in searching the area behind where Spud was fishing. We were hoping to find his cache of salmon, but met with no success. Moorhens and coots were now beginning to greet the daylight with their *crek, crekking* calls to each other and at last there was sufficient light to see the rod. It had sunk as far as our hearts now sunk; it wasn't too far from the bank but it was in at least ten feet of water.

Graham and I briefly discussed which one of us would strip off and go in for it, but discretion overcame valour. A strong tree branch was the answer and we found one of sufficient length and with the bonus of a smaller branch growing out of one end that we trimmed to form a sort of grappling hook. My colleague, being taller and having longer arms than I, was clearly the better choice to wield this primitive tool, and after a couple of abortive attempts the evidence in the case Procurator fiscal versus Spud was landed. As we knew there would be, there was a lump of lead and a large treble hook on the end of the line, and the breaking strain of the line was at least twenty pounds.

The next night we paid Spud a visit. He made no denial of the events that took place since he knew both of us at least as well as we knew him. He was resigned to his fate and had expected the inevitable 'chap at the door'.

•

I had a second poaching encounter with Spud several years on, when I was a sergeant. After repeated complaints from the owner of a private stank about fishers taking trout during the night, my fellow sergeant and I hatched a plan, but first I'll explain the legal position with a stank.

A stank is an old Scots term for a loch or pond that is stocked with fish, normally either brown trout or rainbow trout. There must be no inlet or outlet by which other wild fish can access the loch so that the trout, being stocked fish, are accepted by the court as being owned by the person putting them into the loch. Normally fish, birds and animals are considered as being wild and not belonging to anyone, but in this case, or in the case of a gamekeeper rearing pheasants or partridges in a pen, he is considered to be the legal owner of the birds up until the point when they are released from the pen and become wild birds. To complete the legal requirements for a stank, there must be sufficient notices placed round the stank showing that fishing is not allowed, usually with the wording 'Private Stank – No Fishing'. If these conditions are applied, then the offence of taking trout from the stank is theft, since it is the removal of property belonging to another person. Modern-day legislation in the form of the Salmon and Freshwater Fisheries (Consolidation) (Scotland) Act 2003 has a specific offence that now covers this type of poaching.

It was the month of June and daylight not long after 3.00 am, giving us plenty of time for a foray before our 7.00 am finish. The plan to either deter or catch those who were stealing trout from this stank on the outskirts of Perth was that my fellow sergeant, Jim Macdonald, as soon as it was daylight, would quietly go to a vantage point near the loch, where he could spy round the edge with binoculars. He would then report back to me by radio telling me where the people were fishing, and I and one of the constables from the shift would come quietly in behind them and they would be captured. This plan, unbelievably, worked successfully three nights in succession so we decided to go for a fourth.

On the fourth night the report back to me was that there was a single person fishing on the north side of the loch at the west end, which unfortunately was the most difficult point to access as it meant driving round to the top of an extensive wooded area, parking the car, then navigating through the half a mile of wood that ran from the roadside to the point beside the errant fisher. Negotiating half a mile of woodland, with branches that could be snapped with a careless footstep or cock pheasants that could explode from underfoot with their loud *cuck-cuck cuck-cuck* alarm call was a bit daunting and I wasn't hopeful of success. Anyway it was worth a try.

We parked the police car and set off through the wood. It was woodland comprising mature oaks, beeches, birch, rowan and alder, with just a scattering of pines and larch trees. It was a joy to be in such woodland. I have had bad experiences in dense forests of horrible non-indigenous sitka spruce with low whippy branches causing weals across the face, scratches to the arms and an interminable cascade of needles finding their unerring way between shirt collar and neck. These are a nightmare to navigate and I was relieved on this occasion we were in such a benign and pleasant wood.

We made our way down through the trees to the accompaniment of the soft cooing of wood pigeons above us. The pigeons were okay at this distance from our target but I hoped that there would be none at the bottom end of the wood which could clatter out of the trees and give the game away. We passed a patch of wild garlic with its strong and pleasant scent, and saw several places where, in the last 48 hours or so, a group of roe deer had each scratched away the earth into an oblong-shaped couch and spent its resting daylight hours. Carrion crows had been busy and at one stage when we had the advantage of walking for about a hundred metres along a woodland ride that took us in the direction we wanted to go, the ground was littered with pheasant eggs that they had purloined from their rightful owner and sucked dry.

With about a hundred metres left till we reached the edge of the loch, I was confident from various landmarks that we were on track to come in behind the fisher. I began to worry when a jay started to screech at being disturbed and flew from tree to tree on our right hand side, giving a lovely display of pink and brown body feathers and an intermittent flash of white and vivid blue at each flap of its wings. A chaffinch was also sounding its alarm call, a slow but steady *pink-pink, pink-pink*. If our fisher had his aural senses tuned in and could read the signs of danger very clearly being sent to him by the woodland birds, he should be off. I hoped that he couldn't tell the sound of a chirping sparrow from a croaking raven and was more familiar with the sounds made by slot machines, public bar tills and ice cream vans.

A further fifty metres and I could see our loch-side fisherman had not been tuned in to his surroundings and was still intent on reducing the number of fat trout in the stank. At that point we were making progress virtually from tree to tree. When the fisher made a cast I noticed two things. He was using a bubble float and worm (an especially deadly method of catching trout) and the fisher was Spud! With vivid memories of the Moncrieffe Island escapade, I didn't want the rod to finish up in the loch so decided to close in as quickly as possible before his next cast. There wasn't quite the same need to rush, as a bubble float and worm is a rather lazy way of fishing. An angler using that method is content to let the lure sit in the water for many minutes, watching the plastic bubble on the surface for signs of a nibbling trout before striking at the point he thinks the trout will have the worm and hook in its mouth.

We moved forward as fast as we dared, still minding where we put our feet down, and were gaining ground on our target at a good rate . . . when he started to reel in for another cast. I increased my pace and was about two or three metres behind him when he turned towards me in the course of executing his next cast. He must have learned from the last time on Moncrieffe Island. He continued back with his right hand beyond what was required for the cast, said, 'For fuck sake, not again' and handed me the rod. The bag at his feet held eleven nice Loch Leven trout, the type of trout with which the owner stocked the loch. I had further encounters in future years with Spud in my role as detective sergeant in the Drug Squad, but I think this episode concluded his fishing adventures.

CHAPTER 4

The Buttonless Jacket Gang

The Night Poaching Act 1828 is enforced on a team of rabbit catchers from Larkhall and at Low's Works' Pool the publican's son is surprised twice in the one night.

Considering I was working in a city, poaching was more varied than that encountered in many county police stations. A call one morning from a gamekeeper, Ernie Bannister, just outside Perth alerted me to the fact that he had been visited by a group of professional rabbit poachers. He and his son had been driving through the estate about midnight when they had chanced upon three men climbing over a gate into a field. They stopped and spoke to the men, who told them they had been thinking about poaching some rabbits but now that they had been spotted they were aborting their night's mission. The men had no dogs, no guns, no ferrets – and no buttons on their jackets. This could only mean their intention was to use a long net.

A long net is just as it sounds. It is a fairly fine net, made from cotton or twine, usually either twenty five or fifty metres in length and about three feet in height. It is set along the side of a wood on sticks placed about four or five metres apart. The top edge of the net is normally set about eighteen inches high with the bottom edge on the ground. There is therefore plenty slack in the net in which rabbits can become entangled. The whole length of a field can be covered, depending on how many nets are employed. If the net is set quietly the rabbits are undisturbed and remain feeding out in the centre of the field. Normally two people, each holding the end of a long string stretched between them, walk from the other end of the field towards the net dragging the string over the ground so that when the string touches a rabbit it heads towards the net as fast as it can go. Often a third person is left to run back and forward along the length of the net removing and despatching the rabbits before the net becomes too full and too stretched and begins to allow rabbits to escape underneath. Since this is all carried out in darkness and since a lightweight net is easily snagged on anything that protrudes from clothing, it is important to get rid of buttons and substitute them with string if required.

I was pleased at the keeper's attention to detail. I was even more pleased that he drove round to the main road, the A9, and saw that there was a car parked and unattended at a field gateway. As keepers always do, he had meticulously noted the registration number of the car. He had gone even further and parked his Land Rover at a part of the road where he could watch for the men returning to the car. They returned about an hour later, turned the car about in the centre of the road and headed west.

Before the keeper contacted me in the morning he had also summoned the other keepers on the estate and carried out a line search through the wood near the roadside opposite where the car had been parked. This was an astute move since they found the grand total of 99 rabbits, gutted and spaced out to cool on a grassy area just a few yards inside the wood. There was little doubt that the poachers had spotted the Land Rover and didn't want to risk taking the rabbits to their car at that point. It was the month of December so they would come to no harm from blowflies and ground dwelling insects if left out for a night. Our opinion was that the men would return just after dark for their bounty. They had gone to a lot of bother and there was no way that the rabbits were going to be abandoned to the foxes in the form of a vulpine fast food take-away.

In the meantime I had carried out a check on the vehicle registration number noted by the keeper. It came back as an owner with an address in Larkhall. That night the keepers, a police colleague and I set up a watch on the rabbits from just before darkness fell. We had little time to wait, and before long a car came slowly along the A9 from the direction of Stirling, stopped nearly opposite us, dropped off two passengers, then drove off towards Perth. My assumption was that the driver would turn, wait for a few minutes to give his passengers time to collect the rabbits together then drive back along the road to collect them. It would only take a few seconds for the rabbits to be loaded into the back of the car and all would again be high-tailing it back to Larkhall.

We crouched motionless in a semi-circle round the rabbits. We heard the roadside fence grate as the wires on the fence ran through the supporting staples with the weight of the men crossing, then they were there, neatly surrounded by us, and loading the rabbits into bags. We waited a few moments until most of the rabbits were bagged – there was no use in us doing the work if our victims were obligingly doing it for us – then pounced. There was no escape for the two men. Detaining suspects in dark woodland at night unfortunately doesn't include the right to stuff a hankie in their mouth. At that point their colleague with the car drove along the road and stopped almost beside us. One of our two long-netters shouted a warning and before we could do anything about it the car took of with a screech of tyres, the driver abandoning his two pals to their fate.

The charge on this occasion was under the Night Poaching Act 1828. Interestingly this legislation has powers for landowners and gamekeepers to arrest a suspect, but no such power for the police. A power of arrest exists under the Night Poaching Act for the police if three or more persons are involved, which had been the case, but the caveat is that at least one of the persons must be armed with some sort of weapon, even a walking stick. Since we had no evidence of a weapon they could not be arrested under the Night Poaching Act.

Much of the content of Game Acts was devised in the nineteenth century and its aim was to give powers to landowners and their 'servants' to arrest poachers, seize game that they had taken, and convey the poachers to the police station. There they would be kept and appear before the court the following day, where a private prosecution would be taken by the estate factor. Nowadays all criminal cases in Scotland are the remit of the procurator fiscal, the public prosecutor. In any event, when we noted the poachers' details they had nothing which could verify their identity; their pockets were as devoid of contents as their jackets were of buttons. Common sense prevails under Common Law, and police officers can arrest a suspect until such time as his identity is established beyond doubt. This would not stretch to arresting local criminals who are well known to the officers concerned but it most definitely applied to two men from Larkhall, dressed akin to scarecrows, that I had never set eyes on before.

The two were taken to Divisional Police Headquarters at Perth, where contact was made with Strathclyde Police to visit the addresses supplied and ensure that we had been given the correct names and addresses. Once their *bona fides* were established they were released to receive a summons to appear before Perth Sheriff Court in due course, where they were dealt with by means of a fine.

The Night Poaching Act 1828 is an Act which is seldom used nowadays. While I have no doubt that many poaching incidents did and indeed still take place at night most offenders either seem to escape detection or are dealt with under legislation that is more specific to the type of game they are taking, such as salmon, deer or hares. Coincidentally I did meet our Larkhall friends a few weeks later when I caught them ferreting rabbits without permission one Sunday morning on a farm on the east side of Perth. They still wore the same buttonless jackets that were their trade mark. This time they were dealt with under legislation designed to deal with day-time poaching, the Game (Scotland) Act 1832, the offence being to trespass on land by day in unlawful search or pursuit of game. They had amassed a catch of twenty rabbits by the time they were caught and again were fined by the court. I chatted to them about our previous encounter and the third person involved admitted that he had been the car driver who had sped off to safety. The two who had been caught held no grudge, stating that all three had chipped in and paid a third of the two fines each. Honour among thieves – and poachers.

•

As I explained earlier, the River Almond, a tributary of the Tay that amalgamates its waters with the Tay's mighty flow just north of Perth, normally has a fairly late run of salmon. Until there is a sufficient rush of fresh water to allow the salmon up the River Almond, they are obliged to lie in the Friarton Hole or the Woody Hole, a long, deep and fast running pool on the Perth bank of the Tay just short of the mouth of the River Almond. Once rainfall has swelled the River Almond, and the salmon begin to navigate its waters, the first obstacle they encounter is a weir just downstream of a pool named Low's Works' Pool. Low's used to be a dyeworks and the pool associated with this old factory is a large, slow moving pool on a bend in the river.

The weir is only about four feet high and in fact is in the form of a slope rather than being perpendicular. In the right conditions of high water levels it is the type of obstacle where the salmon doesn't come out of the water; it simply swims at high speed up the torrent of water. The fish are not seen until they complete their ascent of the weir, but when they reach their new level there is just a fraction of a second when they are almost stationary. It is as if they drop a gear, with the drag of the water holding them back momentarily until they select their lower gear, engage the clutch and depress the accelerator. A flick of their tail, a dorsal fin nearly always showing above the water, and they are away again in the next stage of their amazing journey between the seas off Greenland and their spawning ground.

Never missing an opportunity, the salmon poachers from Perth, Almondbank (a village five minutes walk away from the weir) and elsewhere further afield, are aware of this vulnerable point in the salmon's journey. The poachers stand out in the river, sometimes four or five at a time, just above the weir, in the manner of grizzly bears on Alaskan rivers. While the grizzly bears use teeth and claws, the Low's Works' Pool poachers have an equally deadly weapon – a gaff. After a few minutes of balancing in the current, the poacher's patience is rewarded with a salmon suddenly appearing juxtaposed to his sodden jeans and trainers. A well aimed strike with the gaff midships on the salmon's body and the fish's fate is sealed.

We were well used to catching salmon poachers with a gaff hidden down their trousers on the path at the side of Low's Works' Pool. The gaff would be seized and its owner would be charged with unlawful possession of an instrument that could be used for the illegal taking of salmon or sea trout. We had a huge stockpile of gaffs awaiting their appearance in court as productions in a variety of cases. We should in fact have been on commission from some of the local fishing tackle shops, where the staff must have wondered why the sale of gaffs probably outstripped the sale of salmon flies and other legitimate lures.

It was seldom that the poachers at this location were caught with fish, as when they gaffed a fish, they continued on to the far side of the river. It was easy to approach them on the side they started out from as we could drive our cars along the path there. My shift wasn't satisfied with this and we planned an ambush from the far bank. This entailed a considerable walk through dark and rough terrain first of all but we were up for it.

My first capture on the far bank was of the son of a local publican. He came running from the River Almond with a decent salmon of about twelve pounds neatly gaffed and wriggling in a futile attempt to escape. He reached the safety of the bank and bent down to remove the salmon from the gaff – right in front of us. He was fairly philosophical about being charged and the gaff and salmon were seized as productions. Typically he made no reply to the charges of fishing without written permission or lawful authority, taking salmon by means other than rod and line, and unlawful possession of a gaff and a salmon. He simply said, 'Well we'll be safe shortly. Your shift will be finished at ten o'clock'. We took this as a compliment that the poachers paid particular attention to whether our shift was on or off duty. We bade him goodnight and he re-crossed the river while we took the longer route with his salmon and gaff, back to the police car.

By the time we had returned to the police station in Perth our shift had just finished. I put the gaff in the production store, the salmon in the freezer, and had a chat with the night shift inspector, who was very supportive of our anti-poaching initiative. I explained to him that there was a good run of salmon in the Almond and that I was happy to stay on and take one of his shift out to Low's Works' Pool to catch a further poacher or at least put in an appearance and disrupt their activities.

So just over an hour later I and one of the night shift officers were back in our ambush point on the difficult-to-access side of the River Almond. We sat in the bushes motionless and silent, awaiting some sound that indicated we were back in business with a poacher, as we could see nothing but blackness. The absence of one sense seems to sharpen other senses and we could clearly hear the occasional *swish* of water as a poacher moved a few feet one way or another at the top of the weir hoping to find a more lucrative spot for his nefarious activity. After ten minutes or so I heard a splash in the river. I could still see nothing but knew from previous experience of the sound that a salmon had been gaffed. This was followed by the *swish, swish, swish* of the poacher wading to the bank, then we homed in on the *thwack, thwack* of the fish being killed and made our move to capture the poacher.

It was the publican's son again, complete with replacement gaff. This time his language was more choice. He seemed to think it was unfair that I had come out to the river again after I should have been off duty. He had lost two gaffs in the one night. With the expense of the gaffs and the cost of two fines his profit for the night would be gone. After the formal cautioning and charging, which was somewhat bizarre in the pitch dark when I couldn't see to write in my notebook, he observed the usual abstinence from reply and waded back into the river to return to the far bank. He did reply from the safety of the middle of the river. It was quite a lengthy reply though not particularly relevant to the charge – more a graphic description of what he thought of me and my cheating methods of sneaking back when I should have been off duty. I never noted the reply. I couldn't spell most of the words anyway.

Chapter 5

The Cage at Horseshoe Falls

Big Daddy, a new informant, gives the low-down on a large-scale salmon poaching venture and a last-minute deal is struck to jail safebreakers.

If Low's Works' Pool is the first problem for salmon making their way up the River Almond, Horseshoe Falls is the next. As its name suggests, this is a waterfall in the shape of a horseshoe. It is not much higher than the weir at Low's Works' Pool but, due to a partial collapse of the rocks in the centre of the falls, the highest volume of water cascades over this central part. Since this is the easiest route for the salmon, most ascend the falls at this point.

Just before this incident I had developed another very good informant. He was a huge chap with a weak voice that was in inverse proportion to the bulk of his frame. To look at him, anyone would expect a very gruff voice when he spoke and it was mildly amusing when the words were emitted in a sort of soft squeak. Like Mr X, I had given him a warning shot across the bows for a relatively minor infringement of the Salmon and Freshwater Fisheries (Protection) (Scotland) Act 1951 when he really could have been charged. He was relieved, if not grateful, and said he may be able to help me from time to time. Since he went on to be a professional wrestler I'll refer to him as Big Daddy.

Big Daddy had passed on one or two pieces of information that were of moderate interest. So far, rather than ease the passage of his fellow poachers into court, he was giving me intelligence that added to the overall poaching picture. As is the case with most aspects of crime, there are comparatively few crimes where the police do not know the identity of the perpetrator, but knowing who has committed a particular crime and being able to prove this beyond a reasonable doubt are two completely different things. In the meantime Big Daddy was increasing my knowledge of The Complete Guide to Poaching and Poachers in Perthshire.

It is uncommon for police officers to give out their home telephone numbers to informants, but I had developed a degree of trust with Mr X and Big Daddy. Weighing up the odds of them causing hassle to my family, and deciding that the risk was in my favour, I passed them my telephone number. Had I not done so they only had to consult the telephone directory in any case as, unlike some police officers, I had never felt the need of an ex-directory telephone number.

I was night shift at the time of a particularly interesting phone call from Big Daddy. He made contact one evening as I was in the middle of dinner and said that he could give me a good job when I came on duty that night. The first point of interest was that he knew I was night shift. I suppose I was mildly flattered that he knew my shift pattern: it reinforced the view that of the four shifts – or teams of police officers covering the Perth area – our shift clearly posed the biggest threat. His information was that two salmon poachers, both well known to me, would be using a cage at the Horseshoe Falls that night. Policing is a lot more efficient and effective when reliable information of a crime is received before the occurrence of the crime. It allows planning to take place, assessment of the risks involved, assessment of the likelihood of success, the number of officers required to deal with the particular crime, and the fine tuning of proactive measures to catch those that are involved.

To gauge the veracity of the information my first question to Big Daddy was, 'How do you know that these two will be at the Horseshoe Falls with a cage tonight?' The reply surprised me but satisfied me that he was telling the truth. 'I was with them last night. There was a great run of fish on and we had over a hundred. It was a good night's work but I left the sale of fish to the other two. When I got my cut this afternoon they had fiddled the money. They said the price had dropped as some of the fish were starting to go red. I knew this was crap as most of the fish were fresh-run and silver. I said I couldn't make it tonight. They've just pissed me off so you can have them.'

I had only once encountered a cage and realised that it was a very efficient tool with which to take a large quantity of salmon. The cage is made of wire netting or gridweld mesh and although dimensions can vary, the most efficient size to operate would be roughly four feet square and about eighteen inches high. The principle of the cage is that the fish enter by a funnel in the centre of the side of the cage that is facing downstream, rather like the entrance to a lobster pot. They must keep their heads facing into the current or they will drown. They therefore can't locate the route out and are trapped. If a cage is situated with the funnel entrance facing downstream and at the point where most of the fish are running up the river, the operator will have a bonanza. In the case of the Horseshoe Falls the optimum place to station the cage was at the broken part right in the middle.

I phoned my inspector, Fred MacAulay, at home, explained the position to him, and asked if I could come out that night in camouflage gear along with another officer. I got the green light and immediately contacted another shift officer, PC Peter Murray, to ensure he came to work suitably dressed.

By 11.00 pm, an hour after we had started our shift, the inspector had dropped off Peter and me at the side of a country road about two miles from the River Almond and the Horseshoe Falls. It was a lovely night, mid November, cold but not frosty, enough cloud cover to keep us well hidden but just enough light to allow us to navigate reasonably well through the fields towards the river. I knew this area reasonably well and knew that the hardest part would be descending through the larch wood that lay between the last of the fields and the bank of the River Almond.

The fields posed few problems. At that time of year, apart from the odd field of turnips, crops had been harvested and some were even re-sown with winter wheat or winter barley. They were flat and made easy walking. One problem arose in a grass field when we were besieged by a herd of Friesian heifers. This was unfortunate; had they been older cattle they would have been content to munch the grass, chew the cud or whatever they were up to at that particular time. Even if they had been some of the Continental breeds such as Charollais, Simmental or Limousin, these breeds are usually so flighty that they would have taken off in the other direction. It was just our luck to have the attention of twenty or thirty snorting, slavering Friesian heifers surrounding us. We tried to shoo them away but this made the problem worse. They ran off like bucking broncos straight out of a wild-west rodeo, kicking up their heels and farting and coughing loudly with the effort, before returning to exhale their horrible breath on us and cough their snot on us once again.

We were still a field-width away from the wood leading down to the river, which was a relief in view of the noise these damn beasts were making, and thankfully by the time they had spotted us we were reasonably near the boundary fence of their field. When we reached the top of the woodland that stretched 200 metres or so down to the river we watched and listened for a while. There was not a sound and for a few minutes there was nothing to be seen either. Then the faintest flash of a torch on the river assured as that our quarry was there. We gave it a further fifteen minutes and a second flash of a torch in the same place confirmed that our targets were fairly static and gave us a direction to take. Neither of us was looking forward to the fairly steep descent through the wood. Apart from the real risk of us creating a noise that would give the game away there was also the danger that we could lose our footing. One or both of us clattering down the banking and we would have no chance of catching our poachers. We quietly discussed the options and decided that we had plenty of time to move really slowly through the wood, tentatively testing every step before we put the full weight on to the leading foot. The river was still in flood so we also realised that the rush of water over the falls would cover some of the noise we made provided it was not excessive.

Our progress was painstakingly slow and from the top to the bottom of the 200 metres of steep larch woodland took well over an hour. Even the snails seemed to be overtaking us. As we neared the end of the wood we began to see the two men more clearly. Though they were mostly grey ghosts an odd flicker of their torch was sufficient to show us that every fifteen minutes or so they were emptying their cage and piling the salmon up on the riverbank between the cage and the point that we had reached. From then on we began to crawl rather than walk. We had the backdrop of the wood behind us and what there was of a moon was to our right so we were in no danger of being silhouetted. Nevertheless keeping close to the ground obviated the risk of the poachers seeing any sort of shape that resembled a person.

It was then that a major obstacle brought our otherwise steady progress to a standstill. As we moved closer to the two men we suddenly realised that there was a very wide, very dark, and probably very deep ditch or lade between where we were and where we wanted to be. The two poachers were operating from a strip of land between this stretch of water and the main part of the river. Neither of us knew about this beforehand yet I am sure it just didn't appear that very night to thwart our operation. Since we hadn't known of its existence we had no idea how to get across. We considered wading it, but didn't know whether wading would turn into swimming. I had a fleeting vision of the two of us with our feet stuck in several feet of clinging mud that lay in wait for the unwary under the water, while we were ridiculed by the poachers as they continued their night's work in safety.

Rather than throw caution to the wind we started to crawl downstream. I was thankful that we did so as we had only gone about fifty metres when we found a bridge made of two old railway sleepers with some planks of wood roughly nailed between them. What a relief. I thought afterwards about what we would have done had we not found a crossing point. In the variety of possible solutions the common factor always included getting wet.

Now that we were on the same part of dry land as our targets the rest was comparatively easy. A fifty metre crawl while the poachers were otherwise engaged in the river and we were nearly there. We could see the pile of salmon on the bank and it was a case of getting to an ambush spot as close to them as possible. Ten metres away there was a fairly substantial elder bush which offered enough shelter. The time then really seemed to slow down and it seemed forever until the two men emptied the cage again and began the short journey from the cage to the riverbank, then from the riverbank to their stash of fish. They were laying their latest catch out on the pile, by good fortune with their back or at least their sides facing in our direction. It was enough time to slip from behind the elder bush and literally bid them good morning. There was no scramble to grab them and handcuff them; had they run off we knew who they were anyway so a chase would have been pointless. One made a futile attempt to rid himself of evidence by throwing a gaff he had in his hand into the river but, unlike the rod with the treble hook and lump of lead thrown into the Friarton Hole, there was no need to retrieve it. It was a reaction to the surprise he had received and I didn't blame him.

The two were quite matter of fact when they were caught and in fact reminded me of two other men I and another colleague, DC Ian Cantwell, caught after a tip-off Ian had received that they would be breaking into a certain office. We had staked out the office and watched the two men, regular 'customers' of ours, enter the common close. We heard the office door getting kicked in and gave them enough time to enter the office before walking quietly up the stairs. When we entered the violated office we split up to search the rooms off the hallway. I had checked the last room on my side of the corridor and Ian had just entered the last room on his side. I came into the office two steps behind him, in time to see our two housebreakers rifling through drawers and files with their socks on their hands. They were bare-footed and their trainers were lying in the middle of the floor. The response of the first one to spot us was to say, 'Hi Ian,' just as if we had met them socially in a pub. A greeting like that from our two salmon poaching friends would not have surprised me in the least. It was a good rapport to have with criminals. We played fair and they respected us for that.

With the salmon poaching convictions that they had accrued, and the fact that the use of a cage on such a scale was obviously a commercial enterprise, it was inevitable that the two poachers would receive a jail sentence. Nevertheless, criminals always want to defer a jail term for a long as possible. When we got them back to the cells at the police station at Perth one of them offered me a deal to release them to receive a summons for court rather than be kept to appear in court that morning. If the deal was good I would be happy to oblige as in fact it would save me sitting and hurriedly compiling a report that morning. The deal was that he knew of a safe-breaking job that was about to come off and he would give me the time, location and those who were to be involved once he could confirm the details. He and his *socius criminus* would have to be released there and then and I would have to trust him. I had trusted him in similar circumstances before and he had kept his word. I had nothing to lose, while he had much to lose: if he failed to deliver it would be the last time that I or any other police officer would trust him.

I let him and his co-conspirator out to receive a summons. The safe-breaking came off and the three involved were arrested and jailed. Our two salmon poachers had a few months' grace before their case came up. They pled guilty and were jailed for 60 days each. Everyone involved, apart from the safe-breakers, was pleased with his particular part of the deal, and I was sure we would all meet again in similar circumstances.

Chapter 6

Balaclavas on Moncrieffe Island

Local deer poachers remove to Mull for a change of scenery and the Moncrieffe Island crew resort to desperate measures to conceal their identities.

My next piece of valuable intelligence on deer poaching came from Mr X. Three Perth poachers had branched out from Perthshire and had gone to Mull to take red deer. Mr X gave me their names and the details of the vehicle that they were using, which was a Land Rover. I was particularly interested – though not surprised – that one of the poachers was Big Daddy. It looked like I may have to arrest my informant, but if informants are not closely linked with crime they are unlikely to have the knowledge to be able to regurgitate any worthwhile information. Another of the poachers was Wyllie, the telephone box man. The third was a man whom I knew but not for poaching activities. Mr X's information was that the three had a shotgun with them and were intending to shoot red deer from the roadside. He informed me that in the south-west of the island there were plenty of deer grazing at the roadside and not a house for miles to hear the shots.

After North Uist, Mull is my favourite of the isles to the west of Scotland and I knew what he was telling me was likely to be accurate. As a regular user of a shotgun I was well aware of how unsuitable this weapon would be against red deer, even with the heaviest of ammunition. If they were shooting from the roadside it would be a fair bet that every second deer that they fired at would run off injured and would die a lingering death. Of all the poachers I had caught to date, I wanted these three jailed more than any of the others.

Very few informants, unless they are actually taking part know every detail of the crime. Though I prodded and prodded Mr X for more information, especially details of when they would be returning to Perth from Mull, what he had given me seemed to be the limit of his knowledge.

That day my colleague, Iain MacLeod, and I sat on the A85 Crieff to Perth road every spare minute of our shift. So determined were we to catch this crew we sat through our meal break watching car after car going past, our hearts beating just that bit faster every time a Land Rover approached. Perth being a market town, Land Rovers were ten a penny and it's a wonder we didn't have heart failure.

Both of us were thrawn characters who hated to be beaten and our perseverance paid off in the end. Just after midday a Land Rover passed us, we recognised its occupants as Big Daddy and Co and the chase was on. To call it a chase is an overstatement as the Land Rover stopped immediately we caught up with it and put on our flashing blue light. The Mull mob had met their match.

Big Daddy and the third person – for simplicity I'll just call him the Third Man – were quiet and polite. Wyllie, on the other hand was arrogant and cocky, but this was exactly his style and what we expected of him. We told them why they were being stopped and our powers under the Deer (Scotland) Act 1959 entitled us to search them and the vehicle. All five of us then moved round to the rear door of the Land Rover, which I opened slowly in case the deer fell out on to the road. No deer fell out. The Land Rover, apart from some deer hair and blood, was completely empty. A thorough search under the seats and in the receptacles on each side of the vehicle under the window shelf also proved fruitless. Thoughts of a conviction for taking red deer with a shotgun were fading, though we knew from the large amount of money they had in their pockets that the suspects had sold a good number of deer. The National Lottery had not been invented so that could not be proffered as an excuse for the wads of notes in the pockets of three long-term unemployed people.

We had the power to detain the suspects for up to six hours, which was our next step. The three were taken to Perth Police Station and put in cells so that we could continue our enquiries. They had obviously disposed of the deer somewhere between Mull and Perth but I couldn't think where this could have been. I was banking on them bringing the deer to Perth and trying to sell them to the local game dealer. I would have had the utmost co-operation had that been the case but then they possibly knew with the good reputation of the local game dealer that he would either not accept the deer or turn them in to the police.

In policing it never pays to put all your eggs into one basket, which is exactly what I had done. I had formed my own unsubstantiated opinion of where the deer were destined for sale and had never asked that question of Mr X. I fervently hoped I could make contact with him. Six hours may seem a long time but it's very short in terms of obtaining enough evidence to secure a conviction. I've absolutely no doubt that for a suspect languishing in a cell, wondering how successfully or otherwise police enquiries are progressing, six hours must seem an eternity. For the investigating police officers, who often have to trace witnesses, take statements, make searches, seize productions, interview suspects, six hours passes in a flash. I often envied our colleagues south of the Border who have 24 hours and in some circumstances can ask for an extension. Having said that, I had never once known of a police officer in Scotland running out of time with a suspect. Building a case against the clock is all about good knowledge of the law, prioritisation of those parts of the investigation that will yield sufficient result to obtain a *prima facia* case that can later be built on, good time management and confident and structured interviews. And of course in this particular case knowing how to make contact with your informant!

I managed to get hold of Mr X again and learned from him that a Dutch game dealer had started a new business on the west side of Crieff. His premises could be a possibility for our three suspects to have off-loaded the deer. That was definitely to be our next stop.

Mr X had come up with the goods again. The Dutchman admitted buying two loads of deer delivered by Land Rover in the last three days. We asked to inspect his venison register, which gave us a Mickey Mouse name and address for the seller of the two consignments but the correct vehicle registration number of the Land Rover. We then asked to see the sales slips, which showed us the weight of the deer sold, the price the dealer paid per pound, and a signature of some name plucked out of the sky to match the fictitious entry in the venison register.

Nineteen deer had been sold in all, and they were still in the game dealer's cold store. We inspected them and found them to be a mixture of stags and hinds, one lot in season and the other out of season since the periods for the legal shooting of different sexes do not overlap. We took possession of all of the deer and arranged for a police van to transport them to a freezing facility in Perth. In the investigation of crimes where animals have been killed, and the manner in which they have been killed is the subject of one of the charges, it is important to retain the carcasses in case the defence disputes the evidence relating to the killing. Even though the defence may not really want to inspect the carcasses, if that opportunity is not available then an otherwise good case can collapse.

We now had exactly what we needed to charge the three suspects. Equally importantly, it would eliminate the smugness and arrogance that Wyllie had been displaying. His gas would be at a peep – a good Scottish phrase evocative of how we wanted him to feel.

Armed with the new evidence, we re-interviewed our suspects and they admitted what they had done. We were then in a position to charge all three with various offences under the Deer (Scotland) Act 1959. Relevant charges were taking deer without permission, taking them by means other than shooting them with the proper rifle and ammunition, two or more persons acting together to commit these offences, taking them during the hours of darkness, and taking some of the deer out of season. Only one aspect of the case had still to be sorted out, that of the origin and whereabouts of the shotgun involved.

We knew the strengths and weaknesses of Wyllie, Big Daddy and the Third Man and knew on whom to put pressure to find out about the weapon. In this particular case it would be unprofessional of me to reveal who gave details, but we learned that the shotgun had been stolen from a farm near Perth and that it was presently buried, wrapped in a polythene bag, on a particular hillside on Mull.

I had been in contact with a police sergeant on Mull and passed him the details so that he and his officers could recover the shotgun for us. I had a fairly exact position with several landmarks and was of the view that its recovery would take a fairly short time. Several hours later there was still no telephone call from the sergeant and I was anxious to know that the gun was safely in the hands of the police. In some circumstances, when I am carrying out a particular task myself, I have great patience. The opposite is the case when I am relying on someone else to do a job for me. I would much rather have gone to Mull myself for the damn gun but that was out of the question.

Exasperated, I telephoned the police station at Craignure, where I had last spoken with the sergeant. It was one of the constables who answered and he sounded very excited. I suspected the good news of the recovery of the shotgun but this was not forthcoming. The reason for the constable's jubilation was revealed. He gleefully related that the sergeant had slipped while crossing one of the hill burns and had fallen headlong into a deepish pool of black peaty water, probably destined at some stage in its downhill journey to become an ingredient of Tobermory or Ledaig malt whisky. It was obvious that the constable had a good day out. And the shotgun? 'Oh aye, we got that awright.' It must have been the first occasion when the recovery of a shotgun was the second prize.

Wyllie, Big Daddy and the Third man got the booby prize. All were jailed for their episode on Mull.

•

I had another interesting adventure with Iain MacLeod, slightly earlier in our service than the Mull adventure, in the late 1970s. Iain was in one of the beat cars – aptly named Panda cars because of the white doors contrasting with the dark blue of the vehicle – while I was undertaking a spell of duty as office constable. We were night shift and I had received information that an individual in one of the rougher areas of Perth was poaching deer, and that he just left them in his car boot overnight before selling them on. Since I had no 'wheels' I asked Iain to come back and pick me up about 3.00 am when it was quiet and we'd go and have a quick peek into the boot. We had a large box of car keys in the office, their main purpose being to help people reacquaint themselves with the inside of their car if they had locked themselves out or lost their keys. I selected the most likely handful and awaited Iain's arrival.

When we reached the street concerned, we parked the panda car in front of the suspect's vehicle, quickly hopped out of our vehicle and closed the doors silently. It was a street with tenement buildings on both sides. The type of street where many windows remained lit throughout the night and even at three in the morning it was unusual to drive along the street and not see someone leaning out of a window – even on a third floor – and conversing loudly with someone on the street. It was a street of nocturnal inhabitants, night owls.

We went to the boot of our suspect's car and tried the first key. Unbelievably it opened the boot. We began to lift the boot lid. And the alarm went off. In the quiet of the night it was bedlam: a klaxon that would almost wake the dead. We slammed the boot shut – which thankfully silenced the bloody din – and bolted for the police car. Iain had it started and away in seconds but not before one or two faces began to appear at windows, including our suspect's window.

We retreated to the office and I had barely taken my jacket off when our suspect came marching into the police station. He either must have been sleeping with his clothes on or his pyjamas were under his coat. I went to the counter to ask if I could help him.

'There's just been two of your cops at my car boot. They set the alarm off. What the hell's all this about?'

'Ah, they'll be checking the cars in the street,' I replied. 'At muster the sergeant told the officer who covers that beat to make regular checks of the parked cars as there's been a spate of thefts from unlocked cars in that area. It could be that your boot wasn't properly shut.'

'But they cleared off in their panda car fast,' he countered.

'Yes, that's right,' I responded. 'There was a call for any units in the area to help another officer who was struggling with a man he was arresting.'

'Oh well, that's all right then. I'm glad to see they're doing their job,' was his final word before he left the police station to continue his interrupted sleep.

And the deer in the boot? We don't know to this day; we slammed the boot shut before we could see inside!

•

The advance of modern technology changes all aspects of policing for the better, and the challenge of catching salmon poachers was no exception. The change for us was a piece of equipment that had been used by the Armed Forces for many years. Policing budgets are miniscule compared to those of the military and we, as the poorer relations, have to wait until prices are more acceptable to the public purse. This wonderful and expensive piece of ultra-modern kit went under the name of the image intensifier, now more commonly known as night vision equipment. I had first seen a very advanced form of this equipment demonstrated by the military during a high power NATO conference at Gleneagles Hotel. It allowed us to see landscape on a hillside several miles away in different shades, depending on whether we were looking at woodland, grassland, ploughed land or even cattle grazing the hillside. The Irish song *Forty Shades of Green* came to mind as green was the predominant colour, with a wee bit of purple thrown in. The NATO equipment must also have had a heat-seeking capability. Looking a bit closer we could see rabbits sitting on the grass round the hotel, and I was amazed when they hopped off that their footsteps remained visible three or four hops behind them. Knowing how well insulated rabbits feet are with thick fur I could hardly believe that equipment could be so sensitive as to pick up this tiny amount of heat.

I later used a crude and elementary version of this equipment with a colleague, PC Vince Smith, when we spent a few nights hiding under bushes on a hillside. This was nothing to do with either poaching or wildlife but was in fact during the time in the late 1970s when we in Scotland were under a degree of threat by the Scottish Republican Army. At that time, because of the activities of a relatively few fanatics who, at any cost, wanted Scotland to be separate from the rest of the UK, police were on a raised level of alert. Amongst the threats of this small but determined group was that the oil pipeline running down through Scotland would be blown up. This gave the police additional responsibilities in maintaining regular patrols and checks, especially at the vulnerable points on the oil pipeline where there were valves above ground. Police checks were also regularly made at sites where explosives were stored as they were seen as likely targets to be hit by the Scottish Republican Army in its search for explosives with which it could further its violent aims.

Vince and I were watching one of these explosives stores one night as there had been intelligence that this particular one was to be targeted. None of the barmy brigade arrived but we spent our time watching roe deer, foxes, rabbits, owls, mice and other creatures of the night as they went about their business. It was late autumn and very cold but, between the night-time show and the quaffing of a quarter bottle of whisky we had taken with us, the cold and the time were forgotten as we marvelled at the secret lives of beasties that were unaware of the presence of two pairs of friendly eyes intruding on their privacy. Now having had the experience of night vision equipment I could see another very appropriate use for it.

Shortly after our stake-out in pursuit of the Scottish Republican Army, I borrowed the same piece of kit as we had used and went with another colleague down to the Friarton Hole. Instead of sneaking on to Moncrieffe Island, this time we sneaked down to the Perth side of the river and looked across towards Moncrieffe Island. The bank there was lined with nine or ten poachers, all of whom were casting into the river with their treble hooks and lead and ripping the line through the water with the eventual and inevitable consequence of striking a fish. We recognised most of them and had to pass the single piece of equipment back and forth between us for the purpose of corroboration. We watched all of them at various times foul hooking and landing salmon, and we were astonished how quickly the fish was on the bank. Clearly their line was ultra-heavy duty and none of the sporting 'playing' of the fish that is the real thrill of legitimate angling took place. The fish was hooked and pulled through the water to the bank just as hard as its captor could yank in the line.

We made notes as best as we could in the darkness of what was taking place and by whom, and had a good laugh at our efforts of writing in straight lines once we reached artificial lighting. The cases against those we had observed were almost foolproof since we had witnessed their deeds from start to finish. There was no need to trek on to the island to catch them: we simply knocked on their doors the next day and charged them. They were gutted and we were again accused of using underhand methods to catch them. I suppose most of them thought the whole poaching scene was something of a game and it was fine by them so long as they were only caught occasionally. They were content to be on the winning side but when the tables turned and their substantial financial gains were under threat through technological aids they were pissed off.

Pleased with our success we tried the same technique the following night but what we saw was completely different. The green, almost extra-terrestrial images in our night vision equipment were still there but were wearing balaclavas so that we could not see their faces. They wrongly assumed that if we could not identify them facially they would be safe to continue their nefarious practices. They really hadn't thought through their anti-surveillance measures sensibly. If they had considered whether or not they could identify their brother, father, cousin or uncle from a distance of about 75 metres wearing a balaclava, the answer would have to be in the affirmative. We knew these characters just as well as they would have known their relatives or friends and there was little difficulty in identifying most of them. We knew them by the clothing they wore, by their height and build, by a number of idiosyncrasies that were unique to them, and in one case by the collie dog that regularly accompanied one of them. For a second successive day many of them had a 'chap at the door' that was the forerunner to another court appearance and fine.

The poachers were now on the back foot and their activities were severely disrupted. The situation on Moncrieffe Island became much quieter and any other poacher that we did catch was wearing a balaclava just as an extra precaution.

Chapter 7

The Moon was in the Sky

Good informants are worth their weight in salmon and even tales of housebreaking and drunk driving can bring a smile to the face of a busy desk sergeant.

In early 1981 I was moved to work in the Criminal Investigation Department (CID) as a detective constable. Besides Mr X and Big Daddy I had developed a number of other very good informants. As I alluded to earlier, informants are of little value unless they have a good working knowledge of who is committing what crime. The only way they can have this knowledge is to be on the 'inside'. In other words to be involved in crime themselves or to be a close confidante of criminals, normally by being a family member.

Receiving information about where and when a crime is going to take place and by whom it is to be committed is a huge advantage and makes the detection of crime relatively easy. Even information after the fact is a real bonus, especially if the informant can give details leading to the recovery of stolen property or other items that could link the suspects to the crime. In most cases with intelligence, events are allowed to run their course and the criminals are caught by the police. Occasionally, where there is intelligence that a crime is about to be committed which is likely to pose a real threat to the public, and there is little opportunity of arresting the suspects before the stage that they come into contact with the public, the police may warn the suspects off rather than risk public safety.

When I dealt with informants I managed them myself. Nowadays informants must be registered and can only be 'handled' by police officers specially trained in informant handling. Since there are many risks in dealing with informants, both to the integrity of the officer and the integrity of any subsequent case, this is a sensible route to take. Most of my informants were linked in some way to poaching. The information they passed to me demonstrates how poaching, and indeed wildlife crime as we shall see later, is very much linked to other forms of crime.

The first example of good information originating from poachers on *crime* rather than poaching concerned two men (one of whom was Wyllie, the telephone box man) who were carrying out regular break-ins to houses and targeting money, jewellery and electrical goods. My informant – one I had just recently co-opted to give me information and who appears as a subject of one of the earlier incidents – called me one evening and told me that Wyllie and his pal were intending to break into a house in a rural location that night. They would watch the house with binoculars to ensure that the occupants had left, then break in when they knew the house was empty. I discussed the information with other more senior members of CID and, after contacting the householders to collude with them in the sting, four of us from CID plus a dog handler drove into the householders' garage in an old van. We had been told in advance that we could access the house via the garage, which we did. We had a quick cup of tea with the occupants while we discussed the plan, and they overtly drove away from the house in their car to await our instructions as to when they could return.

Before long two figures appeared in the garden of the house and began to try a series of keys in the lock. We sat quietly inside and I remember marvelling at the dog for refraining from either barking or growling. Having failed with the keys, the men then tried to force a couple of the double-glazed windows, but failed again. I was impressed with the double glazing and on reflection I have attended very few housebreakings where double-glazed windows had been successfully violated unless the glass had been smashed. At one point a car came along the road and the two abandoned their efforts at trying to join us inside the house and hid among the trees and bushes in the garden until the coast was again clear. Eventually they smashed a glass panel in the door leading directly into the kitchen, reached in, unlocked the door and they were in.

I vividly remember in the stramash to arrest them, the German shepherd dog jumping about among us. I knew police dogs were well trained but I wasn't in the least convinced that they could tell the difference between a housebreaker and a police officer in plain clothes. I was of the view that my arse was as likely to get bitten as that of either Wyllie or his criminal friend. I was pleased that no police officer was bitten by the dog but I can't say the same for the two housebreakers.

There were two amusing incidents following the arrest of Wyllie & Co. The detective chief superintendent at Police Headquarters in Dundee had to be updated by telephone every morning by the Divisional Crime Officers, who were of detective chief inspector rank. The detective chief superintendent, Jim Cameron, was known for his pedantic attention to detail and the detective chief inspector, Alf Harding, had ensured that he was aware of every aspect of the case before the morning telephone call. He was subjected to twenty questions and would have been a credit to being questioned on a specialist crime subject by Magnus Magnusson on Mastermind.

Until the last question. 'What was the name of the dog?'

So far as the trial was concerned, I melted into the background. I had been on the job but was not included on the list of witnesses to give evidence as I did not want to be put in the awkward situation in court of being asked the identity of the informant. No-one apart from me knew the informant's identity so there was no risk that he could be identified during the trial and therefore be placed in a position of real threat. I followed the course of the trial from the public benches.

During the trial (despite being caught in the act many people still waste the court's time pleading not guilty) the defence QC was questioning one of the detective officers involved, DC Roy Sommerville, as to how he could identify the two accused while they were still in the garden, in the dark. 'That was easy,' said the officer, 'there was a moon.' This was perfectly correct and each of the men was recognised by all of us long before they broke into the house. The QC wanted a bit more detail, by establishing where the moon was in relation to us and to the men in the garden. Unfortunately he phrased his question rather badly by asking, 'Officer, can you please explain to the court where the moon was.' The answer, 'In the sky,' quickly put paid to that line of questioning and the QC sat down.

The second example of information from a poacher related to a case involving terrorism. Even yet the informant would be at risk if I divulge too many details but because of his information, six men were jailed for a total of 53 years. The men had sympathies towards the Ulster Defence Association (UDA) in Northern Ireland and were collecting weapons and making ammunition which they intended to transport over the Irish Sea. This was one of the most interesting cases of my career, particularly as I was one of the team allocated to interrogate the suspects.

Even with a well-organised gang there were incidents that seemed straight out of Monty Python. When the ammunition they were making was tested it was discovered that the gunpowder with which they were filling the bullet cases was very crudely measured, if indeed measured at all. Some of the bullets when fired would just have fallen out of the end of the barrel, while others had enough powder to go twice round the world. Even the means of obtaining their weaponry sometimes left a lot to be desired. One of the accused had been working on Mull on a road building scheme. He had somehow managed to get his hands on explosives used in blowing up some of the rocky areas through which the road had to pass. No doubt pleased with his booty he stuffed the explosives down his wellies for the duration of his journey to Oban courtesy of Caledonian MacBrayne. Had the other passengers been aware of this he may never have survived to come to court.

•

After a few years as detective constable I was promoted to sergeant in 1985. As detective constable I had dealt with much more serious or complicated crimes than would be dealt with by uniformed officers. Additional training in the form of a variety of detective officers' courses are carried out at the Scottish Police College to equip an officer to deal efficiently with this more complex work. There is also much more freedom in CID work in that detective officers are not getting calls to attend ongoing incidents that need urgent attention, such as breaches of the peace, ongoing assaults and road traffic accidents. This freedom from all but the most serious of response calls allows detective officers to plan ahead, make appointments to see witnesses, continue enquiries outside the force boundaries if need be, and concentrate on putting together evidence to convict someone of a serious, or indeed a series of serious crimes.

I missed the 'hands-on' aspect of my work, which is generally either lessened or indeed lost with each progressive rank. The only exception to this is the rank of detective sergeant, where as well as having a supervisory role, a detective sergeant always investigates his or her fair share of cases. Many popular crime writers have as their main character a detective inspector, who in the book or series spends the best part of each day out investigating some serious crime or other. This just doesn't happen in the real world of crime-fighting. Worse, the investigations are carried out by the fictional detective inspector on his own, and apparently without the noting of any statements. Real detective inspectors, for ninety-nine percent of their time, are involved in supervision, directing, planning, management, policy, decision-making, crime statistics and meetings, all of which makes a very dull story! A detective sergeant as the main character would be much more in keeping with realism.

I was now in a role, along with another sergeant, of running a shift of about sixteen constables. I enjoyed passing on my knowledge of crime investigation to the shift but missed having cases of my own. I managed to get out and about with my shift half of the time, since the other shift sergeant and I shared the office role equally – one month as office sergeant and the next month out supervising the shift. The office duties included being responsible for people who were arrested, checking them through the charge bar, and their welfare while they were with us as 'non-paying guests' in the cells. A quiet eight-hour shift might result in a handful of folk locked up, while a busy shift could result in excess of twenty. Not bad for twelve cells!

I was well practised in booking prisoners through the charge bar, having carried out this duty periodically while I was a constable and an acting sergeant. It was the fastest eight hour shift in any of the different duties I have had within the police service, before or since.

The charge bar staff is at everyone's beck and call – prisoners, advice, car keys, found property, productions, complaints, even to release folk stuck in the police station lift. There was never a dull moment and many surprises, some welcome and others definitely not so.

It was one of the latter that I encountered one late shift in the Spring. The bell at the back door rang, which meant that officers were waiting outside with a prisoner to be booked through the charge bar for some crime or offence. We never knew till the prisoner arrived in front of us why he or she had been arrested. It could be anything from drunk and incapable or shoplifting to murder or rape. In this case it was none of these: it was driving with blood alcohol over the limit. The accused was none other than Mr X.

I booked Mr X through the charge bar, taking and labelling his property and ensuring that he was fully aware of why he had been arrested and of his rights as a prisoner. He was pleasant but clearly very concerned about his predicament, and asked if he could see me privately. I assured him that he could, but the traffic officers who had arrested him had various procedures to go through, first of all in relation to taking samples of breath. Mr X understood the formalities but asked that I come through to the cells and see him as soon as the traffic officers were finished. The procedures didn't take too long, probably as the traffic officers had a very compliant subject. Mr X had already failed the roadside breath test and had now failed the breath test on the more technical equipment in the office.

I spoke with him in the cells and it soon became clear that the drink driving charge was not his main concern. He asked first of all what would happen to his car, though I sensed he knew the answer before he asked. In the case of drunk drivers or other persons whose cars are taken by the police as a temporary measure, the property is taken from the vehicle and logged, so that there can be no allegation that anything has gone missing, and so that there is a signature at the end of the process for everything handed back. 'Oh bloody hell,' he said, 'I've been out at the fishing and I've six salmon in the boot.' I knew that the term 'fishing' was an attempt to make the activity sound legitimate. I knew that the traffic officers would find the fish during their listing of items in the car and ask my advice, knowing my reputation with poachers. I knew that my advice would have to be to contact the water bailiffs and to have them examine the fish. I knew that the bailiffs would find the tell-tale double marks of a large treble hook somewhere on the body of the fish, and an absence of hook marks in the mouth. I also knew that, with the record Mr X had, this could be more serious that drink driving. He was also well aware of that, hence his state of panic.

It was my call and mine alone. I couldn't ask a senior officer as that would have put him on the spot. It would also have blown my informant's cover, which is something that police officers with good informants don't do. Mr X was a good informant and my decision was based on future benefit to the public rather than out of sympathy to Mr X, though there is no doubt that the first factor was complemented by the second.

I had control of the car keys and knew that before too long the traffic officers would be asking for them so that they could list the items in Mr X's car. The decision had been made and within minutes the salmon had been quietly transferred from his car to mine. I replaced the keys then called on Garry Gibb, the superintendent of the Tay District Salmon Fisheries Board and took the salmon to his door, telling him the wee porky that we had recovered the salmon but no-one had been traced for catching them. He emptied the salmon out and they were six bars of silver, fresh run from the sea. We both marvelled at the condition of the salmon. Garry then said, 'Look, you and your shift do a great job in catching a lot of poachers, just take the salmon and divide them up with your officers. They're lovely fish and if you don't take them they'll just sit in our freezer.' Kind offer though this was it was the last thing I wanted to hear. Even though I was acting in the public interest by keeping my informant on board and increasing dramatically the favours that he owed me by way of good information, even though my mouth was watering at the thought of lovely salmon steaks, these were the last six salmon that I wanted. I was desperate to get rid of the fish in a manner that was semi-legitimate, but the fisheries superintendent was equally keen that I and my officers benefit from their recovery.

What a nightmare. We debated back and forth about the salmon and I tried to tell him, untruthfully, that we all still had some salmon from a previous recovery of fish at the side of the River Tay when the culprits had run off. He was insistent that we use these fish up as they could be wasted, when I was saved by the bell. My radio was at almost full volume and the control room operator was asking for anyone available to attend at a fight within one of the Perth pubs. That was my chance and I fled, shouting profuse thanks as I ran down Garry Gibb's path, and that we would get some salmon another time. The pub fight was a saviour. In fact I would willingly have taken on a grizzly bear at that point, especially if I could have placated it with six fresh run salmon.

I never regretted my decision to make Mr X's salmon vanish. So far as a quality informant is concerned it was a good investment and the beneficiary of my doorstep battle to hand over the salmon was the general public. The enigma of why I wouldn't accept six salmon in prime condition for my shift is probably still a matter of concern for the fisheries superintendent.

Chapter 8

A Case of Slack Water

All in a day's work: an intriguing poaching scenario on the banks of the Tay and a drug dealing postmistress in the scenic Highlands.

I was back in CID as detective sergeant when I had a call at home one day from Mr X. He had reliable information concerning four men who would be going out poaching that night to the River Tay at a part east of Perth near the hamlet of Kinfauns. The ringleader would be one of the pair we had caught operating the cage at the Horseshoe Falls on the River Almond. Mr X gave me the names for the other three, who were all well known to me as poachers, as well as being willing participants in other fields of crime when they thought there would be some pecuniary advantage. The information was that the men would be leaving a particular address in a housing scheme in Perth at 3.00 am, and that they would be using a grey Datsun (now Nissan) car. I was given the registration number of the car, which always makes success a bit more viable. So far the information was good, and it was to get better.

The men would drive down the A90 Perth to Dundee road and park off the road where there is access to the Perth – Dundee railway line. The car would be left there and the men would cross the railway line and make their way to the river bank, where they had a dinghy and a net hidden. They would only be there about an hour before heading back home.

Two complications followed. Firstly the men would be wearing balaclavas so would not be recognisable. I thought I could cope with this problem since I knew in advance who the men were. The second complication was that they would leave everything hidden at the side of the river and return to collect their fish about midday. That way, if they were stopped by the police on their return to Perth during the night – as they might well have been – there would be no incriminating evidence in the car. They would take their chance on being stopped during the day but (a) this would be less likely as the police were liable to be tied up with other matters, and (b) only one person would make the run, so on aggregate the fine would be lower and all could pay a share of it. This was not an insurmountable problem and was a tactic of salmon poachers of which we were well aware.

One aspect of the information puzzled me. I didn't know why the time they were leaving the house could be predicted so precisely, and why the poachers would only remain at the riverside for about an hour. It seemed a lot of effort to go to for an hour's work. The reason, once I had been enlightened, was logical. It gave me further evidence that the poachers were tuned into the forces of nature and that this knowledge was essential if they wanted to successfully catch salmon.

I learned from Mr X that twice a day in a tidal river there is a period referred to as 'slack water.' This is a period of about half an hour at each high tide when the force of the water coming down the river is counterbalanced by the pressure of the tide coming up the river, and results in the flow of the river being stopped. When a gill net is put across a river one end is fastened to the bank while the rest of the net is paid out from the dinghy until all of the net is in the water. The floats fastened to the top of the net keep it on the surface and the weights fastened to the bottom ensure that it hangs down into the water like a curtain. Slack water is an ideal time to put the net across the river as it will hang motionless, neither being swept downstream nor upstream. Likewise the dinghy will just sit steadily in the river without any controlling effort by its passenger. If the operators have timed their venture correctly there will be little or no movement of either the net or the dinghy, apart from that caused by the frantic struggles of the salmon swimming upstream that were unlucky enough to have been entangled by being in the wrong place at the wrong time. When the dingy starts to drift downstream, its occupant knows that slack water has passed and it is time for his counterpart on the bank to start to haul in the net.

The information from Mr X was that 4.00 am was high tide,

therefore the poachers would leave about an hour earlier, giving them sufficient time to reach their spot on the river and get organised to catch slack water.

I was due to start at 10.00 pm so I decided to carry out some reconnaissance in the late afternoon to see how best to tackle this job. I came on duty early, at 3.00 pm, not wanting to chance an earlier visit to the Tay at Kinfauns as there was a good chance that the motley crew would have fish to pick up that day around noon. I didn't want to spoil the operation by being seen on my recce.

I parked at a farm steading some distance away, having told the farmer what I was up to and trusting him to keep the information quiet. It was a Spring day and as I crossed the railway line to the area of scrub and trees between that point and the river, I was treated to a lovely chorus of birdsong from its many small feathered inhabitants. Though this avian orchestra would have had many more players at first light, I could hear the easiest of the birds to identify, the chiffchaff, pronouncing its name loudly and clearly, *chiff chaff, chiff chaff, chiff chaff*.

The whitethroat was the next to be spotted since it is one of the few warbler species to sit on top of a bush and sing rather than skulk in the bushes. It chattered away its creaky, grating song, while in the background I heard another of the warblers in full flow. To my shame I'm never sure which of the warblers I am listening to. I think this one was a willow warbler. It always reminds me of a motor bike engine that is not running too smoothly (in a much higher pitch of course). The engine is just about to give up, then it has a new lease of life until the next piece of dirt hits the carburettor and it begins to splutter again. My simile does the bird an injustice as it's really a lovely song and many times on a night shift I have parked the police car in an area I know to be full of these birds, switched off the engine, and marvelled that many of them have flown from Africa to regale us with their sweet music.

In more recent times I had my grandson, Sam, out with me in the woods one day. He was either four or five at the time and I was trying to teach him to recognise bird song. We listened to several birds on our walk, starting with a blackbird, then a mistle thrush, a chiffchaff, a wren and a robin. He was interested to begin with but I had probably overdone his first nature study lesson and he was becoming bored. This fact was confirmed when I asked him if he could tell me the name of the bird singing on top of a young sitka spruce tree beside us. His reply? 'It's another bloody chiffchaff.' Spot on. Bloody good answer Sam!

Back at the River Tay, there was a clearing of several yards between the edge of the scrubland and the river. At one point there was a clump of bushes thick enough to give cover and situated almost beside the river. If I placed someone in the middle of these bushes they would have a good view of what was happening upstream and downstream. I checked first that this was not the hiding place for the poachers' dinghy and net before settling on this as the best available observation point.

On the return journey to my car I almost stood on a young roe deer fawn hiding in the undergrowth. I saw its mottled body just at the last minute and changed my route by a few degrees so as not to disturb it. It was well camouflaged and relying totally on its innate instinct to lie absolutely still unless flight became the better option. As roe fawns are born in May it was probably just a few days old and no doubt had a sibling lying close by, aware of my presence and hoping that the danger of a predatory human would pass quickly. This was my first encounter with a roe fawn. Even yet I have only found one other roe fawn and one red deer calf at that vulnerable stage when they rely on camouflage more than the speed that they will eventually develop.

When I came back to the police station I made contact with the water bailiffs from the Tay District Salmon Fisheries Board and arranged to have the services of two of them. This was agreed and a 2.00 am meeting at Perth Police Station was arranged. A meeting at two in the morning would seem strange to most people, but water bailiffs, like police officers, are used to working round the clock. Criminals respect neither office hours nor weekends, in fact weekends and night-time are often their most productive periods. I intended to remain on duty for the operation, but needed the help of a police officer from the night shift before the trap could be set.

After the 2.00 am briefing, I sent the two water bailiffs, complete with a borrowed police radio, to hide in the clump of bushes I had identified at the riverside. Their remit was simply to wait, watch and report, nothing more. I told them that the poachers would be wearing balaclavas, which was nothing new either to me or to them, and assured them if they were in their place of concealment by 2.45 am they would not have long to wait.

At the allotted time, the night shift police officer who had volunteered to help took his own car and parked near to the target car, which was sitting outside the address given to me by Mr X. Like the water bailiffs, his task was to wait, watch and report. While we had been making our plans for a successful night's work, the men in the house were probably doing the same. It was not possible for both of us to have the result we wanted. As the dawn of the next morning was breaking one group would be disappointed.

Just before 3.00 am, I parked at the farm I had used in the afternoon and walked up the hill for about quarter of a mile so that I had a vantage point overlooking the spot identified by Mr X as the parking spot for the poachers' car. The watchers were in position. We just needed the participants to make their move.

•

Any police officer who has been involved in surveillance, or involved in simply waiting at a given point in anticipation of a crime taking place, knows that in at least half of the instances the long wait is in vain. The rest of the time, a long period watching and waiting may have some form of moderate success and just once in a while everything comes together exactly as planned. I was shortly to move to the drug squad, where much of the work involved surveillance. As examples of how differently things work out, one operation meant surveillance on a ship in Dundee Harbour for two weeks of 12 hour shifts in the expectation that someone was to come to the ship to collect three kilos of heroin that was on board. No-one arrived and we had to allow the ship to sail to its next destination, Rotterdam, where the latest intelligence indicated the transfer would take place.

At the other end of the spectrum, we had received information that a particular vehicle was en route to Dundee from Manchester with a cargo of 5 kilos of cannabis resin. A colleague and I parked near the Tayside boundary at Dunblane to watch for the car on the A9. I had reversed the car into a good spot to watch the road and switched the engine off. The car that we were waiting for was the third one to come along the road. We arrested the person in the car, recovered the cannabis and went on, with me driving the car from Manchester that the dealers were expecting to see, to make the connection in Dundee. We arrested four dealers and recovered a carrier bag with £10,000. If only it worked out like that all the time.

•

'Stand by, stand by,' came the call from the officer watching the poachers' car. 'That's five people coming from the target close and getting into the target car. One is out of the car again, he's walked round behind it. He's pulled up one of the metal drain covers at the side of the road and has put it in the boot.' Five people were one more than we were expecting but so far so good. 'That's an off, off now, down the hill. Brake lights showing at the roundabout and the car has taken the second exit, heading in your direction.'

I updated the two water bailiffs of the position using the UHF channel. (The first message had been passed to me on the VHF channel, which the bailiffs couldn't hear). Less than ten minutes later I saw headlights appearing from the direction of Perth. The car slowed down, turned about on the road and headed back to the parking spot. My radio message to the bailiffs was, 'Stand by, stand by, that's the target car with us and parked up. Occupants leaving the car and walking along the railway line in the direction of Perth. Now lost to my view and should be with you shortly.' I was happy at this as I had walked along the railway line earlier and it took me towards a natural crossing point from the railway line into the area of scrub and trees that led towards the river.

'That's five men wearing balaclavas approaching the river. They're pulling out a baker's board from under a bush. The baker's board has a net on it. They're back into the bush. It's a dinghy this time. They're coming towards the river.' The bailiff's report was welcome news and things were going exactly to plan. I had previously spoken with the night shift traffic crew and had told them of the information and the plan. I asked that they be available about 4.00 am to pull the poachers' car on its way back to Perth. I updated them as to the current stage of the operation and said I would keep them informed so that they could get into position to stop the vehicle once that was required.

Once more the bailiffs were on the radio. 'That's the net getting tied to the bank. They've tied something to the bottom of this end of the net. It looks like a metal drain cover.' So that's what they wanted it for – an anchor next to the bank on the bottom edge of the net to keep it taut. 'That's one of them now rowing out into the river with the net. Looks like a waiting game now for half an hour.'

It's interesting when something happens, like the taking of the drain cover, that's not in the game plan. Some statutes, such as poaching game or throwing away litter, don't have a power of arrest, and often this limits the action that police can take to obtain evidence sufficient to charge the person with the offence. It is always circumspect not to simply look at an offence in isolation but to take a more rounded view of all the evidence available. Occasionally, tucked away amongst the strands of evidence, lies a Common Law offence. Common Law offences range from breach of the peace to murder and include most crimes of dishonesty. All have an automatic power of arrest attached. In this case, had there not been a power of arrest for salmon poaching, the five men could have been arrested for the theft of a metal drain cover. When investigating crimes and offences it is always worth training the mind to think laterally.

'That's the net getting pulled in,' reported the bailiffs. 'They've certainly caught some salmon. They're being knocked on the head. The net's getting put on the baker's board again. That's now everything including the salmon back under the bush again and the targets are heading back towards the car.'

I was immediately in touch with the traffic crew, asking them to get into position to stop the car and to arrest the five occupants. The poachers returned to the car and were making back towards Perth a remarkably short time after leaving the river bank. I left the poachers to the traffic department and went to meet the bailiffs and help with the salmon and the fishing tackle. It had not been a great night for the poachers, only having caught eleven salmon, but being Spring fish, they would have commanded a good price.

Once we were back to Perth I went through to the cells along with the police officer who had kept watch for their car leaving the house at the start of the operation. The poachers were adamant they had done nothing against the law. They admitted they had been out looking for a place that they could take salmon on a future occasion, which accounted for their jeans being wet up to the knees, 'but Mr Stewart, ask the traffic boys. Our car was clean when they searched it. We've done nothin. Honest.'

•

My next three and a half years of policing was as detective sergeant in the drug squad, working from Headquarters in Dundee, with a remit covering the whole of Tayside. It was a job I had never set sights on but it turned out to be a challenging and enjoyable role, and one I could thoroughly recommend to any police officer. I went to Dundee not knowing my way around the streets, not knowing many of the officers who work in Dundee, knowing very few of those serving in the drug squad, and as detective sergeant in charge of detective officers who knew far more about combating drug dealers than I did. Everyone on the squad was supportive, knowing I would take some months to find my feet, and I couldn't have worked with a better bunch. The hours were exceptionally long but it gave me real satisfaction to remove some of the peddlers of misery and death from our streets.

Many of our days stand out in my memory, mostly for decent recoveries of drugs or for the capture of one of the bigger fish in the drug dealing world. One particular day in rural Perthshire stands out because it was initially unusual, but then extremely funny. Our main objective that day was to obtain evidence against the then postmistress at Kinloch Rannoch, which of all the villages in the whole of Tayside is probably the most remote. In the late 1980s it was one of the last places I would have expected to find drug users, far less a drug-dealing postmistress.

The information was that when many of the unemployed young

people from the village and surrounding area came to cash their Giro cheque, they could have part payment in cannabis resin. Our intention was to get hold of some of the more likely looking candidates after they left the shop and establish if they had obtained any under-the-counter goods in the post office rather than what would be traditionally obtained in that outwardly respectable store. If we thought that it was difficult to park our vehicles in strategic and covert positions in Dundee, Perth or Arbroath it was a completely new experience in Kinloch Rannoch. Everyone knew everyone else and a car sitting for an extensive period in the same place drew inquisitive, and sometimes knowing, attention. We might as well have been in marked police cars.

Nonetheless we were tuned in to the people we were looking for and by about midday we had stopped several people who had bought cannabis resin, recovered the drugs and obtained statements as to where and from whom they bought it. We had earlier alerted the Post Office Investigation Branch to our activities and they joined us in the early part of the afternoon. The outcome of the day was that the post-mistress was charged with supplying and being concerned in the supply of cannabis resin. At the conclusion of the post office investigations she was also charged with embezzlement, there being a large sum of money that she could not account for. It was an interesting day out in the country.

Our day wasn't finished and we decided, since we were in Highland Perthshire, to pay a visit to a hotel in Pitlochry where it was known that drug dealers plied their trade. As it happened, more cannabis resin and amphetamine had been recovered in Pitlochry in the previous three months than in the rest of Tayside put together. In the late afternoon we parked up near to the hotel and six of us walked briskly in to the public bar. The main drug dealers and some of their underlings were sitting at a table and we expected a flurry of activity from them as we approached, ditching their drugs on to the floor so that we could not make the link between the drugs and the person or people who dropped them. Not a movement, in fact they turned and grinned at us. It was a bizarre situation

We surrounded the group, announced who we were, and began to search them for drugs, recovering drugs of varying types and quantities on most of them. We were still amazed that they had just sat still, grinning like Cheshire cats as we surrounded them. The reason, we soon learned, was that they were expecting a visiting darts team to play them in some competition or other and they mistakenly took us for their opponents.

•

Shortly after this I was back in Pitlochry again, this time running a very small incident room during an investigation into the death of a newly-born baby that had been found near the roadside north of Dunkeld. When serious incidents like this occurred the drug squad was sometimes utilised either to carry out enquiries into the incident or to staff the various posts within an incident room. In this case, instead of an incident room with a staff of about twenty working in shifts, the complete staffing amounted to me as detective sergeant acting as office manager, statement reader and action allocator, and a policewoman acting as indexer and receiver.

As I arrived one morning I met two uniformed officers going out of the office. They told me that during the night a call had come in from the parent of one of two boys who had been playing in a wood. The boys had earlier found a large biscuit tin concealed in a gully that bisected the wood and the general opinion was that it contained a large amount of cannabis resin, probably somewhere between two and three kilos. I stopped them in their tracks and said that as there was a suspect staying in a caravan in the wood, they couldn't go to the wood to recover the tin in their uniforms as they would be as well with flashing blue lights on their heads. I would contact Headquarters and have drug squad officers attend.

An hour or so later two drugs squad officers attended and I briefed them. I wanted them to go to the tin, recover the contents without damage to fingerprint evidence that may be on the packaging (DNA wasn't in such common usage at that time), replace the contents with stones, and let me know by radio when that was done. They were then to hide nearby and I told them I didn't think they would have to wait too long for some action. I then contacted a local gamekeeper, advised him of what had been found, and told him how he could be a tremendous help to the enquiry. He appeared within a very short time for his briefing at Pitlochry Police Station.

Before long, the officers contacted me by radio and told me they had recovered three kilos of cannabis resin from the tin and had replaced the cannabis with some stones. They were now well hidden in a spot not too far from the tin. I told them to stand by as we were about to coerce the suspect to collect his tin.

The gamekeeper, in his tweeds and deer-stalker hat, called at the caravan and knocked on the door. It was answered by our suspect and the conversation went along the following lines.

'Well Moses, [that really was his name] how are things today?'

'Not bad Charlie. I'm just living quietly.'

'Have you seen any foxes about the wood here? There's normally a litter about this time of year.'

'No Charlie, I've never seen anything at all.'

'Och well I just thought I would pop in and ask. I'm getting half a dozen of the lads together later this morning. We'll give the wood a good scour, though I think the den will be somewhere in the gully. The vixen's probably cleaned out one of the bigger rabbit holes and cubbed there. If she's there I'm sure we'll find her. We'll have the terriers so if you hear any bangs you'll know what it is.'

'OK, thanks Charlie. It's fine that you've let me know.'

Within a very short time of the gamekeeper leaving the caravan I had a radio message from the drug squad officers in the wood that the suspect had just been to the gully to collect the biscuit tin and had been arrested. For good measure he had another twenty quarter-ounce deals of cannabis in his pocket. Good old Charlie.

•

In 1993 I was promoted to inspector. In addition to that role I was also asked if I would like to be the Force Wildlife Liaison Officer and have overall charge of any matters relating to wildlife crime through the Force area. It would be a completely different type of wildlife from those with whom I had been accustomed in drug squad and CID work. I relished the challenge and was keen to get started.

PART II

FRUSTRATING TIMES

'You mean you brought me oot here because somebody shot a KITE?'

CHAPTER 9

Modern Wildlife Crime Detection

A chronology of development in wildlife crime investigation from 1993 to 2007 which sets out the changing role of the police and supporting agencies.

Wildlife crime investigation has seen a sea change since 1993 involving developments in staffing, training and resources that continue to the present time. It's worth pausing for a moment to reflect on these changes since many of them inform the wide range of cases described in the following chapters.

Investigating crimes against wildlife has been the responsibility of the police since at least the beginning of the twentieth century. Much legislation through the years devolves powers to the police and to the police only. Going as far back as the Protection of Animals (Scotland) Act 1912 (which includes offences committed against captive wild animals as well as domesticated animals), powers to enter land, to search and to arrest have been given to a police constable. Similarly in the Protection of Birds Act 1954 (now repealed), the Wildlife and Countryside Act 1981, the Wild Mammals Protection Act 1996 and even more modern wildlife legislation, the police have a variety of powers which they alone can use. This contrasts with some, though not all, of the poaching legislation where I have already described how power is divested to landowners for offences committed on private land.

Until the mid 1990s, the response of the police service in dealing with wildlife crime and animal welfare was disappointing, indeed almost non-existent. The police were put to shame by charities such as the Scottish Society for the Prevention of Cruelty to Animals (SSPCA), the Royal Society for the Prevention of Cruelty to Animals (RSPCA) and the Royal Society for the Protection of Birds (RSPB). Calls from the public reporting offences were being made to these charitable organisations, the officials of which were responding admirably in the absence of any powers. Scottish SPCA can report cases to the Crown and make a tremendously good job of this considering that until 2006, under the Animal Health and Welfare (Scotland) Act, they did not have any statutory power to enter land or premises. They naturally cannot detain or arrest suspects. Even with the increased powers given to inspectors of the Scottish SPCA under the 2006 Act the fact remains they are a charity dedicated to improving the welfare of animals and are not a police force nor do they seek this role. RSPCA, the animal welfare organisation covering England and Wales, hire solicitors and take their own prosecutions, something that cannot happen in Scottish courts. RSPB in England and Wales, until the latter part of the twentieth century, also carried out investigations into bird crime and prosecuted cases in court. They still retain this capability but, in practice, all cases are now reported by the police to the Crown Prosecution Service (CPS) and it is they who take the cases to court. The CPS solicitors are the public prosecutors in England and Wales while all prosecutions in Scotland are at the instance of the procurator fiscal.

Officials of RSPB have no powers whatsoever in Scotland but their investigations staff are a valued and essential part of many police investigations into bird-related or even some animal-related offences. Personally, I do not think that the RSPB investigations staff of three in Scotland should be termed 'investigations officers'. This tends to convey to the public that they carry out investigations into bird crime and therefore crimes committed against birds should be reported directly to the RSPB. I have worked hard in the Tayside area to dispel this myth as time can be wasted by a person waiting to report a crime to an agency that works 9 to 5, Monday to Friday. In addition, the first contact with the person giving information is invaluable. RSPB will obtain details of the alleged crime and then pass these to the police, but they may not obtain sufficient information or question a witness as might a police officer. Some of these calls are anonymous and if as much detail as possible is not gleaned at the time the opportunity is lost and the person cannot be contacted again to firm up on further questions. I would much rather RSPB changed their role title to 'Investigation Support Officers' and make this widely known. This has a precedent in TRAFFIC, the wing of the Worldwide Fund for Nature (WWF) that has the role of monitoring illegal international traffic of wildlife. They do not purport to be investigators but act *in support* of investigators, namely the police and HM Revenue and Customs.

Having questioned the role title, I fully appreciate the value of the work done by RSPB investigations officers, whose experience is utilised regularly by the police. It is not so many years ago since many of the initial stages of bird-related investigations would indeed be carried out by RSPB. At the point when a culprit needed to be arrested the RSPB staff would call at the nearest police station hoping to find a police constable who they could convince, cajole and coerce to come with them, under their direction and guidance, to carry out the rest of the investigation in a manner that would hopefully gather sufficient evidence to convict the culprit. RSPB led the field, the police followed.

In 1981 the then Chief Superintendent Terry Rands of Essex Police, in response to ACPO (Association of Chief Police officers, England & Wales) acknowledgement of a rising problem of wildlife crime became the first UK police wildlife liaison officer. In 1991 – by then assistant chief constable – Mr Rands recognised the increase in his personal involvement and devised a network of police officers carrying out wildlife liaison work in addition to their normal duties. The scheme started with twenty three officers and became a model for other forces, the innovative lead quickly being followed. In Scotland, Grampian Police took the lead by appointing the first police wildlife liaison officer in 1991. Other forces in Scotland followed, with Dumfries and Galloway Constabulary and Tayside Police being next. By the late 1990s all forces in Scotland, and indeed in the UK, had a part-time wildlife crime officer. Several forces in England appreciated the true value of this role and had by this time appointed a police officer in the role full-time. The police had got their act together at last and were prepared to shoulder the responsibility for enforcing wildlife and animal-related law.

Having by 1993 served for twenty seven years as constable and sergeant and now an inspector, my experience was such that I could not blame the Scottish Police Service for dallying over issues relating to animal welfare. The Scottish SPCA was already doing a reasonably good job, even with their hands tied behind their back because of their absence of powers. Policing was becoming more and more stretched, with an increase in specialist departments to deal more effectively with crimes in which additional policing expertise is required to get satisfactory results. Examples include drug crime, armed response units, community policing, child protection, internet crime, specialist crime-reduction advice and staffing major incident rooms. In addition there was the policing of an ever-increasing number of events that had the potential to host huge crowds with the associated risks. Examples in my home force alone are T in the Park and major international conferences at Gleneagles Hotel, the most recent being the G8 summit in 2005. All of these are a drain on general day-to-day policing so it is little wonder that crime being committed against animals, birds, insects or molluscs comes well down the scale of importance for supervisory police officers endeavouring to stretch ever-dwindling resources.

The Scottish Police Service, as public servants, responds to public demand. Times are changing and the public are very much aware of and very much alarmed by the rate of degradation of the environment. Naturally this includes the threat to our wildlife. Ordinary people fear the loss of wildlife that they take for granted. Many British animals – using this in the widest sense of the definition – are becoming scarce or even endangered. Some, such as the freshwater pearl mussel and wildcat, could face extinction and extinction is forever. No going back. Though all of the reasons for the decrease in some species don't necessarily relate to crime, crime in some cases can be a factor – even the main factor. The prevention and investigation of crime are core police functions. The circle was completed therefore, and the Scottish Police Service reacted to public demand and public concern with the advent of the police wildlife liaison officer.

It is a huge advantage to an investigation to have a range of expertise available. In a joint police investigation with, for instance Scottish

SPCA, their inspectors have animal handling skills and in some cases excellent animal identification skills and a first class knowledge of animal welfare needs. It is unsurprising that their knowledge of animal welfare-related legislation surpasses that of most police officers. SSPCA officers can specialise in that narrow field. As will be seen in further chapters, other organisations have a very important role to play in support of police investigations, investigations that would be much less effective without their assistance and advice.

On 20 July 1993, the date I was promoted to inspector, I was also appointed as the force Wildlife Liaison Officer. It was an appointment that gave me a supervisory role over a sergeant and two constables in relation to wildlife crime issues. All four of us carried out these duties as part of our day-to-day policing. I soon discovered that to do the job properly, the demands on our time exceeded our current operational capability. There were plenty of police officers willing to volunteer, so I increased the number of wildlife officers to ten, including myself. This gave Tayside the highest number of wildlife liaison officers of the eight police forces in Scotland. In England and Wales the number of full-time wildlife liaison officers was slowly increasing, as was the number of part-time wildlife liaison officers within many forces.

Tayside was the first police force in Scotland to go a stage further. I had been due to retire in May 1996, having completed over thirty one years service. At that time I was inspector in charge of the Crieff and Kinross Sections. I was thoroughly enjoying the responsibility of being in charge of two sections – a doubling-up of responsibilities which was forced on the police after the flattening of the rank structure in the wake of the Sheehy report on police management. Even without the wildlife duties I had more than enough work to fill my day but I revelled in being busy. I worked on in this triple challenge until July 1997, when, after some encouragement and persuasion by the then assistant chief constable Bob McMillan, the chief constable, Bill Spence, decided to appoint a more or less full-time wildlife liaison officer.

Chief constables have considerable autonomy but in many respects are accountable to the Joint Police Board. This was a new role for the police but it was a role that the public were bound to appreciate.

Nevertheless the early days of the role were tempered by having the addition of some responsibilities for firearm and shotgun renewals and grants.

The job specification was drawn up and the post advertised within the force. I was one of two applicants and succeeded in getting the job. I was still an inspector but would have to retire post-haste to meet the starting date. My retirement took effect at 2.00 am on the starting date for the new job – 20 July 1997. I had been involved in night shift duties at T in the Park. I finished slightly early, went home to have a sleep, and started as civilian wildlife liaison officer at 8.00 am on the same morning. I suppose not too many people have spent the bulk of their time in retirement asleep!

I spent a few months checking in the many hand guns that were compulsorily surrendered in the wake of the mass murder of the Dunblane Primary School children. I then carried out a handful of enquiries pertaining to the grant or renewal of firearm and shotgun certificates but the pressure of wildlife-related incidents and enquiries was mounting and meant that I was working well over my allotted hours. Inevitably the firearm side of the role was relaxed then abandoned and the 35 hours per week I was being paid for – and many more hours besides – were taken up with wildlife crime duties. By the end of 1997 I had become the first full-time wildlife liaison officer in Scotland.

The appointment of a full-time wildlife liaison officer, in my view, was a very forward-thinking move. Crime against animals and birds has tremendous public interest and the catching and convicting of those responsible has huge appeal both from the media and the public. Being a new post, my early exploits were covered in fine detail in newspapers, magazines, radio and television. Unlike many other aspects of policing I was lucky enough that wildlife crime only seemed to attract positive publicity, though I was exceptionally conscious not to make it appear that Tayside Police had changed its remit to Tayside Wildlife Police. I tried wherever possible to put wildlife crime into its proper perspective. I saw it as imperative that it didn't compete with police resources that were directed at crimes of violence, dishonesty and disorder. I was one lone civilian employee, on a salary that wouldn't break the bank, with ten specially-trained police officers available to me for assistance if the exigencies of their other duties allowed. Ground-breaking stuff but hardly diluting valuable resources required to deal with villains who steal old ladies' purses from their shopping trolleys, armed bank robbers, drug dealers or drunks who make a nuisance of themselves in town centres.

The media honeymoon still continues, the public being fascinated by the combination of criminal activity and animal welfare. I am sure the past and present executive within Tayside Police have never regretted the move to put Tayside Police on the map as the front runner in responding to wildlife crime issues in a way the police should have been responding since the advent of the Protection of Animals (Scotland) Act 1912, the Agriculture (Scotland) Act 1948 and the Protection of Birds Act 1954. It only took eighty five years after all.

The Tayside lead of a full-time post was followed by Strathclyde Police in 2003, Lothian and Borders Police in 2005 and Grampian Police in 2006. The Scottish Police Service had acknowledged their statutory responsibility to deal with wildlife and animal-related crime in a professional manner and in a way that was welcomed by the Scottish Executive, conservation organisations and the vast majority of the general public.

Before returning to my original appointment as part-time wildlife liaison officer in 1993, two further developments in the evolution of this role are worthy of mention. The first is the inclusion of environmental crime within the job specification by Tayside Police, Lothian and Borders Police and some forces in England and Wales, particularly Warwickshire Constabulary and North Wales Police. Given that they are inextricably linked, to investigate environmental crime separately means that the synergy is lost and different agencies may be working at cross purposes. This is even more relevant since 2004, at which time the Nature Conservation (Scotland) Act placed a statutory responsibility on the police to investigate crimes committed against protected habitats.

The second significant development is the generic change of role-title to wildlife *crime* officer agreed throughout the UK in 2004. After discussion at a meeting of the UK wildlife liaison officers the consensus view was that the main responsibility of the officers lay in the prevention and detection of crimes committed against various forms of wildlife. This had been a natural and logical evolution from the original concept of an officer who would link in with relevant organisations and liaise regarding wildlife issues. The new title was a much more accurate definition of the new tack that the job was taking and reflected the training, expertise and specialisation that the officers had now attained. Wildlife liaison officers officially became wildlife crime officers – in some cases wildlife and environment officers – but for simplicity I will from this point refer to the officers as wildlife crime officers and begin to look at some of the demands on my time since 1993.

CHAPTER 10

Poisoned Bait, the Laird's Mate

Game management on shooting estates has been responsible for some of the most horrendous crimes against wildlife over many years, and poison has been its weapon of choice.

The laying of poisoned baits has been endemic in game management for over a century and a half. Poisoning of wildlife has been by far the worst crime committed against wildlife – and sometimes inadvertently against domestic pets and domestic livestock – for many years. In addition to foxes and crows, many hundreds of thousands of birds of prey have ended their lives at or near a rabbit, pigeon or game bird carcass laced with pesticide of some sort. There is no doubt that, by 1993, many gamekeepers had changed their ways, but a considerable proportion still relied on the use of poisoned baits spread around their employer's estate in a manner that constituted a real danger to human health, if not human life.

One of the earlier pesticides used went under the trade name Phosdrin. Its active ingredient, mevinphos, was extremely dangerous and could kill by being absorbed through skin. I had heard many accounts of gamekeepers in the past being affected by Phosdrin and quite honestly the prospect of handling it terrified me. Fumes, splashes and certainly contact with the mouth were all potentially lethal. One gamekeeper was admitted to hospital after either inhaling fumes or absorbing Phosdrin through the skin. He was suffering hallucinations and he imagined, amongst other things, that people were walking on the ceiling and that his dog had pups under the hospital bed. His hallucinogenic state became so terrifying that he fled the hospital ward and swam a river adjacent to the hospital to escape his terrors. Quite apart from being poisoned, he almost drowned.

Another gamekeeper told me that in his earlier days of gamekeeping he had been using Phosdrin and had put baits out on the moorland to kill whatever species happened upon them. He was driving down the hill track when he saw the mist suddenly falling. Unable to see through the windscreen of the Land Rover, even with the wipers on, he tried to put his head out the window in order to attain better vision. He suddenly realised that his inability to see was nothing to do with deteriorating weather conditions but had everything to do with Phosdrin. He jumped out of the Land Rover straight into a burn and immersed himself in its diluting water. He reckons to this day that this action, though soaking him to the skin, saved his life.

In 1987 another gamekeeper was not so fortunate. On returning home his wife found him dead on the kitchen floor. He had been using Phosdrin to prepare baits and must have got some of the deadly chemical on his hands. He had rolled a cigarette and had also poured and drunk a dram of whisky, either of which could have caused the tragic result. It was with this background knowledge of Phosdrin that I embarked on my first case of poisoning.

In February of 1995 I had a call from RSPB that they'd had a report from a person who had a cottage on Edradynate Estate near Aberfeldy to the effect that her cat had been poisoned. The woman had found her cat writhing in agony on the doorstep, noticed that it had been sick, and had immediately taken it to the vet for treatment. Remarkably it was still alive and even more remarkably it seemed to have no long-term effects of a meal that is nearly always fatal. It is interesting that the action of the RSPB investigations staff at that time was completely different to the procedure that would be employed now. They had gone out to see the cat owner, collected the cat vomit, made a search of a nearby wood, collected a dead pheasant they suspected had been poisoned bait and a dead tawny owl they suspected had been a victim. All had been submitted by RSPB to the Scottish Agriculture Science Agency (SASA) in Edinburgh and the call I received was RSPB informing me that the cat vomit, dead pheasant and dead tawny owl all had traces of mevinphos, the active ingredient of Phosdrin.

The action by the RSPB in this case perfectly reflects the frustration they had felt for years with the inability of the police to properly investigate crime committed against wildlife. They had in effect carried out a police investigation. They had attended at the scene of a crime, taken possession of a production (albeit an extremely unusual production in the form of cat vomit) made a search of a crime scene and removed a pheasant bait and a poisoned tawny owl. I did not blame them. The police had been for years abrogating their responsibilities because the investigation of wildlife crime was simply not a priority. When I received this information I was embarrassed for myself and for the police service generally. I resolved that this situation would not continue and that Tayside would fulfil its obligations under the Wildlife and Countryside Act 1981 to assume responsibility for the professional and efficient investigation of wildlife crime.

The efficient investigation of wildlife crime, or any other crime, is relatively easy. The *effective* investigation of wildlife crime is another matter entirely. Wildlife victims, even when alive, cannot speak and cannot give statements. They cannot say, 'It was Joe Bloggs who poisoned me. He is the person you are looking for.' By its very nature, wildlife crime takes place in remote or private places, away from the public gaze. Finding witnesses is exceedingly difficult. Even when traced, some witnesses may not want to be involved in a court case as they may be in employment on the same estate and in addition may be in a tied house.

In this particular case, accompanied by other police officers and RSPB investigations staff, I made a further search of the area around the house where the cat of eight remaining lives had residence. Powers are granted to police officers to carry out such a search but the Act, at that time, did not state that other persons may assist in the search. This and other fairly abstract and ill-defined powers under the 1981 Act bothered me. Though I did not know it at the time, I was to have a considerable say in re-defining and strengthening the powers in the future.

The outcome of this search was the recovery of two partially eaten wood pigeons and a very recently dead sparrowhawk not twenty yards from one of the wood pigeons. The eyes of the sparrowhawk were as clear as they had been when it was a living thing. I had seen the eyes of many thousands of animal and bird corpses in my lifetime and knew that the sparrowhawk had its fatal meal from the carcass of the wood pigeon earlier that morning, probably not much more than an hour before we found it. This was a fairly small-scale search, carried out without a search warrant but still within the powers designated under the Wildlife and Countryside Act. All of these corpses were found within a pheasant laying pen full of adult pheasants being kept for their egg production. With hindsight I wish that we had gone for a warrant and extended the search but then hindsight is a privilege we don't possess in real time. The woodpigeons and sparrowhawk all tested positive for the chemical mevinphos. I had a suspect in mind, very much connected with the pheasant laying pen, but wanted further evidence before we moved in on him.

I visited a number of residents on the estate and was absolutely shocked at what I learned. According to the interviews I carried out, my suspect had, at various times, set up a gun with a string attached to the trigger to pepper with wheat any intruder who brushed against the string. He had allegedly driven into Perth to the workplace of a person who lived on the estate, to remonstrate with him after a pheasant had been knocked down and killed by the person's car. He had allegedly poisoned a tenant farmer's collie, and also shot dead the dog of a visitor to a neighbouring estate after the dog had run off and was being pursued by its owner. I was taken aback by the vitriol these people had for my suspect but their hatred was tempered with fear and all interviews were 'strictly off the record'. All those I spoke with were in tied houses and none wanted to become involved in a prosecution. News of my investigation had travelled fast and out of the blue I received a telephone call from a former factor for the estate. He had anticipated the reluctance of those who could potentially help, wished me the best of luck, but doubted that my enquiry would ever result in court proceedings.

Along with other officers I made a thorough search of all buildings associated with the suspect but nothing of evidential value was found.

•

Exasperatingly, there was no power to detain a suspect under Section 14 of the Criminal Procedure (Scotland) Act 1995 for any offence being investigated under the Wildlife and Countryside Act 1981, which is the main piece of legislation dealing with crimes committed against wildlife. The reason for this is that offences committed under the Wildlife and Countryside Act were not (until 2003) punishable by imprisonment. His detention would have to be in connection with culpable and reckless conduct, a crime under Common Law.

For a person to be convicted of culpable and reckless conduct it has to be proved that the actions he carried out resulted in, or may reasonably have resulted in, injury or death to humans. This was the first time that this Common Law offence had been used in a wildlife crime case. The reasoning was that if a member of the public, or even some of the estate staff, had encountered any of the baits or victims and had handled them, they could potentially have been at risk of death or serious injury.

I detained the suspect under Section 14, which gave us six hours to obtain sufficient evidence to charge him. Despite the fact that the baits and all the victims except for the cat were found in pheasant rearing pens associated with his day-to-day work, he denied any involvement. I charged the suspect but knew in my heart that what was lacking in the case was one of the most crucial factors – the identification of the suspect as the person who had committed the various crimes. I discussed the case with the procurator fiscal, who said that if evidence of identification came to light before the case became time-barred in a couple of month's time, he would proceed. Otherwise he would be obliged to mark the case 'no proceedings'. A case can be marked 'no proceedings' by the procurator fiscal for a variety of reasons, though the three main reasons are that there is insufficient evidence, it is not in the public interest to proceed, or the case has become time barred. In this case the time bar was six months from the date of the crime, later extended to two years and it is now three years from the date of the crime. This was fair comment by the procurator fiscal and was beyond what he was required or expected to have done.

The two months went past very quickly and the case was deserted by the Crown, having become time-barred. The following week I learned that another employee had borrowed the suspect's Land Rover but it had broken down. In his search for tools to repair it, he had lifted up the passenger seat to search the compartment underneath as the most likely place for tools to be stored. Instead of tools there were three dead sparrowhawks. I am sure this would have clinched the case but naturally the employee wanted to keep his job and his house and the information came to me via a third party. This was the first of many frustrations in this most difficult area of policing to obtain convictions.

•

Several poisoning incidents occurred in the intervening period and gave us as relatively new wildlife crime officers a chance to sharpen our skills at this type of investigation. The next one was more successful. In June 1995, a field ornithologist was walking on the hills on Farleyer Estate, Aberfeldy when he found two hens eggs lying on a bare patch on the heather moorland. The eggs were in the middle of nowhere and there was not a hen to be seen! The ornithologist was well aware of what to look for in relation to poisoned baits and it was his view that the eggs were baited with a pesticide of some sort and had been left out to provide a fatal feast for a pair of ravens that he had earlier observed in the area.

The witness photographed the eggs and it was interesting that he left one where it was and collected and wrapped up the other one to bring to the police station. There is no doubt that this saved us considerable valuable time in the enquiry but it was a dangerous thing to do. The collecting and delivering of potentially toxic evidence by a witness is something the police would never recommend. If for instance he had made contact with me from the hill, had told me of his suspicions and I had asked him to bring the eggs in for examination there would have been two major flaws in that instruction. The first, and by far the most important, is that he could have run the risk of being contaminated by the eggs during the handling of them. Secondly, he would have removed all the evidence from the scene of the crime – from the *locus* in police parlance – and since he was on his own the fact that the eggs had been there in the first instance would not have been corroborated.

Since under Scots law all main pieces of the evidential jigsaw require corroboration in some form or other, this would have been a bar to using the eggs to any effect in a courtroom. A defence lawyer could easily argue that the ornithologist did not find the eggs on Farleyer Estate at all but had simply injected them with pesticide in his own home and brought them to the police simply to cause trouble. There would be no prosecution argument that could stand against such a theory.

Though he shouldn't have touched the eggs, what the ornithologist did was in fact ideal. He effectively gave us a chance to get a quick test carried out on the egg that he brought in, while leaving the other one to be collected when there was corroboration available. Tests for pesticides are carried out free of charge by the Scottish Agricultural Science Agency (SASA) in Edinburgh. The scientists there are extremely experienced and professional. They are also extremely busy so those of us who put specimens there for examination supply as much information as possible to enable them if possible to home in on the correct chemical on their very first test. We also try not to harass them for a quick result except where this may make all the difference between a successful case and a failure. In this case we were keen for a quick result. We had also spotted a minute quantity of white powder adhering to the egg near where the culprit made the hole in the shell to insert the chemical and mix it with the contents. When we looked slightly later the powder had gone, but it was enough for us to suggest to SASA that the most relevant test to start the series of tests should be for Alpha-chloralose.

Alpha-chloralose – sometimes referred to simply as Alpha or chloralose – is permitted for the control of birds, mainly feral pigeons, by approved persons who are licensed under Section 16 of the Wildlife and Countryside Act 1981. It is also available in a very low concentrate form as a rodenticide for the control of mice indoors. Alpha-chloralose acts by slowing the metabolic rate of the body, causing the victims to suffer thermal shock, and ultimately die of hypothermia. When this chemical is recovered by the police it is never in the low concentrate form and invariably is almost pure. The substance can still legally be used outdoors in Ireland and this is the source of most of the Alpha-chloralose recovered.

The day after the two hen's eggs were found by the ornithologist, we set off to recover the second egg from the hill. The search began almost in the shadow of the magnificent mountain near Kinloch Rannoch, Schiehallion. As I got out of the car the first bird I saw was a female hen harrier flying over from the direction of Schiehallion making for the estate from which we were about to recover a poisoned bait. I couldn't help but wonder if the harrier would breed successfully that year or in fact if it would still be alive in a few weeks' time.

The route in to where the eggs had been found was steep. I was extremely fit on the hill at one time but several years of driving a desk had taken its toll. I managed to keep up with the others but at the expense of keeping quiet, listening to the conversation and saving the valuable energy that I had for breathing rather than speaking.

The journey up the mountainside was exciting in respect of bird life. Though my lungs were under pressure I could still see well enough and there was enough oxygen getting to my brain to register accurately what I was seeing. Meadow pipits were everywhere and I thought that if the harrier survived, at least it would have plenty food. Meadow pipits to me are the moorland equivalent of wildebeest on the African plains. They are abundant and seem to be the staple diet of many of the moorland predators. I remembered sitting on a hillside one day and seeing a merlin gliding along two or three metres off the ground. A meadow pipit chose the wrong time to fly up from the heather and took off when it saw the merlin. The merlin seemed to have the ability to switch on turbo-charging and it just accelerated up to the pipit, grabbed it neatly in one talon and that was the end for the pipit.

The other bird that was much in abundance, especially as we were following the line of an old drystane dyke up the hill, was the wheatear. Male wheatears, in their resplendent grey and black, look like they have just come out of a tailor's shop, complete with their coat and tails reminiscent of a morning suit for some posh event or other that they are just about to attend. Seen close up they are incredibly smart, and this image is enhanced when they fly off in their typically undulating flight displaying their brilliantly white rump, flashing like a beacon between alternate periods of wing-beat and glide.

The last highlight was a wren – probably with a mate on a nest somewhere in the drystane dyke – that chattered its warning call as we approached, bobbing up and down like a small brown version of a dipper and with its short tail sticking up at right angles to its tiny body. The sheer volume of the song (and also the warning call) of the wren always leaves me lost for words. It is incredible that one of our smallest birds can be such a noisy wee devil. As we passed the nest, the wren flew out in a semi-circle to land behind us again chattering at heaven knows how many decibels in defence of its nest and its mate. I realised how easy it would be for egg collectors to find rare birds' nests and plunder their eggs since most birds have an inbuilt defence mechanism that unfortunately betrays their most treasured possessions. It is strange that one of our smallest birds could be so brave as to defend its nest, while one of our largest birds, the golden eagle, would slip off the nest without a sound while approaching humans were still half a mile away. It would watch from a distance but would display none of the aggressive and threatening behaviour of the brave wee wren.

At the top of the hill I managed to draw breath. There was even a short distance when we had to go downhill, which was a real treat. The hen's egg was exactly where the map drawn by the ornithologist indicated it would be. It lay there on a small grassy patch surrounded by heather, a domestic entity completely incongruous in surroundings that were almost wilderness, a trickle of albumen bubbling from the small hole in the shell through which the poison had been inserted.

The egg was photographed *in situ* before being carefully wrapped in packaging and placed in my rucksack. As is still the case, this is the point that I finish what is left of any sandwiches and coffee in my rucksack. This serves the joint purpose of making space for any new arrival in my rucksack and ensuring that the nourishment I get will be beneficial rather than detrimental to my health.

As often happens in these cases we had a strong suspect already in mind. A new gamekeeper had been employed on Farleyer Estate but before his arrival there we had been alerted to several suspicious or illegal incidents on the estate where he was formerly employed. Taking all the circumstances together there was sufficient evidence to allow a sheriff to grant a search warrant and we paid our suspect a visit eight days later.

Many investigations into wildlife crime are carried out as joint investigations with other relevant agencies. In this particular case the team consisted of another police officer and me, plus two members of staff from the then Scottish Office Agriculture and Fisheries Department (SOAFD) now Scottish Executive Environment and Rural Affairs Department (SEERAD). This government department has a remit to investigate the use, misuse and abuse of pesticides and the experience of their staff is invaluable. With the police and SOAFD staff there is a mix of different experience and skills that maximise any opportunity that arises to obtain evidence to submit a solid prosecution case to the procurator fiscal.

When we called at the gamekeeper's house the place was deserted. A small storeroom adjacent to the kitchen door was open and when we looked in there I saw a pair of hill boots on the floor. Inside one of the boots was a white tub and, remarkably, there was a label on the tub stating that the contents were Alpha-chloralose and that it had been bought in a particular store in a town in Ireland. I gently opened the tub and saw that it was half-full of a white powder that had all the appearances to suggest that the labelling accurately reflected the contents.

At this point the suspect appeared in a Land Rover, which he parked near his house. He was cautioned and agreed that the tub contained Alpha-chloralose and also that it was his property. He was asked about the eggs laced with the substance found out on the hill and immediately admitted that it was he who had put them there.

This interview was too easy. After years of interviewing suspects I have reached the conclusion that no-one tells the truth right away. A suspect always waits till he or she is backed into a corner, has assessed the evidence known to the police by the questions they ask or the information they have, realises there is no escape, then tries to make the best of a bad job by throwing in excuses and reasons that assuage and mitigate his or her involvement. There is one notable exception:

when the person hopes that the police will grab with both hands an admission to a lesser evil then go away quickly, rubbing their hands in the satisfaction of an easy result. To the chagrin of this particular suspect it doesn't always work that way.

We knew that something more serious was lurking somewhere in the wings and a short while later a search of the Land Rover justified our perseverance. On the front passenger seat of the Land Rover was a cardboard box. This box mostly contained shotgun cartridges but also held a bottle of Lea and Perrins sauce. I'm not a great fan of Lea and Perrins sauce but I knew that this was not quite the standard colour – dark green rather than black.

Apart from Phosdrin, all of the pesticides I had encountered up till then were in powder or chrystalline form. I asked him if it was Phosdrin but he said it was Lea and Perrins. A feeble excuse came forth that was related to spicing up Chinese carry-out meals that were a bit bland, but it was a last-ditch attempt that the suspect knew was going to fail. To call his bluff I suggested that I would pour a drop on to my hands and taste it. That was the crunch call and there was a reluctant admission that the bottle contained Phosdrin after all.

This was probably the first-ever successful case of pesticide abuse through Perth Sheriff Court and the penalty was substantial. The gamekeeper pleaded guilty and was fined £2500. I thought this would send out a message strong enough to stop in their tracks those who used this method of indiscriminate slaughter of wildlife. The future showed that this was not to be the case.

•

I feel I must balance the books at this juncture. The use of poisoned baits to kill wildlife is inevitably put down to the work of gamekeepers. This is not always the case and the police must investigate these cases objectively. At the start of an investigation the police must consider who may have a motive to use poisoned baits. This should take account of the most likely intended target of the baits. The answer to this question may point towards a suspect engaged in a particular occupation or hobby. Baits to protect game birds may indicate game management; baits to protect lambs may indicate farming interests;

and baits to protect racing pigeons may indicate pigeon fanciers.

There are variations on this, especially in urban situations. Baits may be to kill a neighbour's cat that is a threat to racing pigeons, aviary birds or even the pride and joy of an enthusiastic gardener. I have even investigated the poisoning of several dogs in an Angus village where the motive was clearly to get rid of dogs that were soiling well-manicured grass. It is also well worth the police officer considering the elements of circumstantial evidence before embarking on any wildlife investigation. This was taught to me at the Scottish Police College in 1966 under the acronym MAGICOP: M for motive, A for ability, G for guilty intention, I for identification, C for conduct after the crime, O for opportunity and P for preparation. If all or most of these can be established the case is normally strong enough to gain a conviction, though one that must always be present is identification.

In defence of the many gamekeepers who work within the law and are valuable allies to the police and therefore to the community, there is a fitting example of help to the police from a gamekeeper in north-west Perthshire. At the time I was working from Police Headquarters in Dundee rather than in Divisional Headquarters at Perth as I do now. The gamekeeper called me fairly late one afternoon towards the end of March. 'There's a tent out on the hill and it's near the eagle nest. I wonder if it might be one of your egg collectors at the eagles?' The timing was spot on. The golden eagles would have laid their full clutch of two – or, extremely rarely, three – eggs. This is the time favoured by egg thieves. The chicks have hardly started to develop within the eggs, which makes the eggs much more easily blown of their contents. It is a much easier undertaking to blow fresh eggs than to try to eject a three quarters grown chick through a very small hole in the side of the egg. An egg at a late stage of development requires to be injected with acid to dissolve the chick, and only after this can the ensuing mush be forced through the hole.

In any case this was good information from the keeper but I told him that I couldn't attend from Dundee as it would be dark before I got there. Instead I'd arrange to have an officer attend from the police station at Aberfeldy. He wouldn't be a wildlife crime officer but the keeper could keep him right. 'Tell the officer to meet me at the bottom of the loch. I'll take him up the loch in the boat and that will save a lot of time. There will only be a half hour's walk at the other end till we get to the tent.'

The police officer duly met the gamekeeper and the two set off up the loch in the boat, one in a suit of tweeds and a deerstalker hat and the other in a dark blue woolly suit with a black and white diced cap. The boat was beached at the far end of the loch and the two trudged the mile or so to the tent.

Picture the scene. The tent was in the middle of nowhere. It was zipped up and appeared to have been abandoned. The deerstalker hat and diced cap stood momentarily outside the tent. The diced cap slowly and deliberately slid the zip from top to bottom to reveal. . . a man dressed in nothing but women's underwear, false boobs, bra and panties. The whole works. The occupant of the tent had not the slightest interest in golden eagles or their eggs, only in the peace and solitude of a Highland glen. A peace rudely interrupted. It is questionable which of the three received the biggest fright. Needless to say the transvestite hill-walker high-tailed it back home to Edinburgh pretty damned quick. In police-speak this was a false alarm with good intent, with a bloody good laugh added in. At least for two thirds of the players in this moorland drama!

•

Much to my disappointment the poisoning of wildlife continued. In 1995 there were a total of seven reported cases including those already described that were found on Edradynate and Farleyer Estates. The others were a baited hare carcass near Aberfeldy, a cat near Methven in Perthshire, a buzzard near Kinross, and, suspiciously, two buzzards found just over the boundary from Edradynate on an estate that has absolutely no shooting interests. The following year was slightly better with five poisoning incidents in Tayside, one of which involved a dead buzzard found on Edradynate Estate. Matters got worse in 1997, when there were eight poisoning incidents. This time two of the incidents related to either baits or victims found on Edradynate Estate.

I was frustrated and angry particularly as we had been unable to charge anyone in any one these cases. Had these taken place today the situation would be quite different. In the 1990s police powers under the Wildlife and Countryside Act, 1981 were poor. It was ironic that we could arrest a person fishing for salmon without being in possession of a permit, but we couldn't arrest someone for killing a golden eagle. As I described earlier, the offences we were investigating were not punishable by imprisonment, only by fine, so a suspect could not be detained and taken to a police station for interview. Lastly – and most importantly – we were still relatively new to these investigations and had little of the experience we now have under our belts.

To go back a step, I was always of the view that the fight against wildlife crime was more than just about bringing people before the courts. We had to ensure compliance with the law through a variety of means. Coercion, peer-pressure, guidance, advice, and understanding by police wildlife crime officers of the reasons behind the commission of some of the crimes all had a part to play in making a change. It was a carrot and a stick philosophy. We had only used the stick so far. Now it was time for the carrot.

Chapter 11

Hen Harriers: the ecstasy and the agony

A pioneering education project to build understanding of this most splendid, and most persecuted bird of prey and Operation Artemis, a unique venture into building unusual partnerships.

Hen harriers are as welcome on a grouse moor as a thunderstorm at a summer barbeque. If they ate only voles, mice, young rabbits and meadow pipits they would be tolerated and probably even welcomed. It is the fact that their diet also includes grouse, especially chicks, that makes their presence incompatible with the job of the grouse moor keeper in producing a maximum shootable surplus of grouse. The law protects all wild birds, with some exceptions under certain circumstances for pest species. The hen harrier is very much included in this protection. In fact the law protects hen harriers even more than most birds as it is included amongst the birds listed on Schedule 1 of the Wildlife and Countryside Act 1981, the rarest of our bird species.

It is easy to protect hen harriers on paper, it is entirely another matter to put this into effective practice. In Scotland, harriers live and breed on moorland. Committing a crime in a moorland setting is a world away from committing a crime on a High Street. There may be plenty witnesses to the shooting of a harrier on a moor but they all have woolly jumpers and absolutely no interest in intelligible communication with humans. Furthermore, ovines are likely to be unreliable witnesses in court.

It is not the role of the police to expound any conservation or ornithological view or theory but rather to uphold and apply the law as it has been written. Having said this, it may be beneficial for the reader to be aware of some background on hen harriers provided by some scientific papers and by some conservation and shooting organisations.

> 1993 – Research into hen harriers indicates that the bird is heavily persecuted on managed grouse moors, with breeding productivity significantly lower in these areas compared with breeding attempts elsewhere in the uplands. (Bibby, C.J. and Etheridge, B. 1993 – Status of the Hen Harrier (*Circus cyaneus*) in Scotland 1988–89. Etheridge, B., Summers, R.W. and Green, R.E. 1997 – The Effects of Illegal Killing and Destruction of Nests by Humans on the Population Dynamics of the Hen Harrier (*Circus cyaneus*) in Scotland).
>
> 1997 – The persecution of hen harriers by some gamekeepers – especially on grouse moors – is formally acknowledged by many associated in the game shooting industry. (Potts, G.R., 1997 – Global Dispersion of Nesting Hen Harriers (*Circus cyaneus*): implications for grouse moors in the UK).
>
> 2002 – The hen harrier decreased in the north-east of Scotland. The majority of the Scottish population is now found on grouse moors. Some of the symptoms of persecution outlined by Etheridge *et al* (1997) are still evident. This showed that in Scotland there was a significantly lower productivity rate on grouse moors than in young forestry plantations and moorlands not managed for grouse. Between 1997 and 2000 there was no known successful breeding of hen harriers in England. (Joint statement in October 2002 between the Game Conservancy Trust and RSPB)
>
> 2004 – The third census of hen harriers took place. In

> Scotland this showed that harrier numbers had increased to 633 pairs, from 408/594 pairs in 1988/89, and a low of 434 pairs in 1998. The increase in numbers was confined to the west and far north. The number of breeding pairs in the east and south, where grouse moors are prevalent, had declined. (Scottish Raptor Study Groups, 2004)

Obviously these are all excerpts from the reports but they reflect the general conclusions so far as they are relevant to this chapter. Even though very few crimes committed against hen harriers are reported to the police, there was no doubt that in some areas, hen harriers were – and indeed still are – victims of crime. Given the span and content of these papers, together with my own knowledge, I would like to think that in 2006 there has been some improvement. However in 1997 there was sufficient evidence to convince me that the law was frequently being broken. I was determined to devise a plan to try to encourage compliance with the law.

I first identified two rural Perthshire schools, Amulree and Kirkmichael, to participate in a project. The plan was to involve the pupils in a hen harrier project where they would be taught about wildlife crime in class, but in particular would learn something of good upland management. Since both schools were in the middle of moorland areas, grouse shooting was nothing new to them. However I wanted them to have the opportunity to hear of the local economic value of grouse shooting from a grouse moor owner. They could then make up their own minds as to whether or not they accepted this and even whether or not they agreed with shooting. There was also to be a practical side to the project. I wanted to take the pupils out on to the moor to see a hen harrier nest.

The next part of the plan was to gain authority from several landowners for me and another wildlife crime officer to go on to their land and monitor hen harriers to identify where they were nesting. We needed to find at least a couple of nests that were fairly accessible. Accessibility was partly out of concern for the pupils but I also had no idea of the fitness of the teachers who would accompany them.

Authority to go onto estates was readily given and in fact we finished up with twelve estate owners who afforded us access for this project. So far so good, but neither I nor my colleague had much experience of locating nesting hen harriers. This was remedied fairly quickly by a crash course in harrier breeding and nesting habits from Bruce Anderson of RSPB Scotland.

As hen harriers are listed on Schedule 1, a licence from Scottish Natural Heritage is required if they are to be intentionally disturbed at nesting time. I applied for and was granted licences for my colleagues, Constables Graham Jack and Bob Noble, and for myself. Scottish Natural Heritage thought the idea was extremely innovative and were of the view that the inconvenience to one or two harriers was likely to benefit the species as a whole. We were ready to go but there was another idea developing. It was one that I didn't hold out much hope for but after all it was worth a telephone call. . .

The phone call to BBC 'Countryfile' paid off. I spoke with a researcher who said they would be delighted to film such a project. John Craven and the film crew would spend two days with us and we should let them know when we were ready to take the pupils to a nest.

Now we were ready to start.

I spent many days on the hill, some in work time and some in my own time, watching for hen harriers. It was late April and the weather on some of the days still seemed like winter. I was always well wrapped up – it was easy to take off some clothes if the temperature rose a few degrees – but sitting in the heather is not conducive to good blood circulation and the generation of heat through the body.

Some days I saw no harriers but there were always plenty of other interests. Mountain hares provided great entertainment. I often had seven or eight hopping round me practically within touching distance. Most were beginning to lose their white winter coat but an occasional one was still resplendent in its winter finery. It's ironic that with our mild winters and dearth of snow nowadays the mountain hares' winter camouflage – intended to enable them to blend in with the snow – puts them at even greater risk. The buck hares had little on their mind except mating with a doe. The does had little on their mind except keeping just that hop or two ahead of the amorous bucks. My presence was a secondary consideration despite their innate fear of humans. Luckily for them my intentions were benevolent and I was grateful for their company.

It is sad that several years on, mountain hares are being culled on many grouse moors as they are host to ticks, which in turn are blamed for a reduction in grouse stocks. There seems little doubt that a scarcity of mountain hares will adversely affect the golden eagle since it is one of the eagles' main prey items. In many areas, one of the eagle's other prey species, the humble rabbit, has also been thinned out due to viral haemorrhagic disease, a disease even more deadly than myxomatosis. Red grouse and black game remain a prey option to the golden eagle but then are these not what the estates are trying to protect by culling hares? I have concerns that in the long-term, what balance of nature there is left will be seriously and perhaps irreversibly affected. But then I'm a wildlife crime officer and not a scientist, conservationist or game manager.

Male grouse were defending their territories and all around I could hear their calls, *go-back, go-back, go-back*. Despite their protestations I wasn't going anywhere! Every so often a male with a bright red wattle over each eye would explode straight up into the air and come fluttering down again to advertise to its neighbour that this patch was taken and would be vigorously defended if need be.

During my periods of watching and waiting there were many other exciting sights. If the wind was right, red deer would sometimes graze gradually towards me. An occasional ring ouzel, peregrine, osprey, whinchat, short-eared owl or a very occasional golden eagle would fly past. The bird I was waiting for, however, gave me by far the best display.

Male hen harriers fly over their chosen nest site in a fantastic display of aerial acrobatics, often referred to as 'skydancing.' The male flies vertically upwards, then does a back somersault and swoops just as vertically downwards. Just before reaching the ground it turns and repeats the whole manoeuvre. This incredible display can be repeated many times and last several minutes. If by some means the public could be taken to a hide or vantage point on the moor to watch a harrier skydancing, I'm sure the earning potential could be at least as much as brought in by the average year's revenue from grouse shooting. Someday a visionary landowner may diversify estate operations to include the hen harrier as a bird of value rather than classify it as vermin along with foxes, stoats and weasels – a view I heard as recently as April 2006.

Once the site of the skydancing display has been identified, the female is then likely to be seen building her nest amongst long, rank, heather, regularly carrying heather stems in her talons and alighting out of sight in the heather to arrange them into a rudimentary platform into which to lay her four to seven white eggs. It is important not to disturb the bird at this stage or at any early stage of incubation as she may desert, and I had to try to memorise exactly where the nest was without going any closer. This is no easy matter from half a mile away in a sea of heather but there was normally some sort of landmark which I was sure I could identify again in a further three week's time.

In a project like this, where I was going to disturb a rare nesting bird, I was determined to minimise any risk of it deserting. I wanted to bring the pupils to see it shortly before the eggs were due to hatch and at a point in the incubation when it was least likely to desert. If the bird was seen building the nest, the safest period to visit it could be calculated fairly accurately. Disturbance of the bird to allow the pupils to see any chicks had other risks. The female could not be flushed in bad weather or the chicks could die of exposure. Nor could the female be flushed off young chicks on a hot sunny day, otherwise the chicks, with the absence of feathers, could overheat and die of heat exhaustion. I took advice on this at each step of the way from Bruce Anderson of RSPB Scotland.

Intermittently during the search for nesting harriers, PCs Bob Noble, Graham Jack and I were calling in at Amulree and Kirkmichael Schools, giving talks to the pupils and setting them a variety of tasks. The classrooms walls by this time were covered with drawings of hen harriers, birds that they had yet to see close up.

The day arrived when we decided that conditions were right to take the two classes out to a nest. One had been identified on Bolfracks Estate near Amulree so Kirkmichael pupils came to join the Amulree class. The estate gamekeeper helped out by providing transport to the nest. In two groups – one group at a time – with instructions to make no noise and to do exactly as they were told, the pupils saw their first hen harrier chicks. The BBC recorded the occasion for their Countryfile programme. After the build-up in class to this day they were absolutely thrilled but respected the very short time they were allowed to be at the nest.

A later visit was arranged at another nest in Glenshee, when the pupils were taken out to see some older chicks being ringed by Bruce Anderson. This time the visit was filmed by Grampian TV news. The nest was inaccessible by Land Rover and was a considerable walk, but the kids' enthusiasm negated any lack of fitness and there were no casualties. The deal was that they had to be quiet on the way onto the hill but could be as noisy as they liked on the way back. It was a smart move by the adults; the pupils were too tired to be noisy on the return journey.

This project had many successful outcomes. School pupils gained knowledge and had fun while doing so. Landowners received praise for their willing participation and help during the project. Through BBC Countryfile, the public became aware of the police effort to curb wildlife crime, particularly crime committed against hen harriers. Lastly, some trust developed among all the organisations and estates involved in the project. The seeds of a unique partnership yet to come had been sown.

A welcome by-product of the hen harrier initiative came out of the blue. Entries were invited for a competition being run jointly by Scottish Natural Heritage, Grampian Television and Shell UK. I was contacted by the administrator of the competition, who was canvassing entries. There was a choice of three categories to enter, one of which was *Understanding the Environment.* I was reluctant at first and thought that our wee project had no chance, but I was persuaded by the then assistant chief constable Bob McMillan to give it a go. Nothing ventured. . .

All projects were rigorously assessed in the run-up to the announcement of the winner. In our case, since we had nothing tangible to show to the assessor apart from the pupils' work on the classroom walls, interviews were conducted with many of the participants in the project to elicit their new-found knowledge.

Our project was one of three short-listed for the category *Understanding the Environment*. Four participants from our project were invited to the Grampian TV studios in Aberdeen. There the final decision would be made and the winner would be announced for each of the three categories, all of this being filmed for a half-hour programme on Grampian TV. The four from our project comprised a teacher, a pupil, PC Bob Noble and me.

In the studio, a summary of the three best projects in each group was given and I could see that we were up against very stiff competition. The other two categories were dealt with first and the winners announced. As if to test our nerve, our category was last to be decided.

Our turn finally came and I was completely floored when it was announced that the best project in the category *Understanding the Environment* was the Tayside Police Hen Harrier Project. I stepped up to receive the award from Donny Munro, lead singer of *Runrig* at the time. The prize was a bronze golden eagle, apparently worth £3000, on a beautiful light grey stone base, plus a cheque for £800. We gave the £800 to the two schools involved and the golden eagle sat proudly at Tayside Police Headquarters until it was unexpectedly presented to me in 2006 to keep. We had achieved a wonderful conclusion from a project primarily aimed at reducing crime committed against the hen harrier.

The project was also a very pleasant end to my career as a police officer. It was a few weeks after the visit to Grampian TV Studios that I hung up my police inspector's hat and took on my new wildlife crime role as a member of Tayside Police support staff.

The hen harrier issue has gone a stage further since our 1997 project. I related earlier that scientific studies show that the hen harrier still breeds less successfully on grouse moors than elsewhere. Even to a layman, this appears to indicate that there is some form of interference by game managers which could range from shooting the birds or destroying the eggs to moving the birds on before they start to build their nest. In early 2007, as I write, the truth is likely to be some sort of sliding scale of these options.

The situation is considerably worse in the north of England than it is in Scotland or Wales. Hen harriers have been almost exterminated there and this is of serious concern to conservationists, especially Natural England and RSPB. Police wildlife crime officers throughout the UK are also well aware of this disgraceful situation and resolved to do whatever is possible to reverse this illegal trend and to bring some of the culprits to book.

At the National Police and Customs Wildlife Crime Conference in October 2003, a decision was made to enforce wildlife crime on the basis of conservation priorities. This is not a new concept but an adaptation of Policing by Objectives. Objectives (or conservation priorities) are set and a policing plan is set to achieve the objectives. A date was made for January the following year for key people to meet and decide what species were affected by such a high level of crime that would make them a conservation priority. I was nominated as a member of the group, which met at the Joint Nature Conservation Committee offices in Peterborough. Apart from the police, there were representatives from Scottish Natural Heritage, English Nature (now Natural England), Countryside Council for Wales, RSPB, Kew Gardens, the National Wildlife Crime Unit and several more. There was never a doubt that the hen harrier would feature on the list of conservation priorities as its breeding record on many grouse moors was nothing short of a national disgrace. We decided on the three conservation priorities as crime against hen harriers, crime against bats (mostly as a result of development and timber treatment) and the illegal wildlife trade in endangered species.

•

In relation to the hen harrier, the operational response was Operation Artemis, which was launched the following month at Kew Gardens by the Environment Minister. Almost immediately there was a backlash from one or two grouse moor interests alleging that the police had more important issues to contend with than investigating a lack of hen harriers in the north of England. Could this be read as *better trying to catch armed robbers than trying to catch us?* There was also a complaint from the same group that public money would be better spent on other criminal issues. In fact the whole of Operation Artemis, from its inception in 2004 until the beginning of 2007 as I write has cost the police little or nothing, with funding coming from conservation organisations.

In Scotland we went down a slightly different route to our southern colleagues, and consulted with relevant organisations before our press launch. Because we spoke beforehand with the British Association for Shooting and Conservation, the Scottish Gamekeepers' Association, Game Conservancy Trust (Scotland), and the Scottish Rural Property and Business Association – which represents landowners – we took the sting out of the operation and made it plain that all the police were asking for was compliance with the law.

Operation Artemis in Scotland was launched by the then Deputy Chief Constable Ian Gordon of Tayside Police, who had the Association of Chief Police Officers Scotland (ACPOS) portfolio for wildlife crime issues. We were pleased that there had been no confirmed cases of hen harrier persecution in 2004, the first year of Operation Artemis. In the following year we were able to produce a leaflet on the Operation the content of which was endorsed by all ten of the diverse organisations involved. This I considered a major achievement. To those who might still be bent on committing crime against hen harriers, this leaflet demonstrated that the principles behind Operation Artemis had backing from a wide range of rural, shooting and conservation organisations.

In the Spring of 2004 and 2005, all estates having habitat that could be suitable for nesting hen harriers had a visit from a wildlife crime officer. Hopefully, at least in Scotland, we are making some progress. During these visits I judged my own success on whether or not I was offered a cup of tea, which turned out to be the case almost every time. Many estates do not hide the fact that they would rather not have harriers on their grouse moor. I can sympathise with that view and it is a view that I can live with provided the estate staff stay within the law. In the north of England, however, the situation is dire and despite Operation Artemis, hen harriers sustain only a tenuous foothold. I suspect that the situation will not alter much unless and until an example is made of someone caught and convicted of killing a harrier and the person receives a custodial sentence.

Chapter 12

The Scourge Goes On

Frustrating times investigating poisoning offences, a licensing slip up by Scottish Executive, a tea party and an about-turn by a defence lawyer.

Poisoning of wildlife continued in the year 1998, this time with four separate incidents. The slight reduction was welcomed but I was incensed that one of the incidents, a poisoned buzzard beside a baited wood pigeon, was yet again on Edradynate Estate. The pigeon had been laced with the pesticide Yaltox, which is the trade name for the pesticide with the ingredient carbofuran. In the late 1990s carbofuran was cropping up more and more and had clearly become the preferred pesticide. It was probably more effective than Alpha-chloralose in the sense that the victim was mostly killed near to the bait; hence it was easier for the criminal to gather up and dispose of all the evidence. It was also far easier to obtain than Phosdrin, which had been banned by that time for more than a decade and was scarce. The legitimate purpose of Yaltox – or carbofuran – was as an insecticide on root crops. It was able to be bought in multi-kilo quantities by farmers and since a tiny amount of the dark blue granules on bait was easily sufficient to kill an animal as large as a dog, I was concerned at the potential to stockpile carbofuran for years to come.

The suspect for this latest Edradynate Estate incident was again visited and interviewed. He stated that he had nothing to do with the setting out of the dead pigeon and denied using poisoned baits. This made yet another undetected wildlife crime on this estate, but as always in these situations, I just had to be patient. If there was to be a recurrence I hoped there might be evidence the next time to secure a conviction. There is a saying among police officers that criminals have to be lucky all the time, the police just have to be lucky once.

In another of the 1998 poisonings, a hill walker was on West Glenalmond Estate in Perthshire in October of that year when he chanced upon the shepherd for the estate. They exchanged pleasantries and the conversation came round to birds of prey. During the chat the shepherd told the hill walker that he had earlier that day found a dead golden eagle. The eagle apparently appeared to have died in the past few days and the shepherd told the hill walker that he suspected that it had been killed rather than having died of old age or disease.

A couple of weeks later the hill walker was on the estate again. This time it was his turn to find evidence of poisoning, which was in the form of a dead buzzard lying near to part of the carcass of a mountain hare. He was highly suspicious and reported his find to RSPB. RSPB investigations officers had still not quite got used to the police fulfilling their statutory responsibilities in the investigation of wildlife crime. Instead of reporting this incident to the police, they went on to the estate, recovered the bait and the victim, and had them examined for pesticides.

To repeat the point, a charity carrying out a police function is a situation that was entirely unsatisfactory but in many ways the police in Scotland had brought this about themselves. A working protocol has since been agreed between the Scottish Police Service and RSPB Scotland, SEERAD, Scottish Natural Heritage, Scottish SPCA and Scottish Badgers, all organisations with which the police work in partnership on wildlife crime issues. Such a situation would not occur now except in extreme circumstances when police resources were unable to attend and the matter was one of urgency.

I was informed that the buzzard and the mountain hare both tested positive for the pesticide carbofuran and began an investigation. My first point of contact was with the shepherd, from whom I gleaned the story about the dead golden eagle. He also told me that a couple of weeks after he had found the eagle he was gathering sheep in the vicinity of a crag where peregrines traditionally nest when he noticed one of his dogs sniffing at a dead grouse. He went over to examine the grouse as it looked alive. He was amazed to see that it was dead, but sitting up in a life-like position with a length of wire stuck into the ground and under its head.

He suspected that the bird would be a poisoned bait to attract the peregrines, since they prefer to kill their prey rather than take carrion. In fact this type of poisoned bait had been found before, and was usually laced with a pesticide of some sort on the back of the neck, as peregrines take the head off their victim before starting to eat it. Pesticide in this position would be ingested by the bird and would most likely kill it. Though all of this was not known to the shepherd, he knew enough to realise that one of his valuable dogs could have been poisoned. He told me that he was absolutely raging and went straight to the gamekeeper, whom he suspected of setting out the bait, and asked if he would pay for a replacement dog if it had been poisoned.

Along with several police officers I made a search of part of the estate for the dead golden eagle and for any other baits or victims of poisoning, but nothing further was found. Though I had been given the rough location of the dead golden eagle, after several hours searching we had to admit defeat, suspecting it had been found and disposed of. Enquiries continued and at their conclusion, the gamekeeper on the estate was charged with setting out the poisoned mountain hare carcass, killing a buzzard and attempting to kill a peregrine by setting out a baited grouse.

By the following July the trial of the gamekeeper had not started, a delay which is regrettable but not unusual. I had been keeping in touch with the shepherd as he was seriously concerned that his job and his tied house would be at risk now that he was involved in a case against another estate employee. When I phoned him one day, by coincidence he had been on the part of the hill where he had originally found the dead golden eagle the previous October. Coincidentally he had chanced upon it again. This time he marked the exact location and that evening took me and a police colleague, PC Graham Jack, to the spot.

There was little left of the body of the magnificent eagle, though most of the feathers were still intact and attached to the body. We photographed it and collected it as gently as we could so as to keep it relatively intact, putting it in a large polythene bag. It was then transferred to SASA in Edinburgh, where the scientists incredibly managed to find sufficient traces of carbofuran to conclude that the bird had been poisoned. As the carcass of the eagle had been lying out on the hill in all weathers for nine months this was an amazing result. The finding of the golden eagle also meant that there was an additional and extremely serious charge.

The day of the trial eventually came. I had discussed the case several times in the preceding months with the procurator fiscal. He was of the view that as cases go, the evidence was slim but might be sufficient for a conviction if everything went well. He was aware of the predicament of the shepherd and intended to call him as first witness. There is nothing unusual in crucial evidence, albeit from the weakest link, being led first when the evidence of that witness is pivotal to the success of the case. If this witness fails to provide the necessary evidence then valuable court time can be saved by abandoning the trial at an early stage. This is preferable to leading the evidence of strong witnesses first and the case failing after several hours because of poor evidence from a key witness.

The shepherd gave evidence-in-chief, which is the evidence as led by the procurator fiscal. His evidence in court fell well below the level of evidence given to the police in his statement and it was clear to all that he was trying to save his livelihood and his house. The case was immediately deserted by the fiscal without the need for cross-examination by the defence solicitor.

Police officers are philosophical and realistic. All of us are aware that evidence has to be presented in court to prove a case beyond reasonable doubt. This had not been the position here so the accused had walked free.

The shepherd remained in employment for a further year – then was made redundant. Having no job had the inevitable consequence of having no home.

•

Much of what I have written so far tends to show shooting estates in a bad light. This cannot be said of the majority of estates and many are veritable havens for all species of wildlife, including game birds. As is the case in all walks of life, there is a preponderance of landowners who get on with doing a job that ranges between mediocre and very good. Those who are carrying out a mediocre job are sometimes simply constrained by money, but nevertheless they do their best and stay within the law.

Then there are those landowners and game managers at the bottom of the heap who are a disgrace and an embarrassment to their colleagues. All manner of illegal practices are likely to take place on these estates and the motive is purely and simply to produce more game at the expense of everything else. As I write, one estate in Tayside is now completely enclosed by a deer fence powered by mains electricity. Deer and mountain hares have been removed and all those who have walked on the estate tell me that it is a desert with nothing other than a few grouse, and with no nesting birds of prey of any kind except for a pair of ospreys, which are no threat to grouse in any case. Conservationists who visit the estate – normally without revealing their presence – think that it is completely wrong and immoral that anyone can be allowed to ruin natural biodiversity in the pursuit of a gain to a single species.

At the other end of the spectrum we have shooting landowners who spend vast amounts of their own money improving an estate. It may be that their principal aim is to improve the shooting but nevertheless they are conscious that all forms of wildlife benefit. One particular landowner in Perthshire has made significant improvements especially for black game but many other species cash in on the improved habitat. Other landowners try hard, against difficult odds, to improve the lot of the few remaining capercaillie on their estate. Many have also planted hedges, shrubs, shelter belts and game crops, all of which help to feed and shelter a variety of wildlife.

In short, shooting estates normally benefit most forms of wildlife, and offer additional food, shelter and protection from predators that are less likely to be present on land that is used solely for agriculture. As one who works regularly with the British Association for Shooting and Conservation, the significance of the name of the organisation should not be lost. Shooting and conservation can and should go hand in hand. It really is a pity that one or two landowners detract from the good work done, in varying degrees, by the majority.

•

Our final poisoning incident of the Millenium year took place at the beginning of November and was an example of the sloppy and unprofessional game management and illegal pest control procedures that so often go hand in hand with the abuse of pesticides. The investigation was sparked off by the finding of a dead buzzard and the sighting of another buzzard that seemed to be lethargic and over-tame, allowing the farm worker who reported the matter to drive his tractor almost alongside it. No healthy wild buzzard would admit humans so close and I am in little doubt that this buzzard was affected by pesticide after feeding on bait. The dead buzzard was collected and on examination found to have died as a result of eating bait laced with carbofuran. When we collected the dead buzzard there was no sign of the one that had clearly been ailing. Surviving a dose of carbofuran is almost unheard of. It may have been carried off by a fox, which would probably end up as a secondary victim.

As in earlier cases, I carried out the investigation alongside my colleague Willie Milne from SEERAD, using his powers. I knew this area of Perthshire well and knew that Glendoick Estate lay directly uphill from where the dead buzzard had been found. We started by looking uphill to try to identify the most likely spot for a bait to have been placed, then drove nearer to that location and started our search.

Years of experience paid off and within half an hour of commencing our search we had found a further two buzzards lying under half a dozen ash trees growing on a knowe at the edge of a field. During a search like this it is always worth having a look under a single tree, a clump of trees or even a telegraph pole. If a buzzard feeding on a bait makes it off the ground, it is likely to land in the first tree or telegraph pole that it comes to and is unlikely to move again except to thump on to the ground in due course as the pesticide takes effect on its cardio-vascular system. The buzzards in this case had been dead for about a month, which tended to indicate a sustained autumn campaign against buzzards. They later tested positive for carbofuran.

Despite a search round the area for any baits, none was found. However our search led us to a crow cage trap two hundred metres to the west of where the dead birds had been found. These traps are normally constructed of posts and wire netting and are roughly three metres long by two metres wide and two metres high. They operate on the same principle as does a lobster pot, where the birds enter via a funnel or similar aperture in the top section to access the bait inside the trap, but can't find their way back out again. The use of crow cage traps is sanctioned under a general licence issued annually by the Scottish Executive. To be legal, various conditions need to be observed. First, the cage needs to be used by an authorised person, who may be a landowner or someone acting on the landowner's authority. Second, only the pest species listed on the general licence may legally be taken in the trap, though all members of the crow family other than the raven and chough are included in this list. Lastly the pest species may only be killed for certain reasons, though the reason 'to protect other birds' satisfies the reason for game management purposes.

Cage traps for game management purposes are normally used in the Springtime and are effective in thinning out a local breeding population of carrion crows which can, if left, seriously decimate the eggs and chicks of ground nesting birds.

By the year 2000 we had just come through a period when other conditions of use had been added as caveats of their legal use. The conditions were that the traps must be physically inspected on a daily basis, any non-target species must be released and all target species must be humanely killed at each visit. When not in use, the cage must be made incapable of catching or holding any wild bird.

All of these additional – and sensible – conditions had resulted from an incident when a golden eagle had been caught in a trap near Enochdhu in Perthshire in 1997. The immature eagle had gone into the trap, possibly to examine some old sheep bones that had formerly been bait when the trap was in use and had been left within the trap. Having got in, the eagle couldn't navigate out again and was destined to a death of starvation. The owner of the estate was distraught when he found the dead eagle and the whole circumstances were unfortunate as the gamekeeper who operated the trap had either left or retired and no new keeper had yet been taken on who would be checking the trap. It had been left in a 'set' position, which was neither an offence at this time nor a particularly uncommon practice and this had been the consequence. The death of the immature golden eagle was made even more poignant by the fact that it had been the first young golden eagle in a decade to fledge from a particular nest in west Perthshire that was regularly robbed of its eggs by egg thieves, and had only made it beyond the egg stage that year because of the selfless work of an army of volunteers who mounted a 24-hour guard on the eyrie. I suppose the young golden eagle had not died in vain as the outrage expedited a change to the general licence condition that had already been recognised and recommended by the RSPB: that of ensuring a cage trap must not catch or hold birds when not being used.

Back to our cage trap that we had just encountered and were standing beside. It was a fairly new cage trap, in good condition. In the month of November it is extremely unusual for anyone to operate a crow cage trap (I have never seen one operated in November in half a century.) No effort had been made to block access to birds via the entrance, and instead of the door being tied securely *open* to allow any birds entering to escape, it was tied securely *shut* with fence wire which had been twisted tightly with pliers round the top and the bottom of the door and had the ends snipped off. This was just exactly the opposite of the new conditions of use passed by Scottish Executive. Inside the trap a buzzard flapped about, having been enticed to enter by some bits of rabbit fur inside the trap. Like the sheep bones in the trap at Enochdhu, this would be what was left of dead rabbits used as bait when the trap had been used in the Spring. No food or water was present inside the trap, further confirmation that the trap was not in current use.

I photographed everything that was relevant but we were now faced with two problems. How could we get the buzzard out of the trap because of the wire binding the door, which was impossible to open without having pliers ourselves? If final evidence was required to prove that the trap was not in current use this was it. I think even the most inexperienced sheriff in the ways of traps would agree that no trap operator would go through this elaborate and unnecessary wire-twisting and un-twisting on a daily basis.

We solved the first problem by ripping some of the netting off the post in a corner of the trap, the only possible solution. The second problem was whether to simply release the buzzard or to catch it and take it for a veterinary check up. There was no way of knowing how long the bird had been trapped, though there seemed to be plenty life in it as it flapped from perch to perch quite ably. I wasn't worried about it being hungry so much as not having had water. It could soon feed itself up again but if it had been deprived of water for too long its kidneys might have been irreversibly affected and we could be releasing it to certain death. On balance we decided that it was not worth stressing the bird further by catching it and subjecting it to veterinary inspection and that it would have to take its chance back in the wild again. We walked round to the back of the cage and the buzzard slipped quickly through the gap we had made in the netting and back to freedom.

I'm not given to anthropomorphic views on birds and animals but it was interesting that the buzzard landed on a small tree a hundred metres away, gave a vigorous shake of its wings, looked back at us as if to say, 'Thanks for your help, guys,' and soared away.

Because of police powers under the Wildlife and Countryside Act 1981 being inadequate prior to the provisions of the Nature Conservation (Scotland) Act 2004, and in many ways open to interpretation and challenge by defence solicitors, I decided that we had seen enough for the day and that we should now apply for a search warrant. This would be an option taken less often nowadays because of considerably strengthened powers but reliance on a search warrant is never a bad thing provided there is sufficient evidence to convince first of all a procurator fiscal then a sheriff. Search warrants are not granted lightly by the court and certainly not for 'fishing expeditions'. The police must present a case that there is reasonable cause to believe that specific items may be found on the premises or lands identified as being the subject of the search. If items not listed on the search warrant are found there are other options available, one being to apply for a further search warrant to seize the items and the other to take the items anyway and argue the legal issues afterwards.

All of which reminds me of a search in which I had taken part on behalf of Northern Constabulary in the early 1980s when I was a detective constable newly back from a detective officers' course at the Scottish Police College. The course was six weeks long and a considerable part of it was reading case law. It was boring at the time but absolutely invaluable in the type of work that detective officers undertake. In this particular search, which had taken place in Perth, I had applied for a search warrant to look for stolen items. Northern Constabulary CID had information that these items were to be found at a particular address. I have no recollection now what these items were but for the sake of argument let's say it was stolen cheque books and credit cards.

I obtained a search warrant and accompanied by my detective sergeant at the time, Stan Gerrard, began the search. We found no trace of the stolen items we were looking for but found twenty or so almost new library books with dates stamped on them showing that they should have been returned long ago. The value of the books amounted to hundreds of pounds and the householder could not give an account of why they were in his possession. We therefore seized the books and charged the suspect with theft or alternatively reset (receiving stolen property).

The accused, as everyone seems to do, pleaded not guilty and the case went to trial in Perth District Court. I gave my evidence-in-chief as led by the procurator fiscal, then it was the turn of the defence. The defence agent was a sleazeball, both in looks and manner, and we had crossed swords many times before.

'Detective Constable Stewart,' he asked me, 'I understand from the evidence you gave when questioned by my friend (the legal term by which defence and prosecution refer to each other) that you were searching for stolen cheque books and credit cards?'

'That's correct.'

'And that this was on behalf of another police force, Northern Constabulary to be precise?'

'That's correct.'

'We have seen the search warrant produced to the court, which was in respect of the aforementioned items.'

'That's correct.'

'Was there any mention of books of any sort on the warrant?'

'Yes, cheque books.'

'Apart from cheque books were any other books mentioned?'

'No.'

'But you found and seized a number of library books from the house?'

'I did, yes.'

'With no power under the warrant to seize them?'

'That's correct.'

'Was this not an unlawful seizure of these books?'

'I don't think so, no.'

'If you *don't think so* where did your legal right to seize these books from my client's house come from?'

'I based my powers on the stated case *HMA vs Hepper.*'

'Detective Constable Stewart, please explain to the court the basis of *HMA vs Hepper.*'

It's as well during trials that only the spoken word and not thought processes can be heard by the Bench, but the Justice may well have been able to interpret my giving the V-sign with my eyes as I responded, 'The principle of *HMA vs Hepper* is that if items believed to be stolen are stumbled upon during a legitimate search for specific other items, balancing the interests of the suspect against the public interest, the police may seize them without warrant.' (*Up yours* being added under my breath.)

Defence agent Sleazeball was silent for a moment, then asked for a short adjournment of the court.

Ten minutes later, clearly after obtaining and reading the case to which I was referring (the same as maybe even had been done by the clerk of the court on behalf of the Justice on the bench of the District Court) defence agent Sleazeball re-entered the court, which shortly after reconvened. I was never recalled to the witness box. Mr Sleazeball addressed the Justice and stated, 'Your Honour, my client now wishes to change his plea to one of guilty.'

Getting back to the wildlife investigation in hand, in this particular case we had a suspect and a search warrant was granted for his premises and for the lands of the estate. Search warrants granted under the Wildlife and Countryside Act 1981 can cater for persons from SEERAD and RSPB. They were therefore also named on the warrant to assist in the search, which took place a week later.

As I often do, I took part in the search of the land rather than the premises and in this investigation teamed up with the senior investigations officer from RSPB Scotland, Dave Dick. We had been searching no time at all when I found a dead roebuck caught in a drag snare and called Dave over to corroborate. The drag was simply a fence post with the snare fastened to the centre of it by a staple. The common thread of this particular investigation was sloppy and illegal pest control procedures, or un-professionalism and corner cutting. This was a prime example of all of these things.

The use of snares is legal provided particular criteria are observed. One of the main conditions of legal snaring is that snares are checked at least once on a daily basis (since 2004 checks have to be made at least once in every period of 24 hours, which is slightly different). Attaching fox snares to drags, (something which the fox is able to drag behind it so as not to destroy a run on which foxes are regularly caught and therefore put other foxes off using it) is a legitimate practice but if the fox is able to disappear with the snare and the snare cannot be found in order to be checked then it becomes illegal. In this case the wood in which the snared roe deer was found was about 100 acres. Finding a fox (or in this case a roe deer) which had made off with a very light drag snare in 100 acres is extremely difficult and success could in no way be guaranteed.

I took photographs and also took possession of the snare and the fencepost as evidence. There was little else of evidential interest in the part of the wood that Dave and I were searching, though we did find several more fence posts with a staple in the centre of their length lying at the side of a woodland ride, obviously having been used as drags at some time. Another pair of searchers had found a further two dead buzzards, almost skeletal, which had been stuffed in a rabbit burrow in another small wood near a pheasant release pen. Lastly, the team that had gone to the suspect's house had found nothing of evidential value but informed me that they were now at Perth Police Station with the suspect, who had attended there voluntarily.

Having an almost useless power of arrest under the Wildlife and Countryside Act 1981 (a suspect must fail to give his name and address or the police officer must believe it to be false before the suspect can be arrested) was an incredible frustration. Equally frustratingly, a suspect could not be detained and taken to a police station for interview since wildlife offences at that time were not punishable by imprisonment. We were left with this third option of asking a suspect if he would please be so gracious as to attend voluntarily at the police station so that we could interview him.

Anyone who has been in an interviewing situation is well aware that the more pressure placed on an interviewee then the more likely that person is to tell the truth. I remember a sheriff's comments to the defence solicitor in a case where I had charged a shop owner with resetting several thousand stolen cigarettes. The defence was making the argument that the accused shop owner had only admitted the offence because I had put her under undue pressure, and was ticking off a series of points by way of demonstrating this. When he had come to the end of the list, the sheriff looked at him dismissively and said, 'Please remember that Mr Stewart did not invite your client to the police station for a tea party.'

With no power to hold our suspect in this case and being unable to put him in a cell to contemplate for a while, he may as well have been at the police station for a tea party or even cheese and wine. He said very little that was going to help our case in any way at all, ended his period of voluntary attendance, and had to be taken back home. It is fair and proper that a suspect has a right to remain silent. What is not fair is that the police are hamstrung by having insufficient powers to carry out an investigation in a reasonable manner and in a way that takes account of the public interest as well as the rights of a suspect. This was an issue our Partnership for Action against Wildlife Crime (PAW) Legislative Working Group successfully addressed but it was still some way off.

At the conclusion of the investigation, a report was submitted to the procurator fiscal charging the suspect with setting a cage trap to catch birds, setting a snare and failing to inspect it at least once every day, and killing four buzzards by the use of the pesticide carbofuran. Of these charges, the evidence relating to the use of the cage trap seemed very good, the evidence relating to the failure to check the snare seemed reasonable but the evidence regarding the poisonings was pretty thin, there being little to link the suspect with the act.

At this point I had decided to obtain a copy of the crow cage trap general licence so that the procurator fiscal would be aware of the conditions of legal use of the trap, in particular the condition that stated the trap must be made incapable of catching or holding birds during any period that it was not in use. I thumbed through a file where I had several of these and discovered to my horror that a general licence that would allow the use of crow cage traps for game management purposes was issued by two separate departments of the Scottish Executive. One of these licences contained the relatively new conditions tightening up their use but the other was unchanged. I telephoned each of the departments, neither of which had realised this mistake. We were now in the position of having two general licences for crow cage traps with contradictory wording.

Even though it was extremely unlikely that the suspect would be aware of the existence of the two general licences it was something that we had to draw to the procurator fiscal's attention. We knew equally well that this would sound the death knell for the whole case. The suspect had to get the benefit of the doubt on the licences, after all one of them made no mention about having to make the trap incapable of catching or holding birds when not in use. It stands to reason that if one legal piece of paper says that you must carry out a particular course of action and another legal piece of paper implies there is no need to do so, a conviction would be impossible. We had been hoping that each of the charges would give a measure of support to the others but our joker was now lost from the pack. Throw in the cards and deal a new hand!

A new hand was almost dealt on the same estate the following year when another poisoned buzzard was found and a further two buzzards were found flying around with a Fenn trap on their leg. We suspected the same person but, despite a thorough investigation, we were unable to obtain any evidence to link him with the three birds.

Every second day I wonder why I do this job! Wildlife crime is unquestionably much more difficult to detect than any other sort.

CHAPTER 13

Badger Baiting

A brief look at the foul and evil crime of badger baiting for which the author reserves some of his strongest approbations.

Many wildlife investigations are the result of predator/prey relationships but in the winter of 1998 a case of quite a different kind was brought to my notice. A gamekeeper contacted me to tell me that someone was trying to snare badgers in one of his woods. I was aware of badgers in that area as a badger sett had been dug out some years previously and it looked as if at least one badger had been taken away to an unimaginable destiny.

Badger digging must be one of the cruellest pastimes of anything remotely associated with wildlife crime. Badgers are dug from their setts and either, there and then or at another destination, made to fight with terriers. Badgers have amazingly strong jaws and could hold their own with any terrier in a straight fight.

An encounter when a terrier happens to meet a badger by accident would be rare or possibly non-existent. These encounters are artificially manufactured by the cruellest of the human species. How can a person who calls himself a member of the human race dig out a badger, maim it by breaking its jaw or something equally incapacitating, and in a confined space from which it has no escape, set on it anything from one to four dogs? Cruelty to animals invariably equates with cruelty to humans. What kind of life must the kith and kin of badger diggers have?

I went to have a look at the snares. The snares were of the kind that, if set for foxes, would be legal. In other words they were not self-locking. Self-locking snares are banned by law as their design does not allow them to slacken off when the captured creature stops struggling. They remain tightly closed and the captive animal is normally strangled. The snares in this case were set on runs that could catch badgers but the runs were not badger runs, which are runs coming from badger setts and used exclusively by badgers.

This was an interesting scenario. It is an offence under the Protection of Badgers Act 1992 to attempt to snare a badger. But the snares were not on badger runs so this charge could not stand. It is an offence under the Game (Scotland) Act 1832 to try to snare game, but this was not the intent of the snares, nor could badgers be considered to be *game.* Had the snares been set higher off the ground to catch deer, this would have been an offence under the Deer (Scotland) Act 1996. The only mammal left was a fox. No matter what legislation I looked at it was not an offence to come on to land without the permission of the owner of the land to try to snare a fox. It *may* have constituted an offence under the Protection of Animals (Scotland) Act 1912 – the legislation that prior to 2006 dealt with cruelty to animals – once a fox had been caught, but we were not at that stage.

I was frustrated, as was the gamekeeper who was keeping me up to date with the position in the wood. He knocked the snares over every time he found one so that it could not ensnare any sort of animal, but this was not the answer to the problem. We both wanted the culprits caught before they managed to get hold of a badger and subject it to an agonising death.

I had a suspect, a man we had caught a few years before when he was residing in Angus. He had been convicted on various charges of cruelty. He had dug up fox cubs in the countryside, took them home to an artificial fox den he had created at the back of his house and set his terriers on them to kill them. He had also tied a ferret on to the end of a length of orange baler twine and set a terrier on it to kill it. Finally he had caught someone's ginger cat, put it in a cage and set two terriers on it to kill it. How did we know it was orange baler twine and a ginger cat? The man had photographed the whole episode and submitted the film to a shop for developing! He had been training his terriers for badger baiting and was fined the surprisingly low sum of £200 for this catalogue of crimes. Since that time he had moved house and was now residing not many miles from the wood in which we were having problems. As badger-related crime is fortunately quite uncommon in Tayside, it was hardly surprising that this man became the prime suspect. Of interest, the man has since been convicted of crimes of dishonesty, violence and salmon poaching, yet another example of the link between wildlife crime and other criminality.

Over the Christmas and New Year period, the snaring stopped and the snares knocked by the gamekeeper remained on the ground where they constituted no danger to any form of wildlife. In mid-January I had a telephone call from the keeper to the effect that snares had now been set in the wood at head height for roe deer. For some reason the quarry being targeted had changed.

I reflected back to a similar incident the previous winter when nine roe deer had been caught in snares in a wood a few miles from the one we were concerned with now. These snares had not been checked for several days and the roe deer that were caught had died in the snares and were unfit for human consumption. Though we did not catch anyone for that incident I had considered our badger-digging man and wondered at the time if he was just in search of free feeding for his many dogs. In addition to terriers he had lurchers and greyhounds he used for coursing hares and deer. Such a number of dogs are expensive to feed and a roe deer could keep them going for several days.

I thought long and hard as to how to catch the phantom snarer and came up with an idea. I had used ultra-violet powder many times in CID enquiries when money was being stolen. The powder was brushed onto bank notes but was invisible to the suspect as it only showed up under ultra-violet light. It contaminated the thief without his or her knowledge. I was aware of two similar substances available commercially, Cyphermark and Smartwater, but wondered what might be available through our Identification Branch free of charge, as my budget was tight and mostly accounted for.

I was pleased to hear that ultra-violet powder had evolved to ultra-violet paste, which would be eminently suitable for the job I had in mind. I obtained a small amount and passed it to the wildlife crime officer for the area concerned, PC Graham Jack, to paint on to the snares that had been set for deer, firstly having knocked them so that they were safe. This was done, and Graham reported back that he had asked a couple staying in a cottage beside the wood to make contact with the police station if any suspicious characters went into the wood, especially if they had terriers with them.

Four days passed and I began to think that the phantom snarer had given up and resorted to his criminal activities in another part of Perthshire. On the fifth day our plan came to fruition. The residents of the woodside cottage telephoned the police station at Blairgowrie to say that three men with terriers had just gone into the wood. Graham responded promptly and caught the three men coming back out of the wood to their car. PC Jack had with him an ultra-violet lamp, not an item normally carried in a police car but he anticipated its necessity for this particular job. When the men's clothing was illuminated they resembled the Christmas trees from just a few weeks past. They were glowing and iridescent! Their hands in particular were a luminous indigo from holding the contaminated snare to form it into a loop designed to catch the roe deer round the neck. We had not only caught the phantom snarer but had the bonus of catching his two accomplices.

Despite the evidence, the three denied any knowledge of snares in the wood and any complicity in setting them. They pled not guilty and went to trial.

There are many stories about the good news and the bad news. The good news is always delivered first. I had a telephone call from the procurator fiscal after the trial. The good news was that the men had been found guilty. Having heard that I wondered how this could get worse rather than better. The charge was, 'being two or more persons acting together, did without legal right or written permission from a person having such right, attempt to take deer by means of a snare, being a means otherwise than by shooting with the proper calibre of rifle and ammunition, Contrary to the Deer (Scotland) Act 1996, Section 17 (3).' The bad news? The sheriff clerk could find no penalty to pass to the sheriff in order that he could sentence the accused appropriately and legally. Did I know what the penalty was or where it could be found?

The sheriff had deferred sentence for three days to enable the sheriff clerk to establish what the penalty was and where it could be found. I hurriedly opened the Deer (Scotland) Act 1996. The Act had recently been updated from the Deer (Scotland) Act 1959, which I knew well and from which I could quote sections. The new Act was less well known to me but shouldn't be difficult to follow.

I searched virtually line by line but no penalty was to be found in the new Act for a contravention of Section 17 (3). The legislators had forgotten to include it. What an absolute disaster. It was difficult enough to get a conviction for any form of wildlife crime. Enforcing this type of crime was the biggest challenge of my career and the legal boffins had buggered it up. At least one of those involved deserved to go to jail and they were about to get off scot-free. At that point I thought that being a wildlife crime officer was the most frustrating job in policing, if not on planet Earth.

The three appeared for sentence after the three-day deferral. They didn't get off scot-free after all – they had their snares forfeited!

Two improvements in law came from that case. I wrote to the Scottish Executive and advised them of the *faux-pas* in relation to Section 17 (3) of the Deer (Scotland) Act. They were sympathetic but told me that though on the face of it the remedy seemed simple, the amendment to correct the Act would need to be introduced via other legislation and this could take some time.

The other aspect of the case that annoyed and frustrated me was the fact that circumstances existed in which someone could go on to land and set snares without authority and yet still with impunity from the legal process. I was at that time in a position to do something about this myself as I was on a working group of the Partnership for Action against Wildlife Crime (PAW) looking at improvements to wildlife law. The recommendation I put forward was that it should be an offence under the Wildlife and Countryside Act 1981 for an *unauthorised* person to set snares on any land.

In 2004, under the provisions of the Nature Conservation (Scotland) Act, both loopholes were closed. I was pleased that I played at least a small part in the forming of more effective legislation in Scotland.

CHAPTER 14

Visiting Shooters

Recalling the case of the West Lothian Wanderers and overseas visitors toting shotguns shows that crime likes a day out, and even a foreign holiday.

Deer are taken in a number of different ways and two other deer poaching cases took place about the same time as the attempt to snare the roe deer. The first investigation brought back memories for me and involved three men in their mid-twenties from West Lothian. The three had driven up to north Perthshire and during the night were driving round quiet country roads in their car, shooting whatever game they could find grazing at the roadside. I remembered having dealt with the father of one of the men for the very same thing in the 1970s, though pater and his pals in the early days had gone a stage further and had broken into Forestry Commission premises and had stolen a number of chainsaws. I have noticed this link over the years between poachers and housebreakers. Criminals arrested during the night with stolen property in their car frequently also had either fishing rods or guns of some description in the car. I was never sure whether the original purpose of the expedition was poaching or theft, but criminals are opportunists and will take advantage of whatever presents itself.

The three West Lothian men had been stopped by night shift officers, who had searched the car and found in the boot three mountain hares in their white winter coats (it being the month of February), three high-powered air rifles and a red deer stag. The men were arrested and in the morning I was asked to assist in the investigation. I examined the three hares and was reasonably satisfied that they had been shot because marks on the rib area of each were consistent with the entry of an air weapon pellet. The red deer staggie was a young beast of almost two years old. Although I could see no obvious cause of death, its throat had been cut to bleed it. I read the interviews of the three accused and found that each of them had stated that the deer ran in front of the car and received only a glancing blow but had gone down like a stone. As it was injured, one of the men had cut its throat. Not wanting to waste the venison, they put the carcass in the boot to join the three mountain hares.

When taking cases to court where a person is charged with taking an animal or bird by a particular means, it is important to exclude all other possible causes of death. There is little point in charging someone with shooting mountain hares where there exists a possibility, albeit slight, that they had picked them up as road kills. A switched-on defence solicitor is likely to suggest that this is how his or her clients came by the hares – or even the red deer – and that, though it may be a technical offence to have picked them up and kept them, it is not an offence with which His Lordship's busy court should be troubled. The police officers giving evidence would be asked if the cause of death had been established, and if the answer was no, the next obvious question would be, 'Do you agree that it is possible that these hares could have been the unfortunate victims of car accidents?' The police officer would state that this was unlikely but the defence, rightly, would be relentless and in the next response, the police officer would have to agree that, while he did not think the hares had been road kills, that possibility could not be excluded. A charge has to be proved beyond reasonable doubt. If a doubt exists then the benefit of that doubt goes to the accused. Case lost.

Similarly if there is an allegation that animals, birds or even fish had been taken by a stated illegal means, they (or at least in certain cases, photographs) must be made available for examination by the defence or an expert used by the defence. This precedent was set in 1976 in the case *Anderson vs Laverock* when a past British and World Championship flycaster was charged with being in possession of twenty six salmon in circumstances which afforded reasonable grounds for suspecting that he had obtained the salmon as a result of committing an offence under the Salmon and Freshwater Fisheries (Protection) (Scotland) Act 1951. At the beginning of the trial, the defence lodged an objection on the grounds that the fish had not been produced and that the case should be dismissed. The sheriff repelled the objection and went on to convict the man. The conviction was appealed and the High Court upheld the appeal and quashed the conviction, stating that neither the accused nor his solicitor had been given an opportunity to examine the salmon. The fish had been destroyed, without the knowledge of the flycaster, Mr Anderson, shortly after he had been charged. This had been deemed unfair as the defence had no chance to look at any marks or absence of marks on the fish and challenge any allegation as to how they had been taken.

I was in no doubt that I had to get the three mountain hares and the deer examined, and arranged to take them to a leading veterinary forensic pathologist that morning. I drove to Lasswade Veterinary Laboratory south of Edinburgh and dropped the beasties off with Professor Ranald Munro, who said he would get to work on them right away since the three West Lothian men were due in court the following morning.

I hadn't quite reached Perth when I had a call from Professor Munro. The hares had each been shot with an air weapon and there was an air gun pellet in the neck of the young staggie. In relation to the deer it was unfortunately another good news and bad news story. Ranald was able to say that the deer had been shot while it was alive and that the pellet, where it lodged, would have put the deer down but would not have killed it. That was the good news – at least for the investigation if not the deer. The bad news was that there was a dislocated vertebra in the neck that could be consistent either with someone holding the deer down with a foot on its neck... or a glancing blow caused by being struck by a car.

This wasn't a fatal setback to the deer poaching aspect of the case. It was important evidentially that none of the three men had mentioned anything about the deer having been shot. In fact all had denied shooting at the deer. We were able to close the gap yet further in that our ballistics lab at Police Headquarters managed to match the pellet recovered from the deer's neck as having been fired from one particular air rifle of the three found in the car. In addition, two of the air rifles were proved to have been capable of producing the level of kinetic muzzle energy when fired that brought them in to the category of requiring a firearm certificate to possess them.

I remember being cited to appear as a witness in this case. This was cancelled as the case was adjourned till a later date and I was re-cited for the new date. This sequence happened at least three times, which unfortunately is all too common. In the end – possibly because the fiscal had been backed into a corner by reason of the series of undue delays – there was an agreement to a very much-reduced plea against two of the men only. These two pleaded guilty to taking the mountain hares during the hours of darkness without the landowner's permission, an offence under the Night Poaching Act 1828. One was fined £200 and the other was fined £250. The much more serious offences committed against the red deer stag and the firearm offences were dropped. It was a totally unsuitable resolution to the case.

It is much less likely that this would happen today. All wildlife or environmental crime cases are now seen by the environmental fiscal for the area, who has – or is building up – particular knowledge and expertise in that field of criminality. In addition, in Tayside, I rigorously monitor all these cases, speaking with the environmental fiscal either before she receives the case papers or just after she receives them to discuss with her the relevance of the charges and the sufficiency of evidence. When the case proceeds to court I continue to monitor its progress to ensure, so far as I can, that everything runs smoothly. Often slip-ups that cause the prosecution to ask the court for an adjournment of trial are based on something that has been overlooked, such as an important witness not being available or not having been cited for trial. This type of problem should be spotted well in advance of the trial date and the issue resolved. Failure to spot this before everyone else involved in the trial has turned up at court can put the case back two or three months and makes it difficult on the next occasion the case is called for the fiscal to object to a defence request for an adjournment. With me keeping an eye on these matters, it is yet another opportunity to avoid this type of problem, which directly or indirectly can sometimes be fatal to the case.

The last deer poaching case of that year took place in completely different surroundings. It related to a dead roe deer found in a garden shed in a Dundee housing estate after the police had received information that it had been stored there by the shed owner, who had used his lurcher to take the deer in Dundee's Camperdown Park. I was particularly pleased at the investigation, which was carried out by a young police officer who had just completed a week's course as part of the in-force training programme, of which I have a half-day input on poaching and wildlife crime legislation. I remembered this particular officer wondering how relevant poaching and wildlife crime training was to him as a city-based officer. Here lay the answer.

From the bite marks to the top of the back legs and the throat of the deer I was happy to give evidence to the court as to it having been taken by a dog, but this was yet another case where a reduced plea was accepted rather than to run the trial. The accused in this case pled guilty to unlawful possession of the deer. The pleas of not guilty to the charges of taking the deer without the landowner's permission, taking it by the use of a dog and taking it out of season (it was a doe taken during the month of August) were accepted. The accused already had a number of non-analogous convictions for dishonesty, drugs and disorder and was fined £250. The sheriff told him that if evidence had been led in court that he had taken the deer rather than simply having it in his possession, he would have been going to jail.

Police officers sometimes suffer frustration at reduced pleas being accepted by the procurator fiscal. However the fiscal is the public prosecutor and his or her role is a mixture of balancing public interest, assessing the strength of the evidence available in a case, assessing whether the penalty would be much different even if a trial were to go ahead rather than accept a reduced plea, and make (or juggle) these judgements against the background of several other trials due to be heard in the same court on the same day. It is easy to be critical but I would have no wish to be in the shoes of a procurator fiscal.

•

On fairly regular occasions wildlife offences are reported where the suspect is a visiting shooter from another country. The first with which

I had involvement in this category related to a man who was using a tape-recorded goose call to lure geese within range of his shotgun near the River Earn at Auchterarder. The use of tape recordings in circumstances like this is banned in the UK. Any calls to lure birds within range to be shot must be an imitation of the bird by a human, or an artificial call of the type that the operator blows into. The man was fined but the penalty was less than it might otherwise have been as the defence solicitor told the court that in his client's country of origin the use of a tape recording was permitted. Neither I nor Dave Dick of RSPB investigations was convinced but by the time we managed to find out the truth and that the court had been spun a yarn, the man was long gone.

Another foreign visitor shot five mute swans on the River Isla near Coupar Angus in daylight, appropriately at a part referred to locally as the Swan's Neck. He claimed that he thought that they were geese, even though at least one of the swans shot was an adult in pure white plumage. In reply to the charge, the man said, 'Nobody said there were swans there. If I had been told this I would have been more on guard.' Some folk blame anyone but themselves.

In another incident, one July evening a foreign shooter was standing shooting wood pigeons under a tree on a farm near Kirriemuir in Angus. An off-duty policewoman lived nearby and could hear the shots. She was aware of where the shots were coming from and at one stage looked toward the tree to see a buzzard fly in and land on a branch. A shot rang out and the buzzard fell to the ground.

The policewoman contacted her colleagues at Forfar Police Station and related the story. Officers attended to deal with the incident and at the same time I received a telephone call at home advising me of what had taken place. I decided to go to Forfar to ensure that the case was being dealt with properly as cases under the Wildlife and Countryside Act 1981 still held some mystique for many police officers, not being offences they dealt with on a regular basis.

On my arrival I was brought up to date with the state of the enquiry and asked if the accused person had returned to his hotel. The answer was no and that he was in a police cell. I asked what he had done besides shooting the buzzard, which caused a look of bewilderment on the faces of the officers, quickly changing to a look of realisation at what they had done.

Under the Wildlife and Countryside Act at that time – 1999 – there was no power of arrest unless the suspect refused to give his name and address or it was believed to be false. It often meant officers had to investigate wildlife crime virtually with one hand tied behind their backs. It is understandable that an interview with a suspect who is detained in a police station is likely to have a substantially different outcome from an interview with a suspect who is in his own home and who may not allow the police over the doorstep.

In any case the situation was reversed here, with a suspect in a police cell without there being legislative power to place him there. He was soon out of the cell and was charged with intentionally killing a wild bird, namely a common buzzard, by shooting it with a shotgun. There was a further charge of being in possession of a thing capable of being used for committing an offence under the Act, namely a Beretta 12 bore semi-automatic shotgun. The accused was due to return to his own country in a couple of days but agreed to present himself at Forfar Sheriff Court the following morning.

In the morning I had a telephone call from the procurator fiscal at Forfar. He explained that the Forfar fiscal was on leave and that he was standing in. He normally worked from the procurator fiscal's office in Glasgow and was not too acquaint with this type of crime. Could I explain to him first of all the difference between a buzzard and a wood pigeon! He was completely devoid of any knowledge about birds but then if someone asked me to explain the off-side rule in a game of football or how many feet from a goal a penalty kick should be taken I would be equally at a loss. Despite initial misgivings, I was still confident that he could prosecute the case better than I could referee a football match.

The accused appeared in front of the sheriff and pled guilty. He was asked if there were any mitigating circumstances he wanted to put forward to the court before being sentenced. The accused said that he hadn't intended to shoot a buzzard. He thought that when the bird landed in the tree, it was a wood pigeon. So much for sportsmanship, letting a bird land before shooting it!

The sheriff looked at the charge of killing the buzzard again and, rightly, told the accused with that particular plea in mitigation he was in effect pleading not guilty. The Crown had to prove all of the elements of the charge, one being that the act of shooting the bird was committed *intentionally*. He was then asked if he wanted to withdraw his plea in mitigation so that he could be dealt with there and then, or if he wished now to plead not guilty and come back for trial. Unsurprisingly he changed his plea to one of not guilty. A trial date was set but no-one expected to see him again. They weren't disappointed.

•

It is exceptionally difficult to prove to a court that a particular wildlife crime was committed *intentionally*. There are many other examples, one in the south of Scotland relating to a person who was charged following the discovery of several poisoned dead buzzards and ravens. The accused had possession of the same poison that had killed the birds and admitted putting the poison on rabbit baits that he had then set out on the estate. All involved thought that the case was clear-cut and a conviction would follow.

When this case came to trial the defence was that the baits had been set out for foxes and that there had been no *intention* to kill buzzards or ravens. Poisoned baits are indiscriminate and will kill any predator or scavenger that eats from the bait. It is unrealistic to set out poisoned rabbits for foxes and intend not to kill anything else. Even small signs *Private Bait – Foxes Only* would be of no help. Nevertheless the verdict of the court was not guilty to the charge of intentionally poisoning buzzards and ravens.

I was furious when I heard this, but the sheriff was absolutely correct. Intent to kill buzzards and ravens had not been proved. It was the Wildlife and Countryside Act 1981 that was badly written and needed changed quickly before more cases like this came to the same conclusion.

On our Partnership against Wildlife Crime (PAW) working group to improve wildlife legislation, we had identified this problem at an early stage and it was one of the recommendations we were putting forward. So far as I was concerned the new legislation couldn't come quickly enough, but it was October 2004 before it was enacted. Now, in similar cases, a person would be charged that he did intentionally *or recklessly* commit the particular act. A reckless act is much easier to prove and had this been available in the last two cases that I have outlined, the outcome would have been different. The public need have no fear of the inclusion of the term *reckless.* The concept of a reckless act has been well tried and tested in Scots law and is completely different from actions that are careless or accidental, neither of which are criminal offences under wildlife law.

CHAPTER 15

The Media and the Message

National recognition for the author (Royal even), and a question of whether the results achieved always justify the hard work of the wildlife detective.

By 1999, the poisoning of wildlife in Tayside had still not gone away. Four cases were confirmed that year, with two of these being on Edradynate Estate. A buzzard and a polecat were found dead in separate incidents, with carbofuran being the pesticide involved. We still had not succeeded in charging anyone in relation to these incidents and the waiting game continued.

We did succeed in charging a 70 year-old retired gamekeeper with several charges in connection with the recovery of four buzzards poisoned by Alpha-chloralose on an estate in Angus and the possession of a tub containing the same substance. Because of his age and the fact he had never been in trouble with the police before, the case was marked 'no proceedings'. It was not in the public interest to proceed with the case.

The following year, following the death in an Angus village of at least two dogs due to strychnine poisoning, enquiries centred on an eighty year-old man. He died before enquiries could be completed.

With such a dearth of successful police enquiries, a reader may be excused for wondering if the work carried out by wildlife crime officers is worth the bother. Tayside police officers were not alone in these frustrating times – the same was happening in every force in Scotland. But our skills would improve, as would the level of support the Scottish Parliament and associated new legislation gave us. In Tayside in particular we were heavily involved in education and preventive work. My own view was that the two-pronged approach, the carrot and the stick, was the only way to progress.

I took every opportunity to make use of the media to reach the public with the messages I wanted them to hear. I wanted the public to be aware of what wildlife crimes were taking place and how to recognise the signs. I also wanted the police to be the first point of contact for someone reporting a wildlife crime. To get these points across I wrote articles, gave radio and TV interviews, produced leaflets and posters and spent many, many evenings giving talks to any group who would sit down for three quarters of an hour and listen. I encouraged the divisional wildlife crime officers to do likewise and, in 1999 and 2000 in particular, we spread the message to every corner of Tayside.

We also started to attend events. We had a stand at the Game Conservancy Scottish Fair at Scone Place, the International Horse Trials at Blair Castle and several other smaller one-day events. At these events we were meeting farmers, gamekeepers, landowners and many other folks from rural environments or from urban environments but with an interest in rural activities. We wanted these folk on our side. We wanted to demonstrate to them the damaging effect that wildlife crime was having on country sports, those who participate in country sports, and even the negative effect that killing off our wildlife could have on tourism in Scotland. We made it clear we were in this for the long haul and that we would give as much help as we possibly could to those who were abiding by the law. But for those who broke the law, especially by the continued use of poisons, we would do whatever we could to ensure they ended up in court.

I must have been getting something right as in 1999 I received the World Wide Fund for Nature (WWF) Wildlife Law Enforcer of the Year award. This is an annual recognition – drawn from all involved in the fight against wildlife crime across the UK police forces and HM Customs and Excise (now HM Revenue and Customs) – of the person who is nominated as having made the biggest contribution for that year. I was thrilled to have won the award and the trophy was presented to me by the then Deputy First Minister, Jim Wallace, at a ceremony at Edinburgh Zoo.

My good fortune continued, and in the New Year's Honours List of 2000 I was awarded the MBE for services to the policing of wildlife crime. This was a surprise and an honour. I never expected such a prestigious award for simply doing work that I really enjoyed.

The award was presented to me at Buckingham Palace by HRH The Prince of Wales. He is extremely knowledgeable about wildlife and in the brief conversation I had with him he asked me how the upland waders in Tayside had fared in their breeding that year. During the twelve years I had carried out armed protection duties, we had met on several other occasions when he was holidaying in Tayside. On one of these occasions I had guarded overnight the Perthshire cottage in which he was staying and had spoken with him during the evening. When my shift had finished it was a lovely morning and I had gone off and shot some rabbits for the freezer – not with the .38 revolver I carried during the night I hasten to add. I had some success and was gutting my catch at the roadside when he passed in his Range Rover and gave me a cheery wave.

One of the factors that may have influenced the nomination for MBE was the extent to which I had developed the wildlife crime project with school children. It had come a long way since the original hen harrier project with two wee country schools in 1997 and was now extended to primary schools across the whole of Tayside. By 1999, about five hundred P6 pupils were involved (by 2006 the number had reached 2000 pupils) and I had them submitting four individual projects, one of which was a nature diary.

I first made a video tape about wildlife crime to give to each class as grounding for their work. The divisional wildlife crime officers and I then went into the schools and spent about an hour with each of the classes involved. Often the session would start with one of two questions to test their knowledge of wildlife. In one Dundee school their knowledge base was quite low. My first question to the two classes sitting cross-legged on the floor of the gym was, 'Can you name three birds you might expect to see on your way to school?' Silence. Not a peep! I re-phrased the question, 'Among the whole class, can we name three types of birds?' Silence initially and I was at the stage that I was expecting someone to say, 'A big bird, a middle-sized bird and a wee bird!' After all they are three types of birds. Anyway the answer was forthcoming – eventually. A craw, a seagull and a robin. So far so good.

My next question was of the same type, but requested the names of three kinds of trees. Collectively, a Christmas tree was all they could muster. I was confident these pupils would benefit from my input over the next eight or nine months.

My last question was, 'Can anyone give me the name of a bird in Scotland that would eat fish?' I looked round the sea of faces ready for a hand to shoot into the air. Arms remained firmly folded or hands remained hidden in pockets. I looked at the two teachers for some indication that one of them was ready to vent her knowledge. There was no such sign. Clearly no such knowledge was available.

Two women were sitting at the back of the gymnasium and I thought that two or more of the kids in the classes may have been their offspring. The meeker of the two tentatively raised her hand to about ear level. She had an answer but didn't know if it was accurate. 'Give it a go, hen,' I thought to myself, though what came out was, 'Do you know the answer?' She should have had the confidence to shout her answer out loudly as it was absolutely correct, but instead she whispered submissively, 'A heron.' I was about to congratulate her superb ornithological knowledge but the woman sitting beside her got in before me. Ridiculing her already self-conscious friend, she stated with authority, 'Naw Jessie, heron ur fish'.

•

I had hoped that in the new Millenium, the scourge of poisoning wildlife might have abated. It was too much to expect it to have stopped but a reduction would have been encouraging. Four incidents were reported that year, but what really worried me were the incidents that were never discovered. Only a very small percentage of wildlife crime is reported. If four wildlife poisoning incidents are discovered it is both reasonable and logical to assume that this is the tip of the iceberg, since those who indulge in this most heinous crime take every precaution to remove the evidence before it is found. In addition to the dogs poisoned by strychnine and recounted earlier, nine buzzards, a crow and a golden eagle were the other victims that were recovered.

One case in early March near Milnathort in Kinross-shire began with a buzzard being found in the garden of a country cottage. The buzzard was near death and was taken by the resident of the cottage to Vane Farm RSPB reserve at Loch Leven. It died and on examination by SASA the pesticide carbofuran was detected as being the cause of death. This is the type of action that worried me. A member of the public, with no knowledge of the danger of pesticides, picks up a dying buzzard. These unfortunate birds, in the last excruciatingly painful minutes of their life, often vomit or slaver down their breast feathers. There is a real risk when handling these birds that this liquid cocktail could get on to the hands of the person trying to do their best for the dying bird. From the hands it could easily get to the person's mouth. Will it take the death of an innocent person who handles poisoned bait or a victim of that bait before those carrying out this awful crime come to their senses?

Where the buzzard was picked up is not an area of Tayside where there is a huge shooting interest and, being objective, I wondered if farming or pigeon interests were behind the crime. As a member of police support staff I had no powers to enter land, but I teamed up with Willie Milne from SEERAD, whose role at least in part, was to investigate the abuse and misuse of agricultural pesticides. SEERAD staff trained for this purpose have statutory authorisation to enter land to investigate the use or storage of pesticides, to inspect premises other than dwelling houses and even to open places that are lockfast. They may also be accompanied by others for the purpose of assisting them in their investigation, which is where I came in.

Willie and I have rural backgrounds and between us amassed over a century of experience of the countryside and farming and game-keeping practices, both legal and otherwise. We quietly drove round the narrow country roads near where the buzzard had been picked up, knowing the contour level at which the bird had been found, therefore keeping a particular eye on land above that contour level. Sick birds are less likely to fly uphill and far more likely to glide downhill from where they feed on a fatal bait and my experience has been to find the bait at a higher contour level than the victim.

The relationship to where bait is found and where victims of that bait are found is a question that invariably comes up in any trial for poisoning offences. There is no prescriptive answer as it depends on a variety of factors including the temperature, the gradient of the terrain, the pesticide being used and the species of victim feeding on the bait. Though victims are normally recovered anything from a few inches to about fifty metres from a bait, a combination of factors may mean that a victim can make it for a few hundred yards or, on rare occasions, a mile before succumbing to the effects of the poison. A factor which seldom, if ever, comes in to the equation is the quantity of pesticide on the bait. Almost without exception there is much more pesticide used than is required. In fact a bait that kills one golden eagle, dog, buzzard, otter or whatever the victim may be, is likely to have enough pesticide on it to kill twenty or more of them.

During our drive round the area that day I noticed blue objects at the edge of a young plantation. My suspicions that they were feed bins for pheasants were confirmed with a quick survey through the binoculars. The location of the feed bins lay about half a mile north-east from where the buzzard was found and, importantly, was uphill. This would be as good a starting point as any.

We parked in the property of the woman who found the buzzard, since it is important not to park the car in a place where it may be noticed by the person responsible for having committed the crime or by someone else who may relay the information back to that person. This is often easier said than done as most often we are in quiet rural areas where anything out of place gets spotted instantly. This is why it is invaluable to have the vast majority of law-abiding country folks on the side of the police: they make first-class witnesses.

About 100m short of the young plantation with the blue feed bins, we walked along the side of a deer fence separating some hill ground with a sprinkling of young trees from the lower arable ground. At the bottom of one of these posts lay a dead buzzard, the skeleton bleached and the body cavity bare of any organs, but sufficient barred tail feathers and curved upper mandible remaining to make a positive identification. At any time, a buzzard falling dead off a post would arouse my suspicions but on this particular occasion I was growing more and more confident that we were on the right track, though this buzzard had been dead at least since the previous autumn.

Just before we climbed the fence to leave the grass field and enter the young pine and larch plantation, I noticed a black object lying fifty metres away which turned out to be a dead carrion crow, probably dead about a month and beginning to smell a bit. No, I understate the extent to which the odour pervaded my nostrils: it was bloody awful. Absolutely stinking.

I made an examination of the crow, a species that can, in most cases, be legally shot. There were no apparent broken wings or broken legs so it was a possible victim of poisoning. It was photographed, bagged and labelled, with Willie and I signing the label, and stuffed into my rucksack... seconds after my sandwiches were removed from the rucksack and stuffed into my pocket. I can live with most dead things sharing rucksack space with my sandwiches but putrid carcasses or items containing maggots are not on that list.

We took stock at that point. Looking uphill from the crow and uphill from where the buzzard bones were lying, and doing a triangulation uphill from both these points to where the lines would cross took us to just inside the top corner of the young plantation, less that seventy metres away. That was where we made for next.

The plantation was about 100m wide and ran downhill for about 500m. It was bounded at the top with a line of mature spruce trees, had a strip seven or eight metres wide down the outside (on the west side where we were) that was almost bare of trees, but which ran into a line of about ten semi-mature beech trees along its edge towards the bottom of the plantation. The trees within the plantation were strips of larch and lodgepole pine alternating, the highest being just more than twice the height of a man. Even before we climbed over the fence we saw three major clues inside the plantation: a circular-shaped scattering of the white breast feathers of a wood pigeon; downhill five metres from that, the remains of a wood pigeon carcass; alongside both, quad bike tracks.

Closer examination of the wood pigeon carcass revealed to us the dark blue granules of carbofuran still sticking to the breastbone and what meat remained on the breast. From what we saw we could interpret the following:

- The carcass had initially been in the uphill position where the feathers now were.
- These feathers had been plucked from the carcass by a bird of prey (not a crow, which does not pluck a carcass as its beak is not designed to do so).
- The carcass of the woodpigeon was only a few days old so had not been the bait that killed the crow and certainly not the one that killed the buzzard that was now a skeleton.
- This point was a regular 'baiting point' and most likely linked to the user of the quad bike.
- This bait may well have been the one that killed the buzzard that sparked off the investigation.

From that point we made a rough search of the plantation and found a very recently-dead buzzard at the base of one of the beech trees near the bottom of the plantation. Just outside the plantation on the bottom side and near to a pheasant release pen were a further three wood pigeon carcasses, all beside quad bike tracks. All of these were photographed, bagged and labelled and joined *Corvus corone,* the carrion crow, now a cadaver in my rucksack. We had succeeded in establishing the source of the poisoning problem and the evidence we had recovered constituted sufficient to enable a sheriff to grant a search warrant. This would enable us to expand our search to include premises and hopefully, this time, get a satisfactory result.

At that point neither of us knew the name of the farm on which we had carried out this brief search. Even though this had been my patch during my spell as inspector in charge of Kinross section it was not one of the farms that I knew, so we still had a wee bit of work to do, but little more than a drive past the road-end to note the farm name. In any event, as it turned out, the abuse of pesticide on the farm was nothing to do with the family farming the ground.

The Scottish Agricultural Science Agency (SASA) did a very quick job for us on the recovered specimens and in each case the presence of carbofuran was confirmed. Exactly a week later, this time armed with a search warrant for the farm and buildings, we came out fielding a bigger team, including several divisional wildlife crime officers, some search-trained officers and two officers from SEERAD. Any organiser of a search that is likely to recover a number of items of whatever sort that will ultimately be used in court as productions is well advised to use search-trained officers. Apart from their practical and methodical approach to searching buildings, they are exemplary in their recording and in their audit-trail of anything that they seize, an aspect upon which trials have been known to founder.

Though, as I said, the family on the farm were innocent, we still weren't aware at that time that they leased the shooting on the farm to a goose guide who reared pheasants and controlled pests. An element of caution is always worthwhile and a knock on the door by two diplomatic divisional wildlife crime officers, DS Neil Macdonald and PC Graham Jack, just prior to the search revealed this. Their check also revealed that the goose guide resided in Fife and that he leased a shed on the edge of the farm in which he kept his equipment. We could have found this out by enquiring at the farm the previous week but there was nothing to indicate that those on the farm were not involved. Further, to make such an enquiry a week before a search would have made the search a waste of time as the Fife goose guide would have been warned off. Nothing in policing is simple.

The goose guide was contacted by telephone and agreed to attend at the farm. He was as good as his word and did so. He was left with DS Macdonald and PC Jack and the specialist search team, while I took the rest of the officers to complete the land search. The land search resulted in the recovery of a further dead crow, five buzzards and a wood pigeon carcass. Again the wood pigeon carcass was beside quad bike tracks.

The search of the shed used by the goose guide resulted in the recovery of a coffee jar almost full of carbofuran. And the presence of a quad bike. Tied on the front of the quad bike was an old game bag, which was also seized for examination. Further, the goose guide, when interviewed under caution, admitted setting out a single wood pigeon bait to deal with a fox. I never noticed on or near to any of the wood pigeon baits that I picked up a notice saying '*Bait for foxes only. No buzzards or corvids please*'.

Once all the samples had been examined by SASA the contents of the coffee jar were confirmed as being carbofuran. Traces of carborfuran were found in the game bag that had been tied onto the front of the quad bike, five wood pigeons were confirmed as having been laced with carbofuran and five buzzards and a crow were confirmed as having been killed by carbofuran. Remember also the ubiquitous quad bike, turning up beside each wood pigeon carcass. All in all I thought we had a very good case.

I'm more confident of success before some trials than others but I hope that I'm never complacent. On procedural evidence, police officers sometimes just have a split second to come to a decision that may make or break a case. A defence agent has months to go over the evidence collected by the police and pick at it with a fine tooth-comb. Statements taken from prosecution witnesses must be made available to the defence well in advance of a trial so a defence solicitor will always know the line that a procurator fiscal is going to take. Conversely however, the line the defence will take is not always known to the procurator fiscal. While it is not the role of the police to say that any of this is wrong or unfair, the public perception is often that the criminal seems to get more legal consideration than the victim of his or her crimes.

The lawyer employed by the goose guide put up a valiant fight. He questioned the search warrant, the right to enter the shed without a search warrant, even though permission from the accused was agreed, the admission (which had been noted by the two officers but regrettably the clipboard paper on which it was written not retained) and the procedures for supervising and corroborating the chemistry work done at SASA.

My comment in the previous paragraph about searching the shed without a search warrant requires explanation. Though we had a search warrant, it was to search the property of the occupier of this particular farm. Though the shed was technically his property it had been leased out to the goose guide and therefore did not fall within the terms of the search warrant. A comparative example in more domestic surroundings would be a room of a house let to a tenant. This put us in the position, if we wanted to search the shed, of either having to obtain a further warrant for the shed or consent being given by the goose guide for the search to take place without a warrant.

There is no question that part of the trial interest of a police officer (or retired-police officer like me) is in the line of defence. I would have been thoroughly impressed by the defence solicitor had he not tried at some stage in the defence to ridicule several of the witnesses, including me. He had sufficient talent, ability and knowledge of the subject to have carried off the defence of that trial without stooping to the depths that we expect from the occasional solicitor who is notorious for those tactics. I learned one or two lessons from the professional parts of his defence. I hope he reads this book and he may benefit from my constructive criticism!

The goose guide was found guilty of several of the charges and was fined £2400. His lawyer appealed against the conviction, an appeal that took the best part of two years to be heard by the Court of Appeal. In the event the appeal was rejected and the conviction and sentence stood. It was a landmark conviction for the abuse of pesticide but my fervent wish was that game management could be carried out without having to resort to illegal practices, especially those involving indiscriminate pesticides.

We were still in the early Spring of the year 2000 when yet another poisoning offence came to light. This time it was a dead golden eagle found poisoned with Alpha-chloralose on the north side of Loch Earn. We expended considerable time and effort into that case partly since the victim was a golden eagle, but came nowhere near to finding the person responsible or even deciding whether the death was related to grouse management or sheep farming.

CHAPTER 16

Operation Easter

Not a fluffy bunny in sight but there is a concerted national effort led by Tayside Police to share data on known egg thieves and closely monitor their movements.

In the Spring of 1997 we launched Operation Easter in Tayside. The operation had been the brainchild of one of the divisional wildlife crime officers, Constable Ian Hutchison, and was an operation (run by Tayside Police as one of the very few national operations in the UK) with the objective of catching or deterring egg collectors. Constable Ian Hutchison was a wizard on computers and put considerable thought and energy into this computerised crime intelligence system. Through RSPB, he obtained the details of the main fifty-or-so wild bird egg collectors in the UK, all of them from England, and set about putting them on a database with the intelligence currently held by RSPB and of each of the forces in the areas in which they lived. Having set the system up, he retired due to ill-health and Operation Easter fell to me to administer and develop.

Though for operational reasons I can't go into the full details of how Operation Easter works, I can say it has been – and continues to be – immensely successful. When I took over the operation in 1998, I transferred it to the Home Office Large Major Enquiry (HOLMES) system, the software being much more familiar to me as I had worked in Incident Rooms on many occasions. By this time I had increased the number of targets to around eighty. The success rate increased since this was really the first time that all police forces in the UK, together with RSPB, were acting in a concerted fashion against egg thieves. Intelligence from every force in the UK came to me and I circulated it in a manner in which it could be utilised proactively with a real chance of catching the egg thieves.

One of the earlier examples related to a man who was visiting Mull and had drawn attention to himself in a hotel there. He was a particularly loud individual and had been asking of the location of various nesting birds, especially white-tailed eagles. As anyone who has visited the Isle of Mull is aware, the islanders are rightly proud of and protective of their birds, especially white-tailed eagles. It is the commodity that brings in most revenue to the island, much more than Balamory. It wasn't long therefore before the island's wildlife crime officer, PC Finlay Christine, got to hear about the Man with the Big Mouth. He managed to get his name and address and contacted me to ask if he was known to Operation Easter. I had never heard of this chap but contacted my colleague from Devon and Cornwall, Inspector Nevin Hunter, and discussed the matter with him. Nevin wasn't aware of him either but said he would make some enquiries.

Within a very short time Nevin got back in touch to say they had sufficient intelligence to apply for a search warrant for the home of the Man with the Big Mouth and intended to search it in the next few days. The result came back from Nevin after the search that they had recovered 3,500 wild birds' eggs, a kilo of cannabis and a handgun. Not a bad result from a Mullach who noticed someone who opened his mouth just a bit too much in a pub seven hundred miles from home.

We obtained results not unlike this several times a year and the egg collectors wondered what had hit them. They had been getting away with robbing the nests of our rare birds for years when each police force, assisted by the RSPB, operated independently and with much less efficacy. Now the egg thieves had something to think about.

•

Intelligence on the actions of those who were already targets of Operation Easter built up steadily, as did the number of targets. By the year 2001, I had over a hundred targets on the system, of which at least ten per cent were getting caught in a year. I had also changed the Operation over to another database, this time to the Tayside Police intelligence system, the most user-friendly system I had ever encountered and which proved its worth time and time again by allowing me to use separate fields for different categories of collectors: those who specialised in taking the eggs of one particular species of bird; egg thieves who visited particular sites; those who travelled abroad for eggs, and many other categories of offender.

The Operation Easter intelligence network had another major result, this time involving Tayside Police officers. In 1999, intelligence was received from the wildlife crime officer in Warwickshire who monitored several egg collectors on his doorstep in Coventry (even though Coventry was in the West Midlands Police area). He related that he had received reliable information that some of the Coventry egg thieves were coming to Scotland the following day to take eggs. He was unfortunately not able to say which of the substantial number of egg thieves from Coventry were travelling to Scotland, which vehicle they were using or where they were going. Needle in a haystack? Not quite.

Between the RSPB database and the Operation Easter database, we were able to work out the most likely species the targets would be after because of the particular time of year. All species of birds lay their eggs at the time of year most suited to them hatching when there is sufficient food around for the chicks' survival. The date fitted a small diving duck called the common scoter. Considering these are fairly rare birds, the name must be something of a misnomer.

Since we thought we had identified the most likely species, it was fairly simple to identify the most likely site, a loch in Inverness-shire where these birds are known to breed and a location that is known to egg collectors. The knowledge of this location is clearly to the detriment of the common scoter, which has lost numerous clutches to egg thieves there over the years.

As Northern Constabulary were not able to supply any officers at short notice to make an early morning visit to this loch the next day, one of our divisional wildlife crime officers, Inspector Gordon Nicoll, agreed to go along with Dave Dick, senior investigations officer for RSPB Scotland. After a long hike to get to the loch, during which time they were eaten alive with midges, they managed to intercept two of the egg thieves coming away from the loch and recovered several clutches of common scoter eggs in their rucksacks. It was intriguing that despite the eggs having been emptied of their contents by the time the two men were caught, no trace was ever found of the small drill that egg thieves use to make the single hole in the egg or of the small tube of lesser diameter than the hole which is used to blow the contents out. Neither was there any trace of the vehicle they had used to get to this Inverness-shire loch or of their associates in crime. It could only be assumed that the others who had travelled with our two accused had used the vehicle to go elsewhere to collect eggs of another rare species.

In April 2000, at Fort William Sheriff Court, the two Coventry men pleaded guilty and were fined £2000 each. One of them, who will feature again – let's call him The Sly Man – told the court that he was finished with egg collecting and would never take another egg.

In May 2000 – a month after the Fort William case – a clutch of osprey eggs was taken from one of several nests in the area around Dunkeld in Perthshire. Despite our investigation, this crime was undetected and would have remained so had it not been for the Operation Easter network.

Nearly two years later, in March of 2002, I had a telephone call from my Operation Easter contact in Merseyside, Constable Andy McWilliam. Andy told me he had just finished a search of a house occupied by one of the Operation Easter targets and had recovered 800 wild birds' eggs. This was only part of the reason he was phoning me. The other part was to tell me that he had recovered the target's diaries and that there was an entry on a date in May 2000 to the effect that The Sly Man had taken a clutch of osprey eggs in Perthshire. Great news, but there could be one small problem in that our case would be time barred after two years (it is now extended to three years because of the provisions of the Nature Conservation (Scotland) Act 2004) and the two years would be up in May. March to May was not a lot of time to gain the evidence required and get it before a court. Of course someone can still be convicted of possession of birds' eggs long after two years has elapsed since the time they were taken from the nest, but the penalty imposed by the court is likely to be less than it would be if it could be proved that the person who possessed them had actually taken them. We are never satisfied with small beer!

Within a day or two of this information I had contacted the wildlife crime officer in West Midlands, PC Andy Hale, who had agreed to obtain a search warrant if we could supply Tayside officers to assist in the search. In many cases it could be difficult to get the authority to take two officers off general policing duties and send them such a distance to search for wild birds' eggs. Middle management within Tayside Police deserve real credit for the support they give wildlife crime officers and for treating wildlife crime just like any other crime rather than the 'furry bunny' crime it is typecast by middle management in some other forces.

Divisional wildlife crime officers DS Neil Macdonald and PC Graham Jack set off to Coventry to join up with PC Andy Hale and to give The Sly Man a surprise visit. Their first success during the search was the recovery of 29 dead rare birds in a freezer. These included chough, corncrake, honey buzzard, stone curlew and hoopoe. Later x-ray examination revealed that most of the birds had been shot with a shotgun.

Eventually a clutch of three osprey eggs was recovered and The Sly Man was asked how he had come by them. He admitted having taken the eggs himself but stated that he took them in 1999, a year too early to be charged with *taking* the eggs but still OK for a charge in relation to their possession. Try as they might, the officers could not get him to shift on that date and to admit he took them in 2000.

By good luck Neil and Graham found a set of photographs in the house, several of which were photographs of Blair Castle at Blair Atholl in Perthshire, and of the Duke of Atholl's private army. By sheer coincidence PC Graham Jack, in his spare time, is one of the Atholl Highlanders in this private army and happened to feature in the photographs. He asked The Sly Man what the photographs were and the reply was, 'Just some holiday snaps that I took of some men in kilts when I was in Scotland in 1999, the same year as I took the osprey eggs.'

Graham quizzed him further on whether he knew anyone in the photos but the reply was in the negative, that they were just holiday snaps. Graham asked him to look again, more closely this time, which he did. His jaw dropped when he recognised one of the images in the photograph as the man standing beside him, albeit minus the kilt. 'Bloody Hell, it's you. You're in this photo aren't you?'

The photos were his undoing. PC Jack was able to tell The Sly Man that the photos were taken for the Millenium Parade in the year 2000, therefore that was the year that he took the osprey eggs in Perthshire. He had no choice but to put his hands up.

It's a funny old thing, coincidence! The Sly Man probably reflected on that during his four months in jail.

•

There have been many more captures of the targets of Operation Easter. The number of targets rose at the height of the operation to a hundred and twenty and is now down to half of that. I have changed database yet again, this time to the Scottish Intelligence Database (SID). It is nothing like so user friendly as the Tayside system but has the advantage that all police officers in Scotland can link in to it.

Some egg collectors who were targets have been forced to give up altogether, some now travel abroad to collect eggs and at least two are known to have moved their egg collections abroad. All of this reflects the success of an operation where intelligence is pooled and police officers and RSPB work together irrespective of force boundaries.

Other major factors came into play in England and Wales in 2002 and in Scotland in 2004 – the fact that wildlife criminals can now be arrested by the police plus the fact that they can also now be jailed for their crimes. The availability of a jail sentence is a partial deterrent but when this is coupled with a realistic risk of being caught it becomes a major deterrent. Any egg collector reading this need not think that we have now become complacent and will rest on our laurels. Operation Easter will continue and in fact is expanding into the illegal world of those who, without the proper licensing, intentionally or recklessly disturb nesting Schedule 1 birds for selfish photography.

Chapter 17

Kids, the things they say!

In which the insightful and often hilarious wildlife and policing perceptions of primary school pupils are shared for the first time.

Despite numerous setbacks with cases not proceeding or not guilty verdicts, the day is often lightened during the part of the year when the schools are taking part in the Tayside Police Wildlife Crime Project. The project was growing year upon year and a lot of my time was taken up marking the four individual projects undertaken by the kids. Though I try to vary the projects from year to year there is one part that is fairly constant; that of completing a nature diary. I much prefer the kids to compile a Spring nature diary. In Spring everything is being renewed after the long winter and changes in our environment are probably more easily noticed by young folks at that time of year. Birds are nesting, lambs are being born, crops are being sown, buds are bursting out on trees and bushes, grass is beginning to grow and there is just a sense of new life everywhere.

The downside of Springtime nature diaries is that there is inevitably too much of a rush immediately prior to the prize-giving, which is normally in early June. In my experience, because of other pressures they are under, many teachers are poor at keeping to deadlines and I am lucky if I have half of a particular project submitted by the deadline I have set. The same criticism cannot be levelled at the children. Some of these 9 to 11 year olds put in a tremendous amount of work and produce first-class nature diaries, even though it may only relate to what they see in a city. They obviously enjoy this type of work and many complete the diary as homework. One teacher was kind enough to write me a short note saying that the project I had set had been the only homework that one boy in her class had ever completed. I was pleased that the kids were enjoying learning about wildlife and its regrettable but attendant crime. I am also of the view that wildlife crime provides an invaluable link between young people and the police. They seem to relate to crime committed against animals and birds and appreciate that the police are doing their best to combat the crime. They seem to empathise with the problems both the police and the wildlife are experiencing. I have given talks to school pupils in the past on drugs, vandalism and 'rules for living'. They turn off pretty quickly as it seems that they are being blamed by the police for this catalogue of social ills rather than being asked what they can do to help, as is the case with wildlife crime.

There are many hilarious moments in the marking of the diaries. I encourage the kids to collect items from the wild and stick them in the diary with a wee explanation of what the item is and its significance. They are normally very good at this but there are always a few disasters, like mushrooms stuck on to a page under a piece of sellotape. By the time the diary comes to me the mushroom is just a black sludge that has soaked the six or seven pages underneath, obliterated any writing and in any case has made the pages stick together so that I wouldn't have been able to read the writing anyway. Another pupil had been catching bluebottles and had stuck four into the diary under sellotape to show me the back view, front view, side elevation from the right and side elevation from the left. I think he was a budding architect.

My favourite entry, though not at the time, was in a diary I was marking during my evening meal. The diary, so that I could read it, had to be next to my plate. It was a very good diary with lots of detail and many interesting leaves and flowers stuck in by way of illustration. One grey, furry, oval object was stuck to the page, with the proud caption, 'This is an owl pellet my dad and I found in a wood'. Owl pellets are grey, furry and oval so the pupil was nearly accurate. Nearly, but not quite. The grey, furry oval object just inches from my plate of food was fox shit!

Another project I set one year was to be entitled, 'A day in the life of a police wildlife crime officer'. I was encouraging the pupils to write about doing my job for a day and to put down on paper what they thought it would be like. They had to use their imagination to investigate a wildlife crime of their own choosing. Most of these stories ran to about two pages and many were absolutely hilarious. I marked many of them on a train journey to and from a meeting on Conservation Priorities I attended in Peterborough and received many funny looks and a few enquiries from fellow passengers as to what I was doing and why I was always bursting into fits of laughter.

Like many police officers, the pupil-officers had due consideration for sustenance and very few stories did not include a stop for a cup of tea, sometimes even specific brews: *I put on a kettle for my Nambarrie cup of tea.* Even after a couple of hours 'work' they felt the need for food: *I stopped to have some stovies at the cake shop* or *I went to have a KFC bucket because I was so hungry.* Most folks have breakfast before they start work, even with an early start, but what about: *PC Smart gets up at 2 am to get an early start at work and to have a glass of wine before his wife gets up.* I know the author of this line's father, an eminent TV cameraman who is *not* called Mr Smart, (the name is changed to protect the innocent – or is he?) In any dealings I've had with the father, the camera has always been rock steady but I teased the life out of him over his son's account of the early glass of wine.

Now that the budding officers had been fed, under Health and Safety requirements they needed the proper equipment for the job: *Having got the call I quickly took off my pink fluffy bunny slippers and donned my wildlife crime suit.* The pupil omitted to say if this allowed her to fly through the air. The kids' language often fascinated me. The word 'donned' is just the perfect verb for this situation. In even more colourful language, another author was describing how he was gathering together all his gear for the wildlife crime job in hand. I considered him a budding professor of English language: *I need all the accoutrements perchance I stumble across a creature in dire straits.*

Once they got under way, the mini-police officers had no mercy when they caught the criminal: *It was Freddy Melville, my twin brother. I arrested him and he got the jail.* Even worse: *After investigating a poisoning incident I found 10 bottles of poison in my dad's shed. I put him in handcuffs and took him to the police station. I said, 'I'm sorry dad but I have to do this.' I then went home and had my tea.* Ah well, at least he apologised to his dad for arresting him.

There were some unusual investigations. One mini-cop was investigating the taking of eggs from a bald eagle's nest at Arbroath cliffs. I suppose it's just possible a pair of bald eagles may have been blown eastwards across the Atlantic without coming to the attention of twitchers! I also learned of a new way to poach salmon: *I saw him giving a worm a poisoned jab and throwing it in the river.* Another sleuth, on having a golden eagle fall from the sky at his feet arrested *a group of poachers that capture rare birds and break one wing and throw them off a helicopter.*

It takes all kinds!

Some ventured into international wildlife crime, though they may not always have been aware of that: *I got a phone call about a komodo dragon that had fallen off an 8 foot high wall and died. The person wanted me to check that it was dead. I went there, took one look and said 'Yes'.* A man of few words but obviously good with a stethoscope. Another 'officer' who had probably strayed slightly off his beat, wrote: *Finally I found a tiger that was poisoned. It was in the east of India. The tiger was creamy and brown in colour and was a male. It had nine cubs.* The fact that a male tiger had cubs intrigued me. I also wondered if the author managed back from India for his meal break.

The previous escapade demonstrates that distance was no object to an intrepid wildlife crime officer. What about this for a day's work: *I was at Stanley Primary School giving a talk when I received a telephone call that a man was stealing eagles' eggs at the top of Mount Everest. I apologised to the pupils and set off for Mount Everest. I didn't have that much time, I had only 4 hours to get there. There was a traffic jam half way there so I had to go the long way round, but it's just 10 minutes longer. When we caught the man I said we had done a good job and should have a drink. We had to go by Taymount Wood on the way home because a badger was caught in a snare. We saved the badger, which was good because it had children. Three of the children had something wrong with them and died. The one that didn't die was the odd one out.* Well. . . what can I say!

Penalties for those caught were sometimes pretty severe. A certain Mr McIntyre *has to serve at least life in prison for this wildlife crime.* Criminals can also be excluded from vulnerable sites by the courts: *The egg thief was fined and banned from all forests, rainforests, woods and jungles.* Sounds to me a good legal definition of any place that has trees! Occasionally justice was meted out by the wildlife victim: *A man called Billy went to an eagle's nest to steal the eggs but the eagle swept him up really high and let him go.* (it gets worse. . .) *So he got lifted again to the eagle's nest and sadly got eaten.*

Lastly, exasperated after a lengthy investigation to catch Horace Huckleberry, the UK No 1 egg collector, the wildlife crime officer-depute corners him. As we all know, the criminal always likes to have the last word: *I was knackered when I eventually got to the tree. I saw the silhouette against the sky and shouted to the egg thief to come down. He said, 'No way. Bug off, I am trying to do some business!'*

Chapter 18

Birds of Prey

A radio chat show prompts a discussion about the emotive issue of winged predators and why people should learn to live in peace with them if not love them.

Birds of prey are an emotive issue. Many people love them. Many people hate them. Very few people are ambivalent to their presence. My job is to uphold the law in relation to all wildlife crime, including birds of prey. Though I have an interest in the conservation of species, which includes that of birds of prey, I must remain objective, fair and balanced in my dealings with those on one or other side of the fence. As I write this chapter, I have just finished listening to an early morning BBC Scotland radio programme, part of which related to birds of prey. A farm worker spoke at length and with an abundance of anthropomorphic sentiment about seeing buzzards killing and eating young lapwings and leverets. He said it was terrible that when a buzzard catches a young leveret it screams out just like a baby. A rat or mouse or vole, much more common prey of a buzzard than a leveret, probably screams out just the same, but is this not so important? I'm sure it's just as important to the rat or mouse or vole. The buzzard is not being deliberately cruel to the prey that it catches; it is simply co-existing with prey species in almost the same manner as it has done for thousands of years. I say *almost the same manner* as any change in predator/prey relationships has in almost all cases been induced by humans. Prior to the Victorian era, the buzzard did not have a countryside supermarket stacked to the brim with pheasants, so it is only natural that now in many areas of the UK its lunch menu is likely to be predisposed towards one of the easier prey items to catch – semi-domestic pheasant poults.

On the radio programme, the farm worker stated with authority that buzzards should be culled and reduced by eighty percent, which would make a big difference to the number of young wader chicks and other ground-nesting birds taken by them. I'm sure it would make a difference but then could a much more substantial difference not be made by a change in farming practices? Every time the farm worker sprays a young cereal crop with an insecticide spray, consider how many millions of insects he is killing that could provide protein-rich feeding for young partridges, lapwings, skylarks and the like. To a ground nesting, insect-eating bird, a field of young wheat or barley must be the equivalent of a desert.

Every time you pass a field of young grass with the dark and light stripes of the roller reminiscent of a well manicured lawn, consider the time of year. If the field has been rolled late in the Spring, imagine how many eggs or young birds may have been flattened in the process. Look also at ploughed fields in late Spring where the land is being left for a later crop, such as turnips or peas. The ploughed land is a magnet to lapwings and oystercatchers and a scan of the field with binoculars is likely to reveal the many shiny black backs of the birds as they incubate their eggs. A week later you pass and there are tractors with a variety of implements going up and down the field and every bit of bird life has been lost. No-one is suggesting that farmers should leave their fields until the middle of summer before they begin their crop cycle but was the farm worker on the programme blind to the damage he has been doing to birds for years and blinkered only against a bird of prey in what remains of its natural habitat?

In my lifetime I have seen a huge change in farmland birds. When I was young I remember arable fields where it was common to have twenty pairs of nesting lapwings and from early March they delighted us as they laid claim to their chunk of the field by rising and falling and tumbling in the sky in their display flight, not unlike that of the male hen harrier. All the while they were making their onomatopoeic *peeeee-weep, weep-weep, peeeee-weep* call that gave them their much more interesting country name of peewit or peeweep. Tractors were much smaller and didn't have cabs, therefore we could more readily spot the nests – a simple hollow in the ground lined with half a dozen bits of straw – and avoid running them over. We then either worked around them or moved the eggs to the side, placing the four conical eggs in a similar hollow made with our heel and marking the nest with a stick so that it could be avoided when we came round with the next implement. This was in times long before the multi-tasking implements of today when a field can be harrowed, sown and the grain covered over all in one go.

Grass fields intended for hay would hold an abundance of curlews, skylarks, grey partridge, wild pheasants and sometimes meadow pipit and redshank. I can't ever remember rolling a grass field yet we still had substantial hay crops. The nearest most of these birds come now to agricultural land is marginal land and their decline was absolutely nothing to do with the buzzard or any other bird of prey.

The next speaker on the programme was an official from RSPB who explained predator/prey relationships and the fact that prey species normally have large and sometimes multi-broods of chicks to compensate for natural loss. He also made the point of changes in agriculture being responsible for the decline of certain species.

The final speaker I could only describe as a clot, who moaned that when he went for a walk in the country, he never saw young lapwings in a nest nowadays (which is little wonder as they leave the nest as soon as their feathers have dried out after hatching). He also lamented that 'you never hear nightingales singing now' (and he was talking about Scotland!) and that all of this, and much more, was down to birds of prey. I have never heard such claptrap.

No doubt, in certain circumstances, birds of prey have a deleterious effect on other birds, and some of the complaints from gamekeepers are justified. For a person who depends on producing high numbers of game birds for his livelihood it must be frustrating to see a buzzard taking pheasant poults or a hen harrier taking young grouse. Nevertheless, these raptors are protected by law and it is my job and that of all police officers to ensure compliance with the law. The police have absolutely no objection to the stance that the Scottish Gamekeepers' Association take on some birds of prey by lobbying for a change in the law to allow some degree of licensed control. This is the democratic route to take, though I have doubts about its success.

It's also interesting, if sometimes slightly confusing, to compare the views of different keepers. Some, like the farm worker on the BBC Scotland programme, would like a drastic reduction in buzzard numbers. Others are of the view that birds of prey don't cause them any significant problem. One grouse keeper took an especially pragmatic approach and said that as long as he can legally continue to control the numbers of foxes, crows and stoats he will be happy, as foxes in particular take far more of his grouse than all the birds of prey on the estate put together.

An issue that almost always arises when I'm giving a talk is the issue of sparrowhawks taking garden birds. I'm often asked for my thoughts on this and can speak from experience as I have a pair of sparrowhawks come into my rural garden on a regular basis and take small birds. Their favourites seem to be greenfinches and siskins with the occasional collared dove taken by the larger female sparrowhawk. There are a couple of plucking posts littered with green and brown feathers yet I can still have thirty birds at a time on the feeders and go through a 25 kilo bag of black sunflower seeds in two weeks or a bag of niger seed in two days. Apart from some disruption to the feeding of the birds, the predation has no long-term effect.

I was once asked by a journalist for a local paper if birds of prey would take pigeons. She had been visiting a pigeon fancier who was bemoaning the fact that his stock of pigeons was being decimated by birds of prey. I explained that peregrines would readily take pigeons that were on a race and that sparrowhawks would take them closer to home, even in some cases entering the pigeon loft to do so. The journalist could see that she now had verification of the pigeon fancier's complaint, but asked, obviously as the next stage in her article, if anything could be done to ameliorate this. I probably surprised her by answering 'Yes'. She seemed delighted that she was going to be able to publish the solution to the problem and asked what could be done.

I replied, 'All peregrines and sparrowhawks would need to be caught up and conditioned to eat grass and turnips.'

'Great,' she said, 'can I print that?'

'Of course you can Maureen,' I replied. 'It's the only solution however impractical it may be.'

Her response, in the next edition of the *Perthshire Advertiser*, an article entitled Birds of Prey Fancy Pigeons. . . 'a police spokesman said!'

Chapter 19

Pearls before Swine

Lesser known species suffer the onslaughts of crime as well as those that are more high profile, which leads the author to contemplating ladies' jewellery – and bats in the belfry.

Not all wildlife crime centres round what we commonly understand as birds and animals. There is a small amount of crime committed against plants, where they are taken from the wild without the permission of the landowner and sold; in the collection of or trade in rare insects; and in the taking or destruction of *Margaretifera margaretifera*. This last creature is arguably our most endangered animal in the UK yet can live for over a century. Scotland has half of the world population. It is disappearing fast and part of the cause of the decline is the crime that is committed against it. The level to which it is endangered is sometimes compared to that of the tiger in Asia. It generates incredible media interest yet it has neither fur nor feathers. *Margaratifera margaratifera* is the freshwater pearl mussel.

The freshwater pearl mussel has been sought-after for hundreds of years because of the pearl that can occasionally be found in one. Many of the more traditional pearl mussel 'fishers' were respectful of their quarry and had a practised eye at detecting which mussel was likely to contain a pearl. They opened the mussel with special pliers, flicked out the pearl and replaced the mussel in the river. They did not break the law as their actions did not intentionally kill or injure the creature. Latter day fishers were much less respectful and piles of shells began regularly to be found on riverbanks, having been cut open with a knife.

In 1997, Tayside Police joined forces with Northern Constabulary and Scottish Natural Heritage to draw attention to the plight of this charismatic creature. Since most of the remaining rivers containing freshwater pearl mussels are in the northern half of Scotland, these were the ones that were being targeted by the pearl fishers. Correspondingly these were the rivers where the remaining stocks of adult mussels – the breeding stock as it were – could be saved if action was taken quickly enough. *Operation Necklace* was primarily a media campaign to highlight what was happening to our most endangered animal. We began the campaign with a press launch at the SNH flagship building at Battleby near Perth. In Tayside, we then took the media out on a short patrol of the River Tay and its tributaries while our Northern Constabulary colleagues did likewise on upper reaches of the River Spey.

No-one was caught illegally 'fishing' for mussels on these patrols but we had made the point, which was grasped very quickly by the Scottish Executive. The law was changed the following year giving the freshwater pearl mussel better protection. It became a fully paid-up member of Schedule 5 of the Wildlife and Countryside Act 1981, and as part of that elite group, it became an offence to intentionally damage or destroy any place the mussel was using for shelter or protection or to disturb it while it was using that place.

Try as we might, we never did manage to catch anyone trying to 'fish' for freshwater pearl mussels, yet the evidence in the form of shells were – and still are – regularly found on riverbanks. It seems as if no-one ever sees the people who are taking them from the river and is yet another frustrating fact of life in being a wildlife crime officer.

What was reported to us not long after the law was tightened up was the presence of a JCB digger in the middle of the River Tay. The operator was moving much of the riverbed around to form croys. Important for salmon fishing, croys are structures made of boulders, rocks and gravel from the river leading from the bank out towards the centre of the river, or can in fact be a wall of boulders, rocks and gravel at a strategic point somewhere in the river, which give added shelter to salmon. I attended immediately along with a freshwater pearl mussel expert from Scottish Natural Heritage and photographed the alteration to the water flow in the river and the new man-made structures that previously had formed part of the riverbed.

Sole impression and spade left a badger sett which had been dug. £1 coin to show scale (See Chapter 13)

Buzzard caught in Larsen trap. It had died of starvation (See Chapter 12)

Buzzard caught in a Fenn trap

Carborfuran, the poisoner's current pesticide of choice (Chapter 22)

Poisoned golden eagle found in the Sma' Glen in Perthshire (Ch 12)

Young red kites being tagged on the edge of a former problem estate (Chapter 26)

Typical dog used by hare coursers (Chapter 29)

Gralloch and legs – all that is left at the roadside after a visit by deer poachers (Chapter 3)

Tayside Police events vehicle at a countryside event

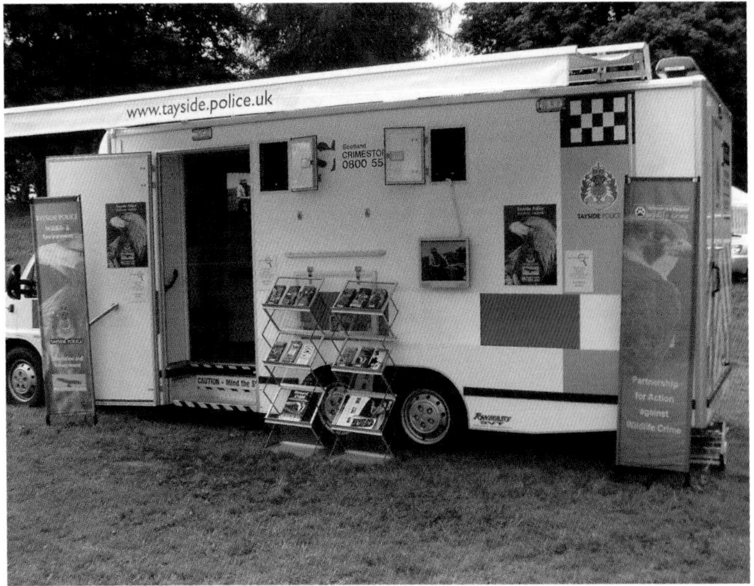

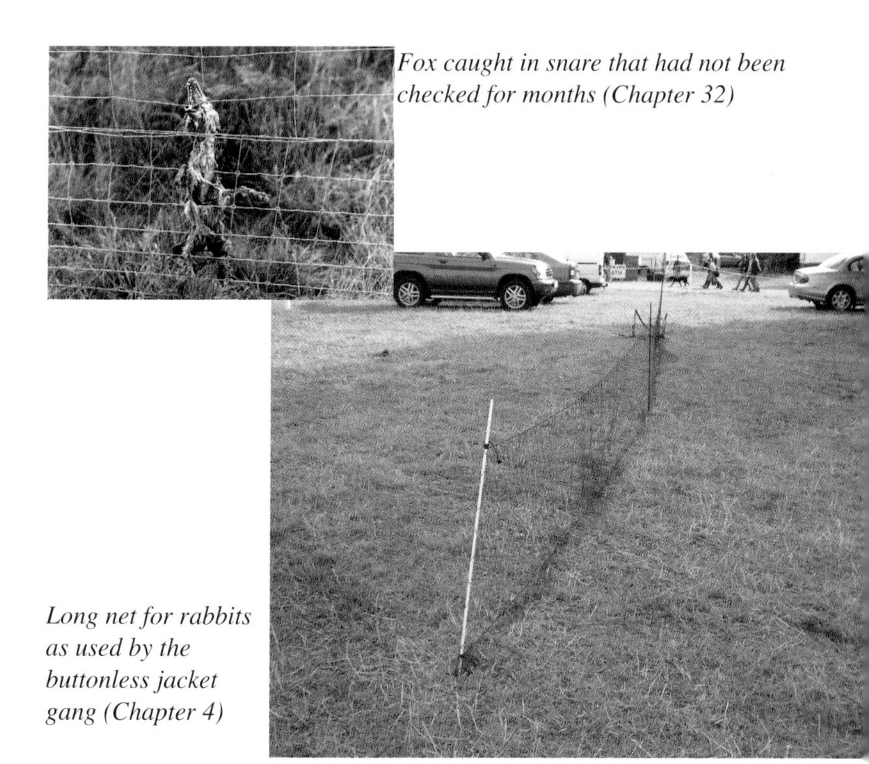

Fox caught in snare that had not been checked for months (Chapter 32)

Long net for rabbits as used by the buttonless jacket gang (Chapter 4)

Snare set at one of the entrances to a 'midden' Chapter 21)

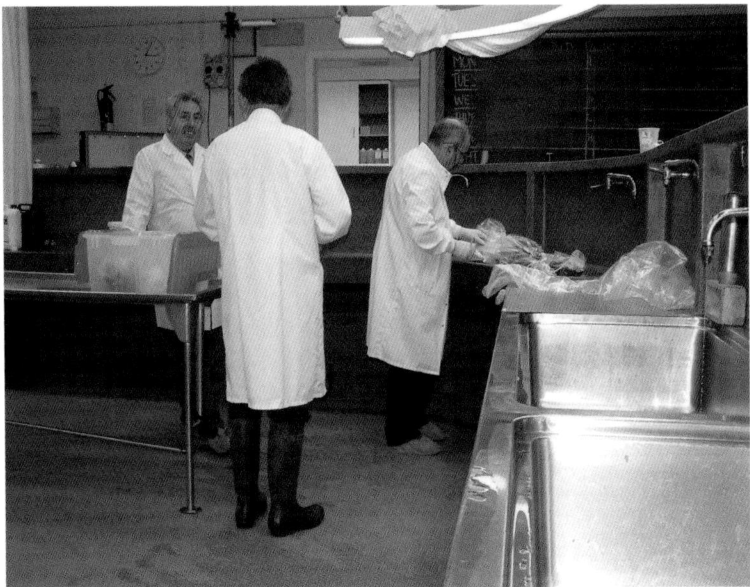

Laboratory – the author (left) with Professor Ranald Munro (centre) and Dave Dick during the Brechin taxidermy case (Chapter 27)

Young hen harriers at an age when vulnerable to mammalian and human predators (Chapter 11)

Sphagnum moss pulled and ready for collection (Chapter 39)

Freshly-opened freshwater pearl mussels at the River Tay near Perth (Chapter 19

Roe deer caught in drag snare (Chapter 12)

Roe that was being eaten alive by an Alsatian (Chapter 35)

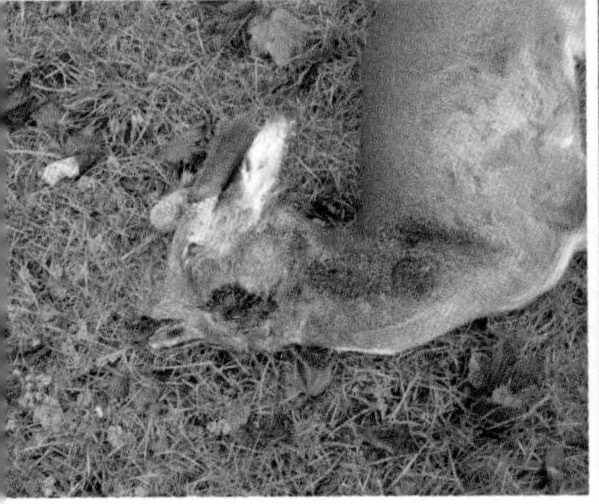

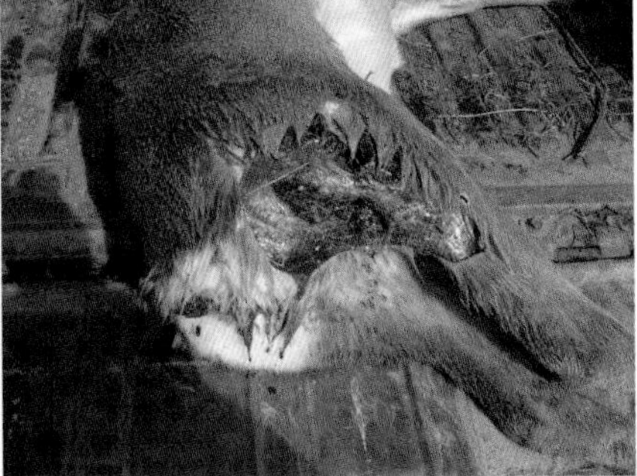

(left) Poacher's rifle injury to roe deer causing a lingering death (Ch 3)

Red deer are easily shot when at the side of a quiet road (Chapter 6)

The clutch of osprey eggs taken in Perthshire and recovered in Coventry (Ch 16)

Typical poisoned bait – a woodpigeon laced with pesticide set out for an unwary victim (Chapter 10)

Phosdrin, the most deadly of pesticides (Chapter 10)

Pine marten caught in Fenn trap (Chapter 34)

Red kite with bottom half of beak and tongue shot off (Chapter 26)

(Opposite) Poster designed by primary school pupils (Chapter 17)

Operation Easter
Hands off eggs
Don't make rare birds
EGGSTINCT?
From posters designed, as part of a wildlife crime project, by Jade Smith (9), and Brooke Elfverson (8) Inverbrothock School, Abroath.
Report suspected egg thieves to the Police
PARTNERSHIP FOR ACTION AGAINST wildlife crime
Printed and Sponsored by:
WOODS
PRINTING SINCE 1830
WOODS OF PERTH LTD.
113-119 GLOVER STREET, PERTH PH2 OJE
Designed by DM Graphics

Salmon at one of the poacher's favourite spots on the River Almond (Chapter 2)

(right) Hang net (Chapter 8)

Typical cage used by salmon poachers (Chapter 5)

Horseshoe Falls on the River Almond, Perthshire. Looking downstream and showing the gap where the cage was set (Chapter 5)

The lade with the River Almond and Horseshoe Falls behind, and the bridge that was a saviour (Chapter 5)

The stretch of bank on Moncrieffe Island at the Friarton Hole on the River Tay where the night vision equipment often revealed a dozen or more salmon poachers (Chapter 6)

The weir on the River Almond at Lowe's Work's Pool. The far side has now been blasted to prevent poaching (Chapter 4)

A view of the River Tay from Kinnoull Hill, Perth, to where the salmon net was set at slack water (Chapter 8)

A common seal (Chapter 30)

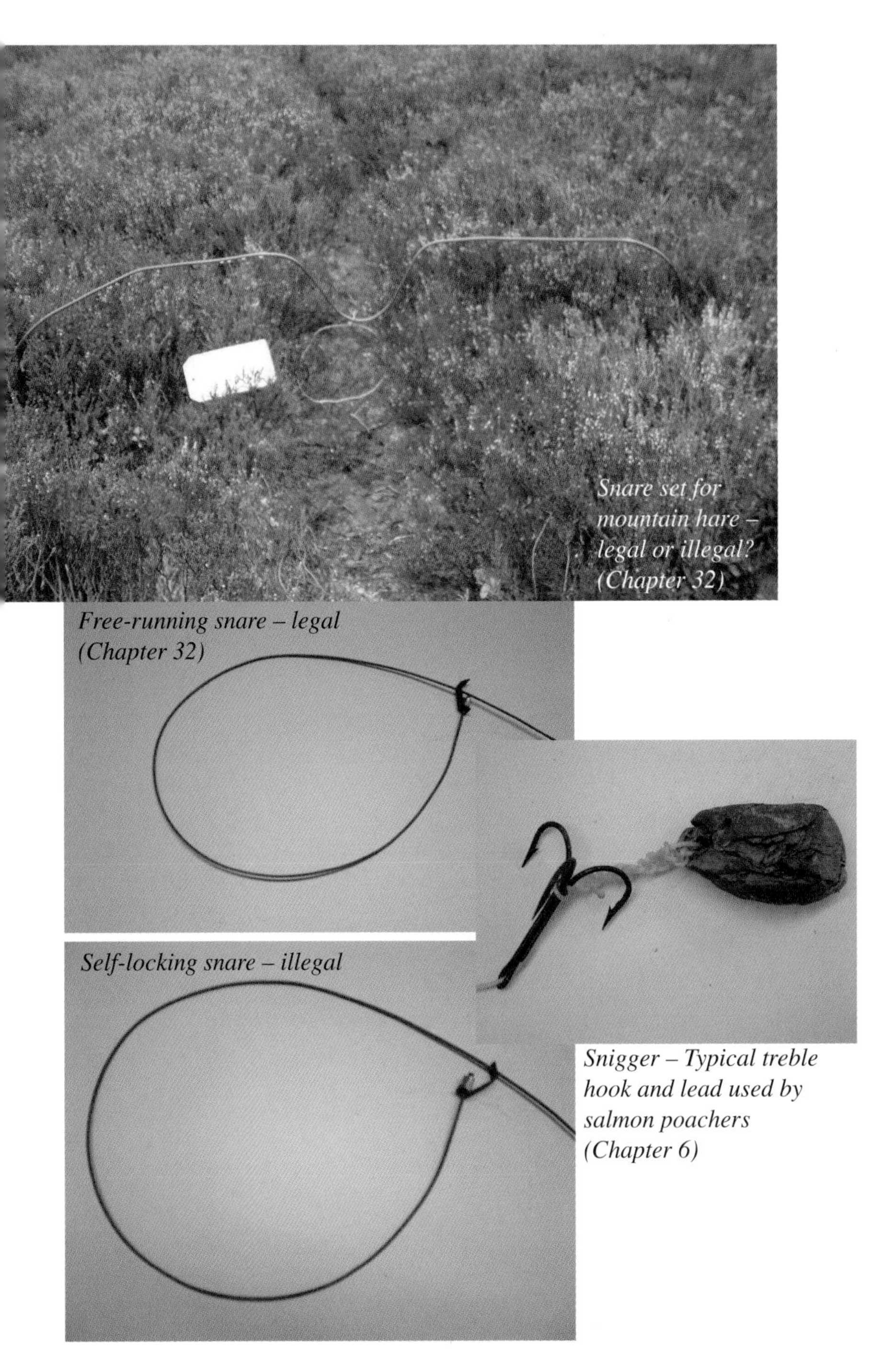

Snare set for mountain hare – legal or illegal? (Chapter 32)

Free-running snare – legal (Chapter 32)

Self-locking snare – illegal

Snigger – Typical treble hook and lead used by salmon poachers (Chapter 6)

The sand quarry with nesting sandmartins just before being flattened

The sand quarry after being levelled (See Chapter 38)

Our investigation revealed:

- planning permission had not been sought from the local council and should have been;
- the area in which the JCB had been working was an area that formerly held freshwater pearl mussels;
- because of the extensive work, it was extremely unlikely that any mussels had survived either being crushed or buried during the re-arrangement of the riverbed;
- a number of mussels had been crushed and killed, which we photographed;
- an expert was able to say that these mussels were twenty to thirty years of age, that their death had *not* been by natural causes, and that they had been killed by some mechanical force;
- freshwater mussels for some hundreds of yards downstream were likely to have been adversely affected by the silt caused by the workings of the JCB;
- the operator who carried out the work;
- the fishing proprietor who had apparently ordered the work to be carried out.

To the lay person there may appear to be more than sufficient evidence here to ensure that someone appeared in court to answer a charge of killing the mussels, damaging their place of shelter or disturbing the mussels while they were using their place of shelter. My colleague, DS Neil Macdonald, and I interviewed the proprietor, who stated that he had not been aware of freshwater pearl mussels in that part of the river. That was effectively the end of the case.

It is incumbent on the Crown to prove all elements of any charge. One crucial element of the charge could not be proved: that any of the foregoing had been done *intentionally*. No-one was therefore charged and though we reported the case to the procurator fiscal for his consideration of a prosecution, we were sure the case could go no further.

If any reader feels frustrated at this point, imagine how we felt after putting considerable effort into investigating this case, including consulting an expert at the Department of Zoology at Aberdeen University. Our frustration was at the legislators for framing legislation that was almost impossible to enforce. It was not until October 2004, under the provisions of the Nature Conservation (Scotland) Act 2004, that the term *intentionally* – a word that caused me and many other wildlife crime officers in the UK no end of frustration – was augmented by the term *or recklessly*. It was only then that we could begin to make progress. We had to move on. Forget the frustrating past. Look to a more promising future.

•

The future turned out to be equally unpromising in the next case, which related to yet another different species, pipistrelle bats. Most people will never think of bats being the subject of crime, but it is surprising how often we now get calls about suspected bat crime. Part of the increase in reporting, like all other aspects of wildlife crime, is because of heightened awareness of the issues. If the public are aware of what is likely to be a crime, especially a crime committed against wee furry beasties, they will be on the telephone in the blink of an eye. The secret is in keeping the public informed. The important aspect of law that the public should be aware of is that bat roosts are protected by law, *whether or not the bats are present.*

Many bats have been destroyed in the past in lofts and attics of buildings when treatment of wood was being carried out. The sprays used often contained chemicals that were fatal to bats. The situation has changed and companies that carry out this work now mostly use bat-friendly (or at least non-fatal) chemicals. This is only one of the problems that bats face. The others are usually linked to development work, where a roof may be taken off a building containing a bat colony, or the whole building may even be demolished. Education is the way forward here, both for the people who monitor bats, so that they can keep detailed records that would be of value in a court case should that situation arise, and also for developers. Many developers encounter bat issues regularly and should know to consult the Scottish Executive with a view to obtaining a site-specific licence issued under the Habitats Regulations should one be required.

Compared to a commercial property, a slightly different situation arises in a dwelling house, though changes *may* be made under the Conservation (Natural Habitats etc) Amendment (Scotland) Regulations 2007, which as I write is before the Scottish Parliament as a Statutory Instrument. If the bats are in the living area, action can be taken there and then to remove them, but if the bats are in a non-living area, such as the loft, yet another set of rules apply.

Bats usually come in to dwellings in the summer to breed, with the average pipistrelle maternity roost containing between 100 and 200 bats. They usually remain in the loft, attic or other crevices until their young are ready to fend for themselves, normally around September. In most cases they will go back to their winter roosts, probably in a tree, until the next breeding season comes round again. Some, however, are known to remain in houses throughout the year, depending on the species and the temperature and humidity of the roost.

To many people, the presence of bats in their loft is not pleasant. Some folks still believe that bats can get tangled in their hair, which is a complete fallacy. In some cases the noise that bats make, especially if they are just through the wall inches from where a family may be sleeping, can be annoying. In other cases there may be a slight smell, but this is normally negligible, after all any excreta are simply the dried remains of insects which quickly goes into dust. In recent years bats have been a further concern after the death from rabies of a man in Angus who had been bitten by a Daubenton's bat. I have had bats in the loft of my last two houses and they caused no problems or worries, even on the occasion when one was whirring round the bedroom in the middle of the night, but then my family are used to animals of most sorts.

The proper, statutory, procedure when a householder has a bat problem, is to make contact with Scottish Natural Heritage. Scottish Natural Heritage will advise on the best course of action, which is likely to include advice on how to exclude the bats *after* they leave for their winter quarters. To try to exclude them without consultation or before they leave is illegal and inviting trouble. Some adult bats are likely to be blocked out and their offspring will die of starvation, while some adult bats are equally likely to be blocked in and suffer the same fate. It was the blocking of a roost that was the reason for our first bat case.

In a case in Kinross-shire in 2001, a householder with a bat roost in the loft missed out the legal requirement to consult Scottish Natural Heritage and went directly to a pest control firm. Pest control firms should know better, yet this one went ahead in early October to seal the attic against entry by bats, detailing the work as 'to remove attic space insulation, remove droppings with sterilisation and replace insulation with external proofing.' The incident came to light because of a person having seen the bat activity in the summer, then having seen the work on the house in October which the witness realised was to exclude bats.

It was unfortunate that the witness mulled over his suspicions until January of the following year before making contact with me. At that time, offences under the Wildlife and Countryside Act 1981 and the Conservation (Natural Habitats etc) Regulations 1994 – both of which can deal with offences committed against bats – had a time bar of six months for reporting offences. This meant that a case must have an initial hearing in court within six months of the date of the offence. An exception is allowed under the Natural Habitats Regulations, where if a bat is killed as a consequence of the illegal activity, then the time bar extends to two years.

Since October 2004, with a time bar of *three* years from the date of the commission of any offence under the Wildlife and Countryside Act 1981, we have a much better chance of obtaining convictions. The three year time bar has one proviso: that the case must be before the court within six months of sufficient evidence being presented to the procurator fiscal. This allows cases to be brought where, for whatever reason, the police are not made aware of the offence until some time after it has occurred.

We investigated the offence and were grateful for the advice and guidance of a local bat expert. Even though police wildlife crime officers are conversant with wildlife law and criminal procedure, we are not experts in all – or even many – aspects of wildlife biology and ecology and depend on experts in a variety of fields. In this particular offence there was no evidence that any bat had been killed. In fact it was likely that the breeding colony had moved out before the work to block up any entrances to the loft had begun. Nevertheless, bat roosts are protected by law whether or not the wee furry beasties are at home. We interviewed a member of the pest control firm with management responsibility, who admitted that he was aware that bats used the attic as a roost, that SNH had not been consulted, that he had issued the instructions for the work to be carried out and that the instructions included the phrase 'sealing the access points.'

The investigation was completed and a case was submitted to the procurator fiscal. The delay in the witness reporting his suspicions had been fatal. Despite the best efforts of the police and the procurator fiscal, the case could not be brought before the court within the statutory six months. A good case bit the dust.

Chapter 20

Poisonous Year End

The twentieth century ends on a higher note on the worst estate in Scotland for the recovery of poisoned baits and victims, but it is not to last.

In the year 2000, no poisoned baits or poisoned victims had been found on Edradynate Estate. This was a great start to the new Millenium but it wasn't to last. In March 2001 a dead buzzard was found on the estate. Analysis at SASA showed that it had succumbed to the dreaded pesticide carbofuran. The usual enquiries were made and the usual suspect interviewed, but his involvement could not be established.

For a case to succeed the identification of the person committing the offence must be proved 'beyond reasonable doubt'. This is the legal standard of proof in criminal cases. In a civil case there is a lesser standard of proof, 'on the balance of probabilities.' In the investigations on Edradynate Estate, we could prove beyond reasonable doubt that baits and dead birds and animals were being found with monotonous regularity on the estate. We could prove beyond reasonable doubt that the baits were laced with particular pesticides and that the victims had been poisoned after having consumed part of these baits. What we were so far unable to prove was who set out the baits. We had no statement from anyone who had seen the offence happening, no admission from our suspect, no trace evidence by way of fingerprints, DNA, sole impressions, recovery of pesticides. Nothing!

Everyone we spoke to in the area told us who was involved but they could not supply any evidence that would help our investigation. To them it was obvious who was responsible and I'm sure they were frustrated that we seemed to be doing so little. I shared their frustration. We were still in times of poor legislation and could not even detain our suspect and take him to the police station.

In December 2001, there was a particularly frightening episode at Edradynate. A dying buzzard was picked up on the public road by some schoolgirls. They lifted the buzzard up and tried to get help for it but its end was probably inevitable in any case and it died while still in their care. It was extremely lucky for the young girls that this particular bird had been poisoned by Alpha-chloralose, which is less toxic than the more usual pesticide of choice, carbofuran. Had this bird been a victim of carbofuran contact with it may well have proved fatal for one or more of the youngsters.

While still investigating this dead buzzard, in March 2002 we had a short foray on to Edradynate Estate and found a dead pheasant that had been laced with Alpha-chloralose and a dead sparrowhawk lying near to it that had appeared to have died after feeding on the carcass. While these were being examined at SASA we submitted a report to the procurator fiscal requesting a search warrant for the lands of the estate and for the premises of our suspect and his assistant. The request was agreed and a search warrant was signed by the sheriff. This would be our second major search of the estate under warrant and we hoped this time to find sufficient evidence to bring to an end the catalogue of poisoned baits and victims that had turned up on the estate with the worst record by far not just in Tayside but in Scotland.

In early April, two divisional wildlife crime officers and two SEERAD staff began a search of the relevant premises on the estate, primarily sheds and buildings associated with game management. PC Graham Jack – the Atholl Highlander – and I began a search of the estate. Two people to search an estate does not seem a lot but Graham and I had been involved in these searches so often that our instinct and experience told us where to look.

In the first half hour of the search we had recovered a dead carrion crow, which turned out to have been poisoned with Alpha-chloralose. Near to the crow we found two rabbit baits lying close together, one of which turned out to have been laced with Alpha-chloralose, the other with carbofuran. It was obvious to us at the time that one of the rabbits had been treated with carbofuran – or at least a carbamate pesticide – as we could see traces of the dark blue granules. Just as clearly we could see that the other bait had no trace of granules and the flesh had not been darkened to the same extent, which made us fairly sure that it had been laced with Alpha-chloralose. It flitted through my mind that it was very considerate of the poisoner to give a victim a choice of death by gut wrenching cramps and ultimate seizure of the cardio-vascular system (carbofuran) or by hypothermia (chloralose).

In a wood close by the two deadly rabbits was a dead buzzard, which had plumped for the carbofuran rather than Alpha-chloralose as its last supper. The carrion crow that we had found earlier must have preferred the Alpha-chloralose. In a field that had in the previous winter been a game crop, and right by the side of the ubiquitous quad bike tracks, lay a desiccated half rabbit. It was one that we may in some circumstances not have bothered photographing and collecting but its proximity to the quad bike tracks made the decision easy. It turned out to be the remains of a cabofuran-flavoured rabbit.

As we walked through the estate, Graham and I commented that we had never seen an estate with so many dead pheasants lying around. If these were pricked (injured) birds left over from the shooting season, the standard of picking-up had been extremely poor. We had both been involved in picking-up with gundogs at shoots and we know how unprofessional it is to leave any unpicked birds either dead, or even more importantly, injured.

We had just finished discussing this slovenly unprofessional practice when we found a carrion crow in a Larsen trap. A Larsen trap is a smallish gridweld mesh or netting and wood cage in which a carrion crow or a magpie can be placed in order to attract other crows or magpies. The trap can be used with other corvids that are on the list of pest species though it is less effective for them, working best with birds that are territorial rather than gregarious.

The trap normally has three compartments, one large to hold the call bird or decoy, and the other two being smaller compartments into which the wild birds are enticed. When a bird enters the catching compartment, its route to get there induces it to perch momentarily on a split stick that then collapses under the weight of the bird, causing the spring-operated door to swing shut and contain the bird in the compartment. The principle of the trap is that if it is used in the territory of a nesting pair of crows or magpies the presence of the intruder in the call bird compartment of the trap often induces an attack by the territorial pair, during which the operator hopes they will be enticed into the catching compartments.

Like the larger crow cage traps, a general licence is issued annually by the Scottish Executive to allow the use of this trap. There are also a number of conditions with which the operator must comply, otherwise the trap is not being used legally. Some of these conditions relate to the husbandry of the call bird, which must have food, water, shelter and a perch. (The list of birds which may legally be taken in a Larsen trap in Scotland, or its conditions of use, may change after the results of a consultation on General Licences launched in January 2007).

The Larsen trap that we were now standing beside had food and shelter. No perch. No water. I was less concerned with the perch than I was with the water. A captive bird will survive without a perch but it will not last long without a water supply. We examined the water receptacle, which was a very light soft drinks can with the top very roughly taken off. There was a small piece of thin wire in one corner of the compartment which may or may not have at one time 'secured' the drinks can in place, but even if it had, the minute the bird started to flap about the cage – as it was doing there and then – the can would be knocked over and the water spilled. It would have been so easy to have made this water container secure but the slovenly operator of the trap had not bothered. In addition to being illegal, it typified the kind of practice that brings the control of pest species into conflict not just with conservationists but with the pubic in general.

In the meantime, those involved in the search of premises were uncovering similar practices. They had found a number of Fenn traps set around the sides of walls in the farm steading beside the headkeeper's house. To be legal, these traps – which are spring traps used for the control of mice, rats, stoats, weasels and grey squirrels – must be set in a natural or man-made tunnel with an entrance only large enough to admit the largest of the species, the grey squirrel. They must never be set in the open or set for birds. There was no question these were set for rats since they were on rat runs along the sides of the walls. I suspect they would be singularly unsuccessful.

My practical understanding of rats is that they will avoid anything new that is placed on their run and will circumvent it rather than stand on it. There was nothing to channel the rats over the traps and nothing to prevent any other species of bird or animal from being caught in the traps.

In a large shed with a door wide to the world, the officers found a pile of proprietary rat poison. One of the conditions of legal use of rat poison is that it is set in a place where only rodents can access it. Normally this is either inside enclosed premises or in a box or a tile. In this shed, all sorts of animals and birds had access, including many seed-eating birds that may well have succumbed to the haemorrhaging effect of the poison.

In addition the officers had taken possession of a knife and a game bag believed to have been used by the suspects. The knife, when swabbed by SASA, showed traces of the pesticide Alpha-chloralose while swabs of the game bag showed the presence of carbofuran and Alpha-chloralose.

As a result of the investigation, the headkeeper and his 20-year-old rookie apprentice were charged with a number of offences relating to what we had recovered. Did we get a conviction this time?

The case was adjourned. And adjourned. And adjourned again. The reasons for adjournment were partly defence requests and partly prosecution requests. After two years the trial had not even started and on the basis of Human Rights, the procurator fiscal was forced to abandon the whole case. It could have been deemed unfair to the two accused that they had been kept waiting on a solution to the whole episode and their human rights would be breached if this continued.

Fair to the public? Had justice been served? Did I still want to be a wildlife crime officer?

PART III
Modern Times

'. . . there's the buzzard . . . right . . . 1,2,3, . . . 'OVER' . . .'

Chapter 21

Cage Traps, Stink Pits and False Alarms

We learn that legal traps can be set illegally, and concerned members of the public sometimes find it hard to tell the difference between a heron and a bunny.

I have always supported the control of carrion crows because of the damage they do to the eggs and chicks of ground nesting birds and, to a lesser extent, by pecking at ailing lambs or sheep that have rolled on to their back or are having a difficult lambing. The use of cage traps is a humane method of controlling crows and is a legal method of doing so. I welcomed the tightening up of the law in the late 1990s in relation to the use of crow cage traps and have made suggestions to the Scottish Executive for further changes. It is unfortunate that a small minority of those who operate these traps take advantage of the fact that they sometimes catch birds of prey and kill the birds rather than releasing them as they are legally obliged to do. In a case in mid-June 2006, a gamekeeper from the north-west of Scotland was fined what appeared to be a paltry sum – £200 – for shooting two buzzards that had been caught in his crow cage. The police discovered another dozen dead buzzards stuffed into rabbit burrows around the cage. The gamekeeper's excuse was that he considered it too dangerous to go in to the trap to catch them! Even if this were true, he could have caught the crow that was in the cage as a decoy, brought it out of the cage and left the door open until the two buzzards had returned to freedom. I was shocked that a defence solicitor would put forward such a ridiculous excuse for breaking the law and surprised that the sheriff seemed to take cognisance of it.

As with any crime, the police have a good idea which gamekeepers can be trusted to operate crow cage traps legally and those who may abuse the privilege. The use of the traps is currently licensed by the Scottish Executive and excessive abuse could risk the withdrawal of the general licence currently allowing their use. Just as there are one or two rogue gamekeepers, there are plenty of responsible gamekeepers and I have frequently telephoned some of those that I trust when a buzzard is seen to be caught in one of their crow cages. I have no doubt whatsoever that in these instances the buzzard is released unharmed.

As many other wildlife crime officers do, I try to warn off visitors to the countryside who are likely to interfere with the traps. It is fairly common for a well-meaning person, ignorant of the reason why crows are controlled, to let a call bird out of the cage, or worse, to damage the trap. This is a crime in itself and lays the person open to arrest for vandalism or malicious mischief. All of the eight police forces in Scotland have agreed the wording of a sign that gamekeepers can attached to a crow cage that explains the reasons for controlling crows. In addition, the sign outlines the law in relation to the legal use of the trap, so that anyone reading the sign not only understands why crow control is carried out but can report any misuse of the trap to the police if the person using it is not conforming to the law.

Having said that, I agree with the control of crows and possibly magpies. I'm not so keen on the control of the more gregarious members of the crow family – rooks and jackdaws. A cage baited with grain will attract both these species in large numbers and a considerable cull can be carried out. Even though this is legal – and I acknowledge the right of keepers or farmers to control these birds – I don't have to agree that they cause a huge amount of damage. The larch wood that I have as part of my property often has a small number of rook nests as an overspill of a couple of larger rookeries nearby. There is no doubt that one or two of the adult rooks take my ducks' eggs. I have also observed that an odd rook specialises in egg-thieving and I sometimes watch such a specialist jumping from tree to tree after I let my ducks out, looking for an egg that has been laid in a nest under a bush or even in the open. They are not nearly as expert as carrion crows and damage to the eggs of wild birds by rooks is moderate by comparison. It is also my view that any damage they cause to the chicks of wild birds is slight. I don't dispute that rooks can cause considerable damage to grain flattened by rain and high winds, but balancing the good that rooks do to agriculture by eating grubs and insects that are detrimental to crops, in my opinion they even the score for any damage they have caused.

In some cases I have seen gamekeepers taking large numbers of jackdaws in cage traps. Though this is also perfectly legal – and those who may not agree with the principle of killing jackdaws should not interfere – I can't say I agree with this type of cull. Again relating it to home, I had a jackdaw almost living with my ducks for nearly two years, and it is still there as I write. The jackdaw is missing part of its tail, and though it can fly, it seems to prefer to hop around most of the time. It roosts in a tree not twenty metres from the back door and goes in to the shed to feed on my ducks' layers' mash regularly during the day. So far as I am aware, it has never taken a single egg during its stay with me and I am always pleased to hear its *chack, chack* call. The strange thing about jackdaws is their strong and distinctive smell, and I can smell it often as I walk through the wood, especially on damp days.

My point in discussing the crow cage traps and some of the members of the crow family is my perplexity over why rooks and jackdaws, indeed also jays, are still vigorously controlled. Are they controlled because the really do damage, or simply because it has been a tradition for the past hundred years? Should we now be bringing our reasoning and responses into the twenty-first century? A consultation by the Scottish Executive on annual general licences was launched on 5 January 2007 and it may well be that once the responses are submitted in April 2007 and account is taken of the respondents views, that jays will be removed from the list of birds that can be controlled and the control of jackdaws and rooks will be limited.

To come back to the point of this chapter, even with new legislation controlling the use of crow cage traps, it takes a long time for the changes to percolate through to the practitioners. Despite the fact that the general licence authorising the use of crow cage traps states that for the trap to be operated legally, birds must be prevented from being caught or contained in the traps when they are not in use, we have had many instances when a variety of birds have died a lingering death due to starvation and lack of water. This is needless, reckless, totally unprofessional and completely illegal. The range of starved birds found has ranged from carrion crows to kestrels, sparrow hawks, buzzards and the occasional small passerine.

In one of the worst cases in Tayside, three dead buzzards were found starved after going into a crow cage to investigate the remains of a dead rabbit used as bait. The gamekeeper operating the trap had been on holiday but stated that he had tied the gate in the open position before doing so. It seems incredible that someone would come along, close the gate and securely tie it with wire, but this was the claim. As you are already aware, police have to prove a case beyond reasonable doubt. Even though it is unlikely that someone would tie the gate of a crow cage shut it is a possibility that can't be excluded, and a possibility for which a suspect has to get the benefit of the doubt. Until the general licence states that a gate or one of the wire panels must be removed when the trap is not in use – and this is a proposal in the January 2007 consultation – I can't see us succeeding with many cage trap prosecutions. It annoys me intensely, not that we can't get a prosecution, but that a minority of gamekeepers who would like to be considered as guardians of the countryside are anything but and in fact let the rest of their profession down by their lack of competence.

Staying with crow cage traps, it is permitted to use a bait of some sort to entice crows to enter the trap. For many years it has been illegal to leave farm animals unburied, and since 1993, fallen farm stock must be incinerated. Even yet, in 2006, I have to remind people using crow cage traps that they can't use dead sheep, dead hens or domestic ducks as bait in a crow cage trap. On the scale of crimes and offences, this must be somewhere near the bottom of the ladder but nevertheless it reflects a lack of knowledge by the operators of their job.

There are many reports when followed up that have a surprising outcome. One caller reported that when he passed a crow cage trap he looked inside and the ground was littered with the skulls of birds of prey. The report was in the autumn so it could have been possible that the trap had been left set over the summer time and a number of birds had been caught. In summer dead animals and birds last no time at all before they are reduced to bones by maggots. The estate on which the cage trap was situated, however, was one where I had never previously had cause to think that any dubious activity was taking place. Anyway I assured the caller that I would have a look.

It was an easy and pleasant walk to the trap past a small loch. A good mixture of waterfowl were on the loch, predominantly mallard, with the drakes just coming in to their winter plumage. A dozen or so teal flew off, circled the loch and landed again at the far end beside the resident pair of mute swans and their four slightly smaller and much more drably coloured cygnets, still very much in their first year brown plumage. Teal are my second favourite duck. They are resplendent in their grey, green and brown colouring and I am always amazed at how they can take off almost vertically from the water in pretty much the same manner as a harrier jet. Having mentioned my second-favourite, the first prize must go to the widgeon. Though it is not quite such a handsome chap as the teal, the sound of these ducks coming in to a pond is magical. The male has a loud whistling call, *whee-yoo, whee-yoo* giving rise to its name of whistling duck. Completing the bio-diversity of this pond was a pair of tiny dabchicks – little grebes to give them their Sunday name – which skulked at the edge of the reeds. This was possibly where they nested in the Spring, though no juveniles were to be seen.

I reached the crow cage trap and steeled myself for a raptors' graveyard as I peered through the wire netting. The ground was littered with skulls, cleaned of flesh and bleached by the rain and the sun. Not a single one was an avian skull; all were the skulls of rabbits that had been used as feeding for the call bird or as bait to draw in carrion crows. I could understand how the lay person could be confused. A rabbit skull, though slightly larger than that of a buzzard, is similar in overall shape, but it is the make-up of the skulls that differ. In a buzzard skull. the curved beak protrudes from the tennis ball-shaped skull. A rabbit skull is elongated, with the nose and the top incisors making a curved shape in a similar manner to the beak of the buzzard. With a little bit of imagination one could be mistaken for the other. I had a good laugh, though I felt a bit guilty at having doubted the integrity of the keeper. I related the story to him a few days later and he took it in good part, recognising though not without being critical of the lack of experience of the person who reported the incident.

Dead animals and birds are sometimes used as baits in a 'stink pit'. A stink pit is a pile of carcasses usually surrounded by a fence or stockade of branches with gaps every so often at which is placed a fox snare. The principle of stink pits – or middens as they are sometimes called – is that a fox is attracted by the smell of the carcasses and gets snared when investigating the prospect of an easy meal. Stink pits are legal provided the snares are not self locking, are checked at least once in every period of 24 hours and the carcasses are wild animals or birds and not domestic livestock.

I had a call to a stink pit one day, where it was reported by a person who had been out for a walk that a badger and a buzzard formed part of the pile of carcasses used to entice foxes. The stink pit was well constructed of brushwood with half a dozen entrances, at each of which a legal fox snare lay in ambush for an unwary fox. As stink pits go this one almost blended with its surroundings, had it not been for the smell. I wasn't in the least surprised that the walker had found it, as the smell could be detected at least a hundred metres away. With a fox's acute olfactory senses, provided it was downwind of the stink pit, it could easily have been attracted from several miles away.

I had a look amongst the dead animals and birds in the centre of the stockade. There were several mallard ducks that could have been remnants of the recently ended shooting season. There were a couple of foxes, possibly victims of the snares or maybe even victims of an accurate .223 or .22/250 rifle bullet fired down a spotlight beam. Much of the rest of the pile of animal remains was made up of heads and legs of deer. All were legal carcasses so far. I then spotted a dead polecat ferret, its fur a blend of cream and dark brown. This must be the 'badger' as there was nothing else that remotely resembled brock. Lying next to the ferret was a hen pheasant. This was the only bird in the pile of carcasses that was anywhere near the colour of a buzzard. Though its beak could never be construed as being hooked, I suppose it was more of a hooked beak than those of the mallard ducks.

I was not in the least surprised at the misinterpretation of the carcasses and in fact I'm convinced that there was no malice intended. It was yet another person stumbling upon something that he or she had never encountered before and assuming because dead animals and birds were involved and because the purpose appeared to be to cause the death of another animal, that it was illegal.

Many people phone me about illegally-set gin traps that they have found when they are out in the country. Invariably they have either sprung or damaged the gin trap before going home and making contact with me. I ask them to describe the gin trap and in what context it was set. The answer is always something along the lines, 'Well it was set amongst some stones. I saw it when I lifted the large stone off the top of the pile of stones. It was a wire trap with a square metal plate. I think the trap would be sprung when the animal stood on the metal plate.' My response would be, 'Would you describe the trap as being a square shape or did the shape more resemble the letter T?' 'It was definitely square.' My next question would be, 'Would you say the jaws of the trap had teeth or were they smooth?' 'I would say that they were smooth. I definitely didn't see any teeth.' The concerned walker had just interfered with a Fenn trap, which was more than likely set in a legal manner in a tunnel of stones to catch a rat or a stoat.

On another occasion, a hill walker contacted me to say that when she had been out walking she had found a large number of dead heron (she used the singular throughout the conversation despite the number of birds being more than one). The birds were lying at intervals along the length of a hill road and must have been there for some time because the flesh had been eaten away but the long necks were clearly visible and that was why she knew they were heron (or herons).

It was a Sunday afternoon that I got the call but I was so intrigued that I went out there and then to see how many herons there were. I walked along the hill track. It was early Spring and it was great to be out and about. Ravens croaked overhead with their distinctive *prruuk, prruuk, prruuk* call, their far greater size and their fan-shaped tail distinguishing them from other black corvids. Frogs had begun spawning and every second puddle on the track was full of spawn that reminded me of a black version of the tapioca that I used to relish as a pudding in my youth. I must have been unusual as a boy in that I liked tapioca and also liked tripe, both foods that would have most kids nowadays (and many even in my day) retching at the thought of putting anywhere near their mouth, far less swallowing.

Further along the track there was a partial skeleton of a rabbit that had succumbed to myxomatosis, probably in the autumn, with little being left of it except the rib and neck bones, the skull and an odd bit of fur. A large female frog hopped from one of the puddles with a much smaller male hanging tightly on to her back in readiness to fertilise the next spawn deposited by the female. They hopped right across another dead rabbit. It clicked then. The vertebrae of the dead rabbits had been mistaken by the walker for the necks of herons. I continued along the track and found many more dead, skeletal rabbits. Myxomatosis must have taken a fair toll of the resident lagomorph population. I had found the answer to the puzzle of the dead heron. But another puzzle was equally intriguing; how can anyone think that the vertebrae of a rabbit can be a heron's neck when it has fur attached to it. Does everyone not know that herons have feathers? After all feathers are what facilitate flight.

In another false alarm with good intent, a lady called me late one March afternoon when I happened just to be finishing a meeting in Edinburgh. She had found a badger's sett that had been dug out and there were four young black and pink badgers lying dead at the entrance. She had spotted the sett at the roadside while she had been taking her dog for a walk. This made me a bit sceptical as badgers are shy creatures and not predisposed to making their setts in roadside verges and ditches. Nonetheless I said I would meet her at the sett first thing the next morning as I couldn't get to the location from Edinburgh before it was dark. I also asked if in the meantime she would mind gathering up the dead badgers so that evidence was not lost. She agreed to do this. Later that evening I had a further call from the woman. She told me that two of the young badgers had disappeared and that she was only able to collect the two remaining. I couldn't understand why that would be but all would be revealed the next morning.

On the following day I met the woman at 7.30 am and was shown the wee badgers. The woman was very concerned that anyone should be so heartless as to dig out and kill badgers. I had great difficulty keeping a straight face when I told her the badgers were young rabbits. Young rabbits are blind and hairless at birth. The top half of the rabbit is dark grey, almost black, and the underside is pink. I could see how the colour could have confused the woman into thinking the wee beasties were badgers but why did their Lilliputian size not make her query her initial thoughts? I asked the woman to show me where she had found them. Rabbits, when they are giving birth, normally dig a short burrow, anything from two to four feet in length, away from the main warren. They make a nest chamber at the end of this burrow which they line with dry grass and fur that they pull from their underside. It is into this cosy nest that the young rabbits are born, completely dependent on their mother for the first four weeks of their lives. In most cases, every time the female rabbit leaves the burrow (during the first two weeks of the young rabbits' lives), she pushes earth forward with her forepaws to block the entrance. This gives extra protection against marauding stoats, weasels and even rats.

The woman took me to a roadside ditch. At the far side of the ditch a rabbit burrow had been dug out, possibly by a fox or a badger. The nest of dry grass and fur still lay exposed on the newly dug earth. The only puzzle remaining was why, after digging out the young rabbits, a fox or badger didn't eat them but left them lying outside the excavated nest chamber.

In all of these incidents, the public were concerned and thought that they were taking the correct action. They cannot be blamed and there are many subjects of which I have little knowledge where my response might have been similar. All police officers are of the view that they would much rather spend time investigating a false alarm than fail to get notification of a situation that is subsequently found to be a crime. All of these false alarms got me out of the office and into the countryside so that has to be an advantage whatever the outcome.

CHAPTER 22

Gamekeeper Pleads Guilty, Gamekeeper on Red Alert

Two cases which illustrate the differing approaches of gamies, and the importance of meticulous evidence gathering to bring English egg thieves to book.

In 2001 the poisoning of wildlife was regrettably still with us. On one particular Perthshire estate a buzzard was found which, when tested by SASA, was found to have consumed bait laced with the pesticide carbofuran. This was interesting, but it is very important to mention that when given this sort of information, the police do not just suddenly jump in with all guns blazing. We await – or seek – further intelligence so that we can try to build a picture that establishes that an identified individual is carrying out an illegal course of conduct.

Sometimes information can be given maliciously. On other occasions information can be given in good faith but may turn out to be inaccurate. On many occasions a gamekeeper, by the very nature of his or her job, is the most obvious suspect. but a police investigation must be objective and take into account any other persons who might happen to have a grievance against whatever species the victim happens to be or, more accurately, was *intended* to be, since these baits are indiscriminate. Even when the information given to the police is accurate it often pays to 'ca' canny' and just wait a wee while longer to see if another link in the chain of evidence emerges that points towards a particular suspect.

On this occasion we didn't have too long to wait. Not long after the recovery of the poisoned buzzard, I received information from an informant that the gamekeeper on the estate was boasting of having killed over thirty buzzards in the past year. This gave us ample justification to carry out a search of the land but I didn't think it would be enough evidence to approach the procurator fiscal to request that a search warrant be sought from a sheriff. We decided to be cautious and have a quiet interview of the suspect in the presence of Willie Milne from SEERAD, who had power without warrant to search land and buildings other than dwellings where there was reasonable suspicion that pesticide was being stored or used illegally. (A similar power to that already granted to SEERAD staff later became available to the police under the provisions of the Nature Conservation (Scotland) Act 2004.)

Under Willie's powers, a search was made of the land by RSPB investigations staff. In retrospect it may have been better if the two RSPB people searching had someone from SEERAD along with them. As it was they were under Willie's control but this was at the end of a mobile phone. It is a point I will return to when I discuss the trial.

Meantime, and simultaneous to the land search by RSPB investigations staff, Willie Milne and a couple of police wildlife crime officers called on the suspect, who was cautioned and made aware of the suspicions in relation to the abuse of pesticides on the estate. A search was made of an outhouse belonging to the suspect and a quantity of strychnine was found, which the suspect was entitled to have for the control of moles. At the same time a film container was found with traces of dark blue granules, which looked suspiciously like carbofuran. In fact the suspect admitted it was Yaltox, the trade name for carbofuran, which he claimed he used as a pesticide on his carrots in his garden.

In the same shed, Willie Milne found an egg collection, which was out of his jurisdiction, that being limited to pesticides. There were also a number of gin traps in the shed, with a small amount of blood and fur being visible on the jaws of one of the traps. Since the investigation of the egg collection and the gin traps were the police responsibility, the police officers cautioned the suspect and asked him about these items. The story of the egg collection was that the eggs had been collected some time ago, prior to the Wildlife and Countryside Act, 1981, except for one egg. This was the egg of a buzzard which the suspect admitted he had taken and added to the collection in more recent times. 'More recent times' was described as since 1982, thereby making the possession of the buzzard egg an offence.

The gin traps were of particular interest. Gin traps are traps with serrated jaws designed to catch a victim by the leg and hold it until the person who set the trap came back to check what he had caught. These traps come in various sizes, with the smallest designed for rabbits, larger ones for foxes, and still larger ones – in countries where they exist – for wolves or even bears. Being leg-hold traps, they are particularly cruel and in the UK were banned for use against rabbits in the 1950s and against foxes in the 1970s. Because of the traces of blood and fur on one of the traps, the officers suspected that they had been used in the relatively recent past, much more recently than 1970. The suspect was cautioned and asked what they were for and declared that he used them to catch fox cubs at dens in the Spring time. This was an activity that had been illegal for about thirty years.

While the search of the shed had been taking place, the two RSPB staff had found a dead carrion crow and a badly decomposed buzzard near to a pheasant pen on the estate. They left them alone and reported the find, by mobile phone, back to Willie Milne. The crow, when later examined by SASA, turned out to have been a victim of a carbofuran bait, while the granules in the film container found in the suspect's shed were confirmed by SASA as being carbofuran.

The suspect was then charged with (1) having an article in his possession (the film container with traces of carbofuran) that could be used to commit a crime against the Wildlife and Countryside Act 1981; (2) setting out an unknown bait laced with the pesticide carbofuran to kill a wild bird; (3) intentionally killing a carrion crow and a buzzard (the buzzard being the one found several months earlier that had raised the initial suspicion); (4) possessing a buzzard's egg; (5) storing carbofuran in a container other than its original marked container; and (6) possessing eleven gin traps for a purpose for which they were unlawful.

To avoid overkill I wasn't present at the search, limiting the number of officers attending to the absolute minimum. Nevertheless,

I knew the suspect – the gamekeeper – fairly well and was not surprised when he made contact asking if he could speak with me. I met him later that day and he told me that he had nothing to do with any poisoning on the estate but was keen to plead guilty to three charges: the storage of the carbofuran, the buzzard egg offence and the gin trap offence. My advice to him was to make contact with his lawyer and tell this to him, as an early plea means that a sheriff must give a discount off any penalty he may otherwise have imposed.

Despite the wish of the gamekeeper to plead guilty to half of the charges, I was not in the least surprised when a plea of not guilty to all six charges was subsequently tendered and a date set for trial. Many months later the trial started and was part-heard, with only one witness – Willie Milne from SEERAD – giving part of his evidence. A further date for the continuation of the trial was set, well over a year from the date of the offence. On this next date, just before the trial started, the defence tendered a plea of guilty to the three charges to which the keeper had originally wanted to plead guilty! The fiscal consulted with me and the reporting officer and asked if this plea would be a reasonable outcome. We agreed that it was a fair result and may well be all that could be proved in any case. The fine the keeper received was moderate – from memory £250 – and may have been considerably less than he would have to pay his lawyer.

From a policing point of view I was disappointed that the trial had not run the full course. This was a new strategy for us, using the powers of another agency. We had then switched half-way through the investigation to police powers in relation to the recovery of the egg collection and the gin traps. The sheriff's comments on our strategy would have been a learning process, may even have been critical but would have clarified whether our action was right or was wrong. We'll probably never know now. Because of the improved version of the law after the provisions of the Nature Conservation (Scotland) Act 2004, the police powers are much stronger and we have no need now to revert to innovative methods to obtain the evidence required.

•

A high proportion of the calls to the police about wildlife crime come to a conclusion other than one where the police charge someone and submit a case to the procurator fiscal. The person reporting may not want to become involved therefore the information can only be treated as intelligence-gathering, there may be absolutely no hope of ever tracing the culprit, the incident may be such that it can be dealt with by a warning, or the enquiry may be on behalf of another police force. All of these outcomes are possible and occur on an almost day to day basis.

In one case I had a call from a man who told me that he had just completed some work at a house near Auchterarder, Perthshire. While he was working outside the stables at the house he could hear a noise coming from the stables that seemed to be a sort of scratching noise that finished with a thump. He looked in and a woman was reaching up to the rafters towards a swallow's nest with a long cane. The cane was scratching along the rafters until it settled on the nest. She was then poking the nest with the cane to dislodge half-grown swallows, which then thumped on to the concrete floor. He asked what she was doing and she replied that she was getting rid of the swallows as they were soiling saddles and other tack that was underneath. The workman was shocked and the fact that a woman rather than a man was carrying out this act left him lost for words. He was surprised – as was I – that the woman didn't simply think to cover the tack with polythene until the swallows had finished their nesting.

It is almost unbelievable that someone living in the countryside didn't appreciate that these swallows fly thousands of miles all the way from Africa to breed. Their epic journey deserves a bit more recognition than the destruction of their chicks for something as petty as the basic act of defecating on items that could so easily have been covered. Even someone with no knowledge of birds must surely feel some sort of empathy with these birds when they see them sitting on a telephone wire, resplendent in their iridescent black and white plumage, set off against their rufous-coloured chin and forehead, long forked tails and twittering their lovely song which is so characteristic of summertime's warm balmy days and long, light evenings.

I was keen for the workman to give a statement but he refused to do so. He said that if he became involved in an issue like this while he was working for a client of his firm he could be sacked. He had let me know what was happening so that we might prevent it happening to the next brood of swallows but that was as far as he could go. I appreciated the fact that he reported the incident and respected his wish that he remain anonymous.

Some time later, when I was satisfied that the reporting of the incident could not be linked to the workman, we visited the woman. She was arrogant, unfeeling, rude and she completely denied the incident. She was certainly not someone I would want as either a workmate or a neighbour.

There have been a number of similar incidents relating to house martins and swifts. Their nests have been deliberately knocked down simply because the birds sometimes soil windows as they land at the nest. In one case with swifts, the person involved cemented over the entrance hole to their nest under the slates. Despite evidence from a neighbour that the cementing had just been carried out in the last few days, the man maintained he had cemented over the entrance during the winter before the swifts returned. He said he did it not only because of his windows being soiled but because he didn't like birds. I would have been pleased had there been just a wee bit more evidence that would have justified us removing the cement and some of the slates to see what lay entombed.

In another incident, a gamekeeper phoned me at home one September evening to tell me that two men had been on the hill and had been heading towards the nesting area of a pair of golden eagles. These eagles have three eyries which they use in a rough rotation. The eggs had disappeared in suspicious circumstances on a number of occasions in the past and we were aware that the site is well known to egg collectors.

Gamekeepers have a good eye for something that is just not right or looks out of place in the countryside, their everyday environment. There are many visitors on the hill in the course of a year and many may have been going in the same general direction as these two, yet these two stood out from the rest of the walkers: they were just that bit different. The main feature that made the keeper notice the men was the fact they were wearing wellingtons. Almost everyone walking the hills wears a good pair of stout walking boots. Occasionally someone in summer will wear trainers if not intending to deviate from paths but no-one, even in the worst weather, would wear wellies!

The keeper got his wife to take a run down the glen in her car to see if she could note a registration number once the men were heading back to their car. She made an excellent sleuth and spotted the car just as the two men were changing from wellies to more sensible footwear. She passed the registration number to her husband, Alastair, who phoned me at home. I recognised the car number right away as belonging to our man from Devon and Cornwall, the Man with the Big Mouth, who you may remember had a badly-timed encounter with the local constabulary when he was in possession of a collection of birds' eggs, cannabis and a hand gun. I circulated the car number but it was not traced.

This was an incident that was put down to intelligence-gathering. There was little doubt that the two men were carrying out an out-of-season recce of the area and I felt sure they would be back in the Spring to take the clutch of golden eagle eggs. We returned a few days later and carried out some forensic measures at the nest site to ensure that we could link the men with any egg theft should they return at the end of the following March. For whatever reason they never appeared and thankfully the nest was successful, with the eggs hatching and a singe chick making it to fledging. It was gratifying that the whole glen was on the lookout for the men in the early Spring. Everyone was determined that they would do whatever they could to protect 'their' pair of golden eagles. On the other hand, maybe the men did come back and we were just not told about it.

In another incident a few months later we found ourselves in a similar situation after we leaned that reconnaissance had been carried out at a Perthshire golden eagle nest site by two English egg thieves, one from Merseyside and the other from Cheshire. These men had been targets of our Operation Easter for a long time and were two of the most active egg thieves in the UK. A week or so earlier – during the month of April 2002 – each had received a visit from Merseyside and Cheshire police, accompanied by RSPB investigations staff. In both cases, substantial egg collections had been recovered and enquiry was under way to see where and when they had collected the eggs. Egg thieves are so fanatical that they keep detailed records of the eggs they take and the circumstances at the time they take them. Recovery of all or even some of these notes is a bonus for the police as a far stronger case can be built, and in many instances the notes can link them to having taking the eggs rather than simply possessing them.

Our two criminals were some of the most assiduous note-keepers in the business and it was their bad fortune that Constable Andy McWilliam, the wildlife crime officer from Merseyside who was involved in both searches, found some of the notes. They showed, amongst other interesting exploits, that the two had been in Perthshire at the end of February 2002 and that they carried out reconnaissance at a golden eagle nesting area on Atholl Estates. This particular pair of eagles has more than one eyrie and it was suspected that they were paying an early visit to see which eyrie was going to be used that year. This could be established by the presence of fresh sticks, heather and greenery on the nest. The knowledge of which nest was in use would allow them, once the eggs were laid at the end of March, to go straight to the nest, take the eggs and make a reasonably quick exit.

There was another snippet of evidence in our favour. Since it was a fairly long walk in to the glen where the nest is, the two men had made it a two-day trip, camping overnight in the glen. As campers do, they had taken several photographs of themselves beside their tent. The photos showed that they had camped at the side of a hill burn. This was also confirmed from their narrative which described how heavy rain during the night caused the burn to rise very quickly and their tent was flooded out. In the pitch dark of a cold and wet February night in a Highland glen this would have made an entertaining spectacle.

One of the older photos showed their tent against a backdrop of the high bank of the burn where at one time, probably several years ago, there had been a landslip. I discussed this photograph with Dave Dick of RSPB and we decided to go to the glen to try to match the photograph with the site beside the burn where the tent had been pitched. This would help confirm that the trip was genuine and evidentially would help the Merseyside case. Out of courtesy, since we were carrying out an investigation on their land, I made contact with Atholl Estates and one of the keepers, Mark Pirie, volunteered to take us as far as he could into the glen with his Land Rover. On the day, this was a great help and saved a couple of hours walking time at least. Mark also volunteered to come with us up the burn to look for the campsite. This would do no harm as he had far better knowledge of the hill than Dave or I. He spends most of his working life on the hill and was much fitter than us, for whom a long uphill trek was only occasional. Mark's speed and agility made him seem like a cross between a mountain goat and a quad bike. We struggled to keep up the pace but with sweat running down my back and down my forehead into my eyes causing them to sting like hell, we trauchled up the steepest part. We had followed the burn most of the way and I for one was glad when, nearer the top of the glen, the terrain became a bit less steep.

In late winter the glen was relatively quiet and was not brim-full of the many small birds, flowers and insects that would spend their summer there. At the start of our ascent I was pleased to see a good number of rabbits. On hill ground, rabbits do comparatively little damage unless young trees have been planted. They are very near the bottom of the food chain and provide a food source for many of the upland predators, anything from weasels and stoats to the larger mammals such as foxes and badgers and of course the larger birds of prey such as hen harriers, buzzards and golden eagles. I would imagine that a reasonable stock of rabbits would limit the numbers of grouse taken by the avian predators so most gamekeepers would be happy to have this ready food supply to divert the appetites of hungry predators away from the keeper's main concern, the grouse.

Apart from a few mountain hares still in their white winter coats and a small herd of red deer, this was the complete mammal count. The bird count was not much higher. Woodpigeons featured near the start as they clattered out of a stand of birch trees they had been using as a staging post between meals. Woodpigeons are so common that I thought it must be quite difficult to go for a walk of any length without seeing them. In days when I did more shooting than I do now, woodpigeons were the perfect quarry – testing to shoot and tasty to eat.

A solitary dipper sat bobbing on a rock in the burn just ahead of us, resembling a small and dumpy female blackbird with a white bib under its chin as if dressed ready to tuck into a hearty meal. It disappeared into the burn with a plop and I would love to have been able to see it half-walking, half-swimming along the bottom, picking here and turning a stone there in its search for aquatic invertebrates. As the dipper disappeared a male kestrel glided over us and a few minutes later began to hover, with absolutely no movement back or forward, before pouncing on what would have been a small rodent in the white grass. It was unlucky on that occasion but there would be plenty more mice or voles to try for before too long. The kestrel seems to have no difficulty in hovering and seems to be able to do this in any sort of conditions. The buzzard can also make a good attempt at hovering but it needs an up-draught and is most successful hovering into the wind at the top of a ridge. It would only ever win a poor second prize.

Much as I had hoped we would see one of the pair of golden eagles, it was not to be. For much of the time I couldn't see anything for the sweat in my eyes but I'm sure Mark would have told us if an eagle had been about.

We had the egg thief's photograph of the tent with the backdrop of the bank of the burn with us and compared three of four likely spots once the burn had levelled out. We hit on the exact spot eventually and every tuft of heather still remaining on the bank after the landslip matched the photograph. It was obvious where the tent had been pitched, on a small grassy area right beside the burn. We weren't surprised that the tent had been flooded as the water level was only a couple of inches below the flat area of grass. I took a couple of photographs as near as I could to the spot where the egg thief must have been standing and was content that this would be another strong link in the chain of evidence.

To complete the day's work, I called at the two local hotels and established that the men had been in one of these for a meal after their adventure. I obtained the credit card slip that the egg thief had signed in payment for the meal and hoped that they had enjoyed their Perthshire steaks.

Evidence was being gathered elsewhere by other wildlife crime officers and when the investigation was completed and the case was put together by Andy McWilliam in Merseyside, it was a very strong case against both men. Because of the extent of the evidence both pled guilty and were given jail sentences. I was pleased to have played my small part in convicting them. It had been a pleasant and very worthwhile day out in the country.

Chapter 23

Calls from the Wild

Could this Tayside falconer have bred golden eagles in captivity, and how many scarce and valuable resources should be used to find out for sure?

Unlike peregrines and some other birds of prey, golden eagles are notoriously difficult to breed in captivity. So it was intriguing when we received information that a Tayside falconer was breeding golden eagles successfully and had sold a number of juveniles. I consulted a number of experts who were of the view that this was extremely unlikely and that it was possible, if not likely, that the juveniles had been taken from the wild and were being passed off as captive-bred.

There was insufficient evidence to expect a court to grant a warrant to search the premises concerned, but there are always other ways to achieve the desired outcome. In this case, the outcome was to establish whether the young eagles that had either been sold or were being advertised for sale were progeny of any pair of captive eagles kept by the falconer.

The simplest and most logical solution was to prepare a team that could handle the birds, take blood samples and agree a provisional date that everyone necessary could attend. At very short notice so as to minimise the risk of any evidence being spirited away, we made contact with the falconer, who had no hesitation in allowing us to come and take blood samples. Had he refused permission that could have added to the evidence and may have swung the balance to allow the granting of a warrant, but I was pleased that it didn't come to that.

On the morning of the blood sampling, we had obtained the services of probably the foremost avian vet in Scotland, Alastair Lawrie, and also a couple of the investigations officers from RSPB.

When we met the falconer, we all agreed that he was one of the most knowledgeable, likeable and straightforward falconers we had encountered. We all had the feeling that we were on a wild goose chase. The feeling I had was just slightly different: I had the feeling that I was on a very expensive wild goose chase.

With some difficulty, the golden eagles were caught and blood samples taken expertly and efficiently by Alastair. What amazed me was the size of the female golden eagle at close quarters and the fact that the falconer could not go into the enclosure alone. He had already been attacked by the eagle and when I saw the size of the talons, almost as long as my fingers, I sympathised with him. Once these massive hooks closed round an arm it would be extremely difficult – and painful – to remove them.

Blood samples were taken from the male and the female eagle and from three young eagles that had been bred from the pair over the past two seasons. The samples were sent off to a university in England that was leading the field in animal and bird DNA and we awaited the result. After forty years of dealing with people, I had a good feel for those who were telling the truth and those who were chancers. I put the falconer in the former category and the result that I expected, however unlikely this was in view of the extreme difficulty of breeding captive golden eagles, was that the young eagles were indeed progeny of the pair of adults kept by the falconer.

After six weeks, the report from the university confirmed that everything was above board. All of us were surprised at the ability of the falconer to breed golden eagles successfully and consistently but we were glad of the outcome. I received a substantial invoice from the university in due course but I was grateful to Alastair Lawrie for attending at the falconer's premises and allowing us to have the benefit of his considerable experience without charge. When I spoke to him later he said that the bill had slipped his mind. I doubt if that was the case and I put the absence of an invoice down to the interest, enthusiasm and calibre of the man.

Expenditure from a policing budget is often incurred to obtain evidence for a conviction. It is seldom that similar expense is incurred to establish that someone is innocent but that reflects modern policing.

An investigation into a complaint should be to establish the true facts, whether they subsequently indicate guilt or innocence.

•

The public interest and support in dealing with wildlife crime is always highly appreciated. In Tayside we have certainly taken every opportunity to get the message across to the public to enable them to recognise wildlife crime, to know what to do in order to preserve evidence, and to realise that they must make contact with the police as soon as possible – even from the site of the suspected crime – and ask if possible to speak to a wildlife crime officer. Our pleas and publicity have been augmented by the variety and professionalism of wildlife documentaries on television. This has raised awareness of wildlife – and in many cases their struggle to survive – tremendously. I have already met and congratulated Charlotte Uhlenbroek on her work. I would love to do likewise with David Attenborough, Kate Humble, Simon King, Gordon Buchanan, Saba Douglas-Hamilton and many more wildlife experts. I know that the public are behind what we are doing to reduce and to detect wildlife crime and I encourage their calls. I have touched on many of these diverse and, by the nature of evidence available, short and inconclusive investigations. Here are a couple more.

A complaint was received one Monday morning in late March about a sand bank containing many sand martin nest holes being destroyed by the loading of sand by a JCB into lorries for use in a flyover under construction on the A90 between Perth and Dundee. From the precise details, I knew the information was coming from one of the lorry drivers involved in the work. It always amazes me how many big butch lorry drivers have a conscience when it comes to birds and wee furry animals. It is a conscience for which I am always grateful, even though the man did not phone me himself but obviously phoned his partner and asked her to contact me.

It was an especially busy morning by way of general policing and I was unable to get anyone to come and assist me. I suspected from the conversation with the lorry driver's partner that the evidence had been lost in any case. Sand martins arrive here from Africa about mid-March and immediately locate a suitable sand bank in which to nest. They peck and scrape at the sand, making an elliptical nest burrow about a metre or so in length in which they make a wider chamber at the end to accommodate the nest and to lay their eggs. As soon as they start their marathon excavation the burrow is protected by law. No-one can legally come along with a JCB and scrape down the sand with a giant bucket and put it into a lorry to be used in road-works. This is the theory. In practice it takes seconds on a Monday morning to eliminate the weekend work of the industrious sand martins, keen to make the most of their short visit to the UK. If their burrow is destroyed so is the evidence that they had been working like wee brown and white feathered drilling machines over two whole days in their individual effort to continue the existence of their species and allow their progeny to accompany or replace them on the epic return journey to warmer climes in early September.

I visited the site, introduced myself, and asked to be shown to the sand face that was being used that morning. I explained the reason for my visit and asked if I could speak with the JCB driver. I have no police powers, hence the reason that I had wanted to take a police officer with me. I was polite and business-like with the foreman. Of course I could have said to him, 'Even though I used to be a police officer I'm no longer a police officer and my role is a wildlife and environment officer for Tayside Police in a support staff role. As such I have no powers to ask you to comply with any particular request. You may help me in my enquiries or you can tell me to get lost.' To tell him this would have been honest, but counter-productive to my purpose. I therefore told him nothing of the sort, which I thought was no less honest!

The foreman took me to the sand face that was being worked and I could see a large number of sand martins flying around, landing on the sand face as soon as the foreman asked the JCB driver to stop and speak with me. The JCB driver denied that the sand martins had made any burrows when he started work that morning but their presence and their keen-ness to get back to the sand face told me otherwise. Unfortunately I couldn't get the sand martins to court to give evidence and I was beaten. Or nearly beaten.

Normally I am a person who busies about, getting things done quickly, and have little time for those who dither and perambulate at the speed of a sloth in low gear. I saw three lorries starting to form a queue to get loaded with sand and suddenly I became that sloth in extremely low gear. I noted the name and address of the JCB driver and much else besides, writing as if I were still in primary one. Once that was finished I saw that the three lorries had increased to about twelve. I then walked round and examined – as if in low gear, four wheel drive – the area under the sand face that the JCB driver had been working on, having a scrape here and a scrape there in a forlorn search for a dead sand martin. There were now about twenty lorries in the queue. I felt I hadn't yet caused sufficient disruption and had some final pedantic questions for the foreman, then for the JCB driver. By this time, the tail end of the queue of lorries was round the corner out of my sight and I had no idea how many drivers were impatiently waiting with their lorries to be loaded by the inert JCB. I eventually relented and let them all get back to work. I just hoped that the sand martins appreciated the moment, for there must have been a considerable financial loss involved for the haulage contractor.

I got a call later in the morning from the partner of the lorry driver who had blown the whistle. She said that the contractor had called a meeting of all the drivers. He knew it was one of his drivers who had contacted the police but had no idea which one. He told them that if anyone else phoned the police about 'bloody birds' they would be sacked. I knew the contractor from dealings I'd had with him when he was in his teens and early twenties when he was an unpleasant kind of chap. If I had upset him and reduced his profit then my visit had been worthwhile.

•

From time to time I get a telephone call from premises that develop films. The query usually revolves round the legality of the film being developed. Some may contain photographs of birds' eggs in nests, a variety of dead animals that may be thought to be protected, or even animals in circumstances that indicate cruelty may have been inflicted upon them. I'm always pleased that shops take the trouble to contact me, even though in many of the cases the person taking the photographs has not committed any offence. One call related to photographs of dead cats. The shop assistant told me she was absolutely shocked at the photos, so I went to have a look for myself.

The photographs were mainly of a christening, with many of the photos featuring a baby surrounded by what I assumed were doting relatives and friends, all in their finery. It was the last four photographs on the roll of film that had caused concern. This first showed a cat and four kittens, obviously shot because of the injuries, and set out on a lawn in the form of the number five on a domino. The cat had pride of place in the centre and a kitten on each corner, as it were. The next photograph had the same dead felines but this time a man was standing beside them with a shotgun over the crook of his arm. In the third photo, the man with the shotgun had been replaced by a woman in a pink top with the shotgun, and in the last image the only difference was that the woman had her fist raised as if in defiance or as a symbol of success. I could see why the shop assistant had phoned me.

'Surely it's not legal to shoot cats,' said the assistant. Of course in some circumstances it can be legal to shoot cats, and I explained the law in relation to ownership of property and the need for the police to prove that anyone participating in the shooting was aware that the cats belonged to someone or that it would have been reasonable to expect that this would have been the case. Anyone who knows me is well aware that cats are not my favourite companion animal. I get exceedingly angry when neighbours' cats dig in my newly sown vegetable garden, destroying the symmetry and orderliness of straight rows of vegetables when the seeds eventually germinate and are growing all over the place. I also get annoyed when young birds fledge, only to become the playthings of someone's moggy – cats that usually sleep at a fireside all day and are then kicked out at dusk to terrorise young birds through the night. Much as I detest the damn things, I can't reach into my gun cabinet, take out my shotgun or rifle and suddenly become the patron saint of garden birds and vegetables growing in straight lines. I am aware that the cats are the property of someone, somewhere, and are therefore protected from my wrath. Cat lovers will probably now be throwing this book in the bin!

The assistant had a puzzled look. 'So you've told me that cats are protected, that they're not allowed to be shot. Why would these people shooting this cat and kittens not have broken the law?' My answer was that if the cats had been feral cats – had not belonged to anyone – then an offence may not have been committed. I would have no idea what the position was of course until I talked to the folks in the photos. One offence the lady in the pink jumper had come very close to committing, irrespective of the status of the cats, was a breach of the peace, by putting the shop staff in a state of alarm. There was no question that the staff had seen nothing like this before. They were appalled.

I managed to get the name and address of the person who had submitted the photos and Constable Graham Jack and I went to give her a visit. She lived in a big house in the country, so any risk to neighbours or to the public from shooting cats here was considerably lessened. The woman admitted right away that she and her partner had shot the cats. The adult cat had been a stray – a feral cat – living in the garden for some time. They had left it alone initially as it was causing them no problem but possibly because it was feeding kittens and needed extra food, it started to stalk and kill red squirrels. She wanted to protect the red squirrels so the cat and kittens had to go. Despite any moral high ground anyone might want to take on the shooting of the cats, neither the woman nor her partner had committed an offence. What I could not understand was why either of the two would wish to be photographed along with the ex-cats and why they did not realise the upset they were bound to cause when they submitted the film for processing. Graham and I had an alfresco cup of tea with the exterminator of squirrel-eating felines, who promised not to take photos of any other pest she had to deal with in her country garden unless it turned out to be something of public interest like a black-footed ferret or a snow monkey!

I had a further encounter with this lady and one which probably caused her infinitely more anguish than the first. I was giving a talk on wildlife crime one evening at a Scottish Women's Rural Institute meeting. There was a fairly large audience and the talk was underway before I saw her. It was the same pink top that she was wearing that was the clue to recognition. I had converted the photographs of the famous five cats into slides and had previously used them in talks to police officers in training. Even then I had blanked her face out. Unusually, the slides were still in the carousel from my last talk to a group of probationary police officers but I had moved them and some other slides I wasn't using in this talk to the end of the carousel, well beyond my stopping point for this evening. Of course she didn't know that. What she *would* realise was that if I did show the slides, she was wearing the same pink top as in the photos. She would also be well aware that everyone in the room would then know that she was the person holding the shotgun and punching the air with her clenched fist. That she was the cat killer. That she may also just have one jumper!

I looked at her later in the talk and her face was brighter than her pink top. She was obviously going through hell and I couldn't help her. She wouldn't have thanked me for shouting out to her, 'It's OK, I'm not going to show everyone in the hall the photos of the cat and kittens you shot in your garden.' I'll bet she couldn't wait till the talk ended. She probably didn't even hear anything that I said, sitting there thinking of an excuse to blurt out as she ran from the hall the minute she saw her image on the screen. 'It's not me, honest. I've seen one or two women who look the spitting image of me. I like cats anyway. . .'

She had no need to flee, and as I described the very last slide I saw the strained look in her face gradually give way to a look of relief. She came up to me after the talk, while I was having a cup of tea and munching my way through the traditional sandwiches and best baking for which Rurals are famed. She told me she had indeed been sitting there terrified all through the talk. She was so thankful that I hadn't shown the photographs as she would never have lived it down in the area. I doubt after her ordeal at the SWRI that she'll chance taking a photo of even black-footed ferrets or snow monkeys now if she has to deal with them in her garden.

Chapter 24

The Fox Hunting Ban and the Dundee Squeaker

The very first conviction under the new legislation banning foxhunting originates from Broughty Ferry of all places, and there isn't a horse, hound or horn in sight.

Foxhunting is a country pursuit that engenders vehement opposing views. For my own part I have never been an advocate of killing animals solely for sport. If the reason for the killing is pest control or where the animals or birds killed will ultimately be eaten I have no problems. Killing foxes for sport is how I see foxhunting on horseback. Though there must logically be a degree of pest control if a fox is killed by hounds during a mounted hunt in my view there are far more effective methods of fox control. I can make the clear distinction between mounted hunts and foot packs. Foot packs, where people on foot with a pack of hounds drive foxes forward to waiting guns and the foxes are shot as a means of pest control, are – at least to me – completely different. I am aware of an instance when nine foxes were driven forward from a wood by hounds and were shot by waiting guns. It cannot be argued that this is not good – and humane – fox control. Though I don't agree with mounted hunts, everyone is entitled to his or her own view so long as it does not colour their objectivity, judgement and fairness, especially in a role such as that of the police.

Lord Watson caused considerable consternation with his Private Member's Bill on hunting with hounds. Though I have no doubt he started off with the intention of banning foxhunting, in my opinion he made the passing of the Bill much more difficult by trying to include the banning of the use of terriers in a fox den to bolt a vixen or to kill cubs. This no doubt doubled his opposition overnight by involving many gamekeepers, farmers and shepherds in a dispute that hardly, up to that point, affected them.

I had sight of the Bill at several stages in its early days. There were three very clear offences: to deliberately hunt a wild mammal with a dog (which included the use of more than one dog); for a person to knowingly allow his or her land to be used for the deliberate hunting of a wild mammal with a dog; for a person being the owner of a dog, to knowingly allow it to be used to deliberately hunt a wild mammal. As in much legislation, the offences are simple. It is the exceptions which complicate something that would otherwise be straightforward. And there were plenty of exceptions – pages and pages of them.

Exceptions permitted the stalking, searching for or flushing of wild mammals with dogs above ground and under control for a variety of purposes but only if the person acts to ensure that, once the wild mammal is found or emerges from cover, it is shot or killed by a bird of prey once it is safe to do so. This allowed the hunting of foxes to continue provided the objective was to shoot the fox rather than to have the hounds catch the fox. We frequently have foot packs of hounds out after foxes in Tayside and this activity remains legal and unaffected by the new Act.

Another exception allowed a dog under control to flush a fox or a mink from below ground for various reasons, provided it is shot as soon as possible after it is flushed. This allowed the bolting of vixens from dens with terriers as has been carried out by gamekeepers and shepherds for generations. A further exception allowed the use of a *single* dog to enter the den after a vixen has been bolted and shot, in order to despatch the cubs. In effect the new Act made little difference to fox control at dens. Though the exceptions I have cited would be the most widely used, there were many others.

I could see one immediate problem. The definition of mammal *excluded* a rabbit and a rodent. Where we did have a problem in Tayside was with illegal hare coursing (before the Bill was enacted hare coursing was legal with the permission of the landowner). Landowners, farmers and gamekeepers were contacting me every week regarding groups of men walking over their land with greyhounds and coursing hares. Prior to 2002, when the men had been challenged there were two standard excuses. 'We were just letting our dogs stretch their legs. They had been cooped up in the car and we thought they need out.' Or 'Our dogs just need the toilet. They just need out for a pee but they ran off. We're doing no harm mister' (or constable as the case may be). I had a variation on this theme in January 2007, when hare coursers alleged that they had to stop and let their two dogs out of the car as they were feeling car-sick. I was intrigued as to how word of this canine malady was transmitted to the human owners? In any event, when we were at the Bill stage I could see a new excuse, 'We're just after rabbits. They're young dogs and they're not fit for hares anyway.'

I made one or two recommendations for changes to the Bill. Some changes were made, possibly on my recommendations, but no change to the rabbit being deprived of its mammal status. Poor wee rabbits, being ousted as mammals by Lord Watson to join the ranks of the non-mammals. Frogs, snakes, newts, lizards, moths, earthworms, blowflies, beetles, centipedes... and rabbits. My prediction came true and a standard excuse now by hare coursers when they are caught is that they are just looking for rabbits. It is still an offence – to trespass on land in unlawful search or pursuit of game – but with a considerably reduced penalty and no power of arrest. At least the rabbits can take comfort that they are still afforded a degree of protection by many of the Game Laws of the 1800s, a privilege denied to worms and beetles!

Mike Watson's Bill was enacted and became the Protection of Wild Mammals (Scotland) Act 2002. Though it could be argued that it did not achieve what it set out to do, and despite my criticisms, it *has* been a benefit to us in policing hare coursing, mainly because of the power of arrest and the increased penalties including imprisonment for up to six months. I was pleased that the first conviction in Scotland under the new legislation was in Dundee. What's more it was for foxhunting!

This remarkable case started off with a call on my mobile phone one evening from a man in Broughty Ferry, which is on the outskirts of Dundee. He told me that on several occasions he had seen someone hunting on Broughty Ferry beach. It was a spotlight that first drew his attention, especially when the spotlight sometimes showed a white light and sometimes a red light. The operator of the spotlight was walking along the beach and the beam was sweeping back and forth. My witness also said that he could hear a squeaking noise like a rabbit in distress.

The reason he had phoned me that particular night was that he had witnessed the man who was operating the light come off the beach on to the road. The man had with him two dogs, a greyhound and a golden retriever. Curious as to what had been taking place, my witness approached him and asked what he was doing. 'I'm after foxes. There's loads of them. I catch them in the beam of the light and squeak them in. When they come in a bit I change the beam to red so they're not spooked. I keep squeaking them in and when they're close enough I let the dogs go. The dogs go after the fox and catch it. They have great fun.'

My witness said that he was disgusted that this was taking place almost on his doorstep and could we do something about it. My instructions to him were to contact the Control Room in Dundee as soon as he saw the man on the beach with the spotlight again. He promised to do so and apologised for disturbing me in the evening.

The next morning I prepared a briefing note for the Control Room and for the police officers covering Broughty Ferry. This was new legislation, it was a type of incident that neither the Control Room staff nor the police officers would have encountered and it was unrealistic to expect them to deal with it efficiently without some basic guidance. The briefing note outlined the type of incident, how it would be reported to the police, the legislation, powers the police officers had and my suggestions as to how best to deal with it.

It worked perfectly. Several nights later, the incident occurred again. My witness took the action I had requested and the police responded quickly, catching the man as he came off the beach. He had a spotlamp, a battery pack and two dogs and was arrested and charged under the new legislation with deliberately hunting a wild mammal, namely a fox, with two dogs. The witness had gone a stage further and had given the police the name of another person who had watched the evening's events. It was an unusual case. No foxes had been seen either being caught or even hunted, though the witnesses and the police officers were able to say that foxes were regularly seen scavenging on the beach.

At the trial I and PC Harvey Birse, a Divisional wildlife crime officer, gave evidence. Over the years both of us had often used spotlamps and rifles to shoot rabbits, and also spotlamps, rifles and squeakers to shoot foxes. We described how foxes could be picked up in the beam of a lamp at a considerable distance and how they could be lured closer by the use of a squeaker that simulated the noise of a rabbit or hare in distress. We also explained the use of the red filter on the lamp, which could be used as the fox came closer. While a fox might be reluctant to continue towards a beam of white light they seem to disregard a light with a red filter which is possibly invisible to them. When giving my evidence, I asked the court if they would like the two squeakers demonstrated. One was a large squeaker which I was sure would be used while the fox was still distant, while the other was a small, quiet, squeaker which would be ideal to encourage the fox to continue coming forward to investigate the intriguing sound for the last 100 metres or so. The sheriff agreed he would like the squeakers demonstrated and I started with the loud one. I unfortunately forgot about the microphone and the loudspeaker system in the court and nearly deafened everyone. The court dispensed with the need to demonstrate the second squeaker, however everyone was wide awake to hear the accused being found guilty. He was fined £250 and his spotlight and battery pack, worth about the same, were forfeited.

I was pleased at the result of this case. Though we in Tayside and one or two other forces have used the legislation frequently, so far as I am aware this remains, at the beginning of 2007, the only Scottish conviction that relates to the hunting of a fox, the remainder all relating to the hunting of hares.

Chapter 25

The March to the Midden

Our investigator is 'in the shit' in the line of duty but there's no way he's going to go home without his wellies.

The road to reducing wildlife crime is extremely rocky and is littered with signs that equate to Slow or Give Way. I have criticised some gamekeepers and landowners already and I have also praised them for the good conservation work that most of them carry out, good work that is spoiled disproportionately by a few. The few rogues could be stopped almost overnight if gamekeepers and gamekeeping organisations threatened to report their suspicions – or in many cases, evidence – to the police. It is unfortunate that this seems too much to expect but some gamekeepers and landowners are beginning to meet somewhere in the middle. Progress has consistently been three steps forward and two steps back but nevertheless, even painfully slow progress is better than retrogression.

As the reader will be well aware, much of my work centres round dead animals and birds found in circumstances that lead the finder to suspect that they have been the victim of a crime. There is no doubt that a gamekeeper *may* be the person who has committed that crime but I emphasise that it is completely wrong to make this assumption without some evidence. I therefore try to encourage gamekeepers and landowners to report dead protected animals and birds that they find, rather than stick them in a hole somewhere in order that they are not unfairly blamed for causing their death. This philosophy is now beginning to show results and at last I am getting phone calls about dead beasties that I would never otherwise know about. Whether or not the animal died naturally, accidentally or as the result of a crime is of less importance than getting the phone call to report or discuss it. It is the trust between gamekeeper and police that I value and try to encourage.

In March 2003 a gamekeeper in Angus called at Montrose Police Station with a dead buzzard he had picked up on his ground. The bird had been recently killed and appeared in otherwise good condition. He left the bird with the police, saying that this was the third dead buzzard he had found in less than a week. I made contact with him, initially by telephone, and he gave me further details. All three birds had been found in the same field and he had buried the first two in a dung midden in the adjacent field. For those not quite so conversant with country matters, a dung midden is an extremely large and rotting heap of cow shit and straw.

I collected the dead buzzard from Montrose and together with PC John Robertson, a divisional wildlife crime officer based at Carnoustie Police Station, went to make a search of the area. We agreed that John would search the woodland edge at the bottom of the field for any dead birds that may be there, while I would make a search of the midden for the two that the gamekeeper said he had buried there. This was a decision I came to regret.

I searched round the edge of the midden first to see if there was any obvious disturbance, which I intended to then excavate further using my green wellies as I had no spade or fork with me. After several unfruitful bouts of burrowing round the fringe, I turned my attention to the top of the midden. The midden had been there for several years and was unusually soft. It may or may not surprise readers that I have been on the top of many middens in my life. All, up to this point, were solid and supported my weight. I soon found that, conversely, this midden was soft and didn't support my weight. If the same conditions were encountered beside the sea, the term would be quicksand. Could this be referred to as quickdung? Quickshit?

Quick was not a term that could be applied to me, except for the quick loss of altitude into the mire. My tempo then changed to very slow, as I became stuck up to the knees. For anyone who has worn wellies they will know that the knees are above the tops of the wellies, which of course means that any liquid above the tops of the wellies can then run down inside. It being early March, the first feeling was a cooling down of my legs below the knees as the vile liquid filled my wellies. My first instinct was to lift one of my legs to escape the midden's clutches but my foot started to come out of my welly.

The wellies were Nora make and over £30 a pair. I didn't fancy leaving them in the bowels of the midden so I shoved my foot back down again. Eureka! I remembered the theory of displacement from physics at school, about the volume of liquid displaced by an object submerged or floating in it. The volume of my foot and lower leg then came shooting up my leg, some inside and some outside my trousers. I saw that the colour of the liquid that came up the outside of my leg was dark brown with a plethora of bubbles. I had no reason to suspect that the liquid scooting up the inside of my leg was anything different. When the bubbles burst they gave an insight into the smell of the liquid. I was now well aware of the texture, consistency, colour and smell of the inner sanctum of the midden. I just needed now to escape from it – with my wellies.

I tried raising one foot a bit, then the other, but the gain with the first leg was negated as soon as I tried to move the second leg. I then tried to completely remove one leg. This was extremely slow but I felt myself making progress. In my determination not to leave my best green wellies behind I had also to curl my toes. This was at last achieving success and after a few minutes steady pulling, my right leg was free. As it became free, I fell on my backside, a position that would have been inevitable anyway if I were to go home complete with two wellies.

I then tried to extricate my left leg from my damp sitting position. Doing this with my left toes curled was okay to start with but as my left leg became slightly higher it became more difficult then became impossible. There was nothing for it but to leave my left welly behind, albeit temporarily. I continued huffing and puffing – in my predicament I still managed somehow to think of the story *The Three Little Pigs* and the wolf's Herculean efforts to blow their house down – and my left leg came free of my welly like a best champagne cork, though the liquid resembled anything but champagne.

It was a fairly simple but very unpleasant matter then to put both hands a few inches into the ripe slurry, gain a grip of my lost welly, and gradually ease it from its tomb. On reflection I should have done that with both of them and my Houdini escape could have been expedited. Suffice to say that the search for the two buried buzzards ended there.

I can also recommend Nora wellies to anyone who intends to or suspects they might sink into a midden. Nora wellies are unlined. I washed them out there and then in a burn, then later washed them out at home with hot water. Being unlined wellies, any smell that would have reminded me of our joint adventure was exorcised.

I took the buzzard to Scottish Agricultural Science Agency in Edinburgh for examination for pesticides. The report received within a few days showed that the buzzard had died from eating bait contaminated with carbofuran. The chemists at SASA were also able to say that the gullet of the buzzard contained what appeared to be pigeon feathers. Since it is normally the bird's last meal that kills it, it is probable that the bait had been a pigeon.

Discreet enquiries were made in the area and suspicion centred on a pigeon fancier who had a pigeon loft on a nearby farm. PC John Robertson and Willie Milne from SEERAD called on the loft owner and told him of the poisoned buzzards. The man denied that the setting out of baits was anything to do with him and agreed to a search of his loft. In the loft, the officers found a small plastic cylindrical pill container with traces of a blue substance, the shade of blue being the same shade as cabofuran. The loft owner claimed that the substance had been for killing rats and mice.

The blue traces in the pill container were sent to SASA for examination and there was confirmation that the traces were of carbofuran. We now had one confirmed dead buzzard killed by carborfuran, two further buried dead buzzards that I really didn't want to think about, and a pigeon fancier with a pigeon loft half a mile from where the buzzards were found and who had a container with traces of carbofuran. The pigeon fancier had to be re-visited.

PC John Robertson and I called on the pigeon fancier a few mornings later and advised him of the SASA findings. He admitted that he had poured the blue granules from the pill container down a rat hole. I advised him that rats would not eat carbofuran on its own;

that it would need to be on some palatable substance that the rats would eat. He then said that he had put the granules on a piece of bacon and put the bacon in a rat hole. There certainly had been a rat problem at the back of the pigeon loft though I didn't fall for his bacon story. He denied putting any carbofuran on a dead pigeon and also said that he was not having any trouble at his loft with birds of prey. In view of his last statement, I wondered why he had a plastic eagle owl stuck on a pole not ten metres from his loft.

Before we left we charged the pigeon fancier with laying out bait that poisoned a buzzard, possessing an article capable of being used to commit a crime against the Wildlife and Countryside Act 1981, namely the container with dark blue traces, and storing a pesticide, carbofuran, other than in its original container.

Before the case came up I had an interesting discussion with the procurator fiscal about the container with the dark blue traces. The fiscal was initially doubtful if the contents of the container were sufficient in volume for a charge, after all it was virtually just a dark blue powdery residue visible in the container. My response was, 'If I filled the container with warm water, left it for a few minutes and gave it to a dog or a person to drink, would there be a risk of death or ill health to the dog or the person?' The answer was in the affirmative and my point was made.

In court, the pigeon fancier pled guilty to the pesticide storage offence only. This was accepted by the fiscal and he was admonished – a conviction that is recorded but without a penalty. He was 68 years of age and had never been in bother with the police before. I thought the result was reasonable taking account of all the circumstances and that he could only be sentenced on the most minor of the charges.

Though I'm sure the last meal of the buzzard we recovered was a dead pigeon, it was not beyond reasonable doubt that the buzzard had picked up a rat that had died or was dying of carbofuran poisoning. If we had managed to recover the other two buzzards from the depths of the midden we may have had a clearer idea. If only the keeper had reported the finding of the first buzzard rather than the finding of the third buzzard. Three steps forward, two back. But still progress.

Further progress on trust from keepers came in late 2006 when a keeper asked for a meeting with me. I was disappointed, though not surprised, to learn that an incoming shoot captain had told him that there were far too many buzzards about and that he would need to take immediate steps to get rid of them. This puts a keeper in an impossible position. He conforms to the wishes of the person paying his wages, which puts him at risk of being imprisoned if caught, or he loses his job. If he loses his job more often than not that includes a tied house that is also lost. He refuses to control the buzzard population and he still loses his job and his house. I have absolutely no doubt that the keeper will not remain much longer on that estate and I will be watching his successor very carefully. I will also be trying very, very hard to bring the shoot captain to book, though employers invariably find a way of distancing themselves from illegality and leave the employee as the fall guy.

Chapter 26

Red Kites in the Sunset?

An assessment of the success or otherwise of the red kite re-introduction programme in Scotland, and some hope for the future.

Like the white-tailed eagle, the goshawk and the osprey, red kites were completely exterminated in Scotland because of man's greed and lack of appreciation and respect for biodiversity. Three were seen as a threat to game management and the shooting industry, while the osprey was seen as a threat to fishing. The white-tailed eagle and the red kite had to be re-introduced from stock from other countries, the goshawk seems to have re-colonised parts of the UK partly from escaped falconers' birds, and we were lucky enough that the osprey considered us worthy of a second chance. A pair of ospreys appeared in the mid 1950s at Loch Garten in Speyside, bred successfully, and have gradually spread throughout many parts of Scotland, especially Perthshire and Inverness-shire.

As I write this on a Sunday afternoon in mid-2006, I seriously wonder if we do deserve a second chance. I have just spent my morning in an Angus Glen carrying out an initial investigation following an allegation of extensive poisoning of wildlife, culminating in the horrendously painful death of a farm collie. 2006 has also been the worst year for pesticide abuse in Tayside for a decade. In addition to the collie, two buzzards and a tawny owl have been found poisoned, and a rabbit, a pheasant and wood pigeon laced as baits with the pesticide carbofuran have been found.

Scottish Natural Heritage and RSPB Scotland are to be congratulated for their work in re-introducing red kites. A considerable amount of hard work and expense went into the programme, to say nothing of the goodwill of the nations who donated their young red kites. RSPB Scotland also worked out a formula for estimating the number of kites that are killed annually at the hand of man. I'm not convinced of their estimate of 30% in some parts of Scotland but I agree entirely that whatever the number is – and it is substantial – it is far too many.

I'm not entirely sure how the formula works but it includes a multiplier of the red kites that are found dead and confirmed to have been shot or poisoned, plus a proportion of those that are missing and the numbers that should reasonably be in a particular release site area based on a similar release in the Chilterns. I'm well aware of the numbers of birds of prey in general terms that we in Tayside recover that show signs of persecution. I know also that the birds recovered are likely only to be a proportion of what has actually been killed at the hand of man. In that respect it may be difficult to argue with the RSPB figures for red kite deaths.

In Tayside, the red kites have not yet spread eastwards to Angus. While I have no doubt that there will be a few red kites passing through Angus, it is not an area in which they have yet settled. In Perthshire, they have gradually spread eastwards from the release site near Doune and are beginning to establish communal roosts in more areas, which lead to (or are the result of) an expansion of breeding areas. To put the persecution into perspective, since the re-introduction programme in west Perthshire, when 103 red kites were released between 1996 and 2001, we have investigated the deaths of five red kites. Of these five, three were poisoned and two were shot.

Let's consider the criminal mind in relation first of all to the two kites that were shot. Shooting a bird in most cases means that the bird is either killed instantly or incapacitated to the extent that it can be caught and killed by the perpetrator of the crime. If a bird is on the ground when it is shot, and it is injured, in most cases it will not be able to take off. It can therefore be caught. It is in the interest of the person shooting the bird to ensure that no-one is aware that a protected bird has been killed so it is likely to be recovered and disposed of in a manner that ensures that the police never become aware of it. If the bird is in a tree, it normally falls out of the tree and is hidden, buried or whatever in a manner in which it is unlikely to be found and subsequently handed to the police. If the bird is flying, it normally falls out of the sky and again, at least in most cases, is easily caught and disposed of. It is fair to say that in most cases a person who shoots at a red kite will be able to get rid of the evidence to avoid conviction. In summary, most red kites that are shot will never feature in a police investigation. I am confident that anyone arguing against this theory will either be naive or biased.

Setting poisoned bait is slightly different. Firstly I would doubt that any poisoned bait would intentionally be set for a red kite, but this does not escape the fact that a red kite, a golden eagle or a collie may be the victim. A red kite feeding from poisoned bait stands the same chance of being killed as any other victim. Since most victims – at least in my experience – die within about 100 metres of a bait, it has a far higher chance of being picked up by the person who set out the bait rather than anyone chancing upon it. I hesitate to give a proportion but I have no doubt that most victims, including red kites, will be picked up by the criminal setting out the bait and will never find their way into the chain of evidence in a criminal investigation. Could our two shot red kites have been the only two red kites shot in Perthshire in more than a decade? I think not. Could they be two out of ten, two out of twenty, two out of forty? We will never know. Could we have been extremely competent in recovering the only three poisoned kites in Perthshire? Again I think not. Three out of twenty? We will never know the true figure but our red kites are increasing at an abysmally low rate compared to those in the Chilterns.

Our two shot red kites had different fates. The first, in the Crieff area, had the lower mandible and tongue shot off so that it died a lingering death of starvation. The crime was almost impossible to investigate as the bird may have been shot near to where it was eventually found dead or it may have travelled a considerable distance after it was shot. The most likely weapon was a .22 rifle and I just have a gut feeling it was a young person let loose with a .22 who was the culprit. We will never know the truth, and it may even be that whoever aimed the rifle at the bird and pulled the trigger thought that he missed the target entirely, though that does not lessen his culpability.

In the second incident, the bird was found hanging in a tree. It was almost certainly shot while sitting in the tree, as its injuries would be almost immediately fatal and it could not have flown into the tree after the shot. It became entangled in the branches almost four metres from the ground, which may be the reason the criminal could not recover and dispose of the body. There was a suspect, who we interviewed shortly after the recovery of the bird. The suspect denied shooting a red kite but stated that he often shot carrion crows out of trees with his .223 rifle. We made comment firstly that .223 ammunition was expensive, but this was countered by the suspect stating that getting rid of a carrion crow was worth the cost. We then commented that crows are black, while red kites are predominantly light brown. The suspect countered – and this was corroborated by his wife – that he was colour blind. He could offer no explanation to counter the fact that, even if both targets look the same to a person who is colour-blind, the kite was wearing a large plastic tag on each wing that would have been clearly visible through a rifle scope. He became very uncomfortable when told that a bullet fragment had been recovered from the red kite and that we were considering gathering in all the estate rifles for test firing to try to match one with the bullet fragment recovered. I intentionally forgot to mention to him that the bullet fragment had insufficient detail for ballistic comparison. That may have had some bearing on why I learned the following day that his .223 rifle had accidentally fallen from his shoulder and over a crag. It was buckled and broken and could not be test fired.

We didn't believe the suspect's story and we were thwarted by the lack of powers to detain him and bring him to a police station, it being prior to the improved provisions under the Nature Conservation (Scotland) Act 2004. It may be that the estate didn't believe him either, as he left his employment and moved out of the area very soon after the incident.

Two of the poisoned red kites were found on the same estate. In addition, they had died as a result of taking the same pesticide, chloralose. This tended to point to the same culprit. In this case the estate owner was the suspect and he had been interviewed after the discovery of the first red kite. As is invariably the case when there is little evidence, the suspect denied responsibility. We made further enquiries but all roads led us back to our initial suspect. The suspect was a pleasant chap and we had a coffee with him, but the investigation had reached an end.

To those who have never conducted an investigation into a crime, the crime should never be taken personally. The police role is to find the evidence to inculpate or exculpate a person who may at some stage of the investigation become a suspect. If that person is cleared of suspicion, as is sometimes the case, then the police can re-think or re-assess the evidence and move on to a new suspect. Even if a person remains the only suspect but cannot be charged through lack of evidence, there is no need for the police to fall out with or take umbrage at that person. The whole legal process is a challenge – some may say a game. It begins with the police investigation, then passes to the drama of a courtroom. In court the prosecution witnesses may experience a hard time from the defence solicitor, very often with a challenge to their recollection of facts or even sometimes implying a slur on their integrity but none of this should be taken personally, especially by police officers. At the investigative stage, I have always made a point of doing my best to obtain the evidence required for a prosecution, but recognise the point when I know I am on the right track but have come to the end of the road. It's a cross between Sir Harry Lauder's *Keep Right on to the End of the Road* and Vera Lynn's *We'll Meet Again.* I simply mean that a criminal has to be lucky all of the time.

After the finding of the second red kite on this estate, I went to see the suspect again, this time with Willie Milne from SEERAD. Unsurprisingly, the suspect denied responsibility for setting out poisoned baits and may have been taken aback when I gave up easily and suggested he put the kettle on. We chatted for about half an hour about many subjects, including game rearing in general, his thoughts on the RSPB, his thoughts on the Scottish Executive and many more subjects. As he gained in confidence, he made a fatal slip. He told me that he was a bit unpopular in the nearby village because of some antic or other with his microlite aircraft. I could see that this was my chance and suggested to him that he would be even more unpopular shortly. When he asked why this would be, I produced a photograph I had taken of the latest dead red kite hanging from a tree. It had obviously landed in this tree after taking its fatal dose of chloralose, had become increasingly unwell and had slipped down the tree until one of its legs had become entangled in a branch. It had then hung upside down till it died. I told him I was about to give the photograph to the media and say that this was the second red kite found dead on this particular estate.

His comment and the photograph were the catalysts I needed. He said the release of this information would make him extremely unpopular, with the addendum of course that it was nothing to do with him. I threw him a lifeline and said that I didn't have to give the photograph and the story to the press but that in exchange for my silence I would need to recover the pesticide involved. My addendum this time – I would need a phone call within two days maximum leading me to the recovery of the pesticide. The ultimatum prompted the response, 'Well I'll ask around and see if I can find out anything.' My response, 'You need ask no further than your own conscience.'

Two days later the suspect called me with the question, 'Are you working on your own today Alan?' I replied in the affirmative and he said, 'I've managed to get hold of the pesticide. If you come out on your own, I'll give it to you.' I made my way to the estate and met the suspect, who handed me a bottle containing a white powder. 'There you are,' he said, 'that's the chloralose.' I replied, 'I never mentioned chloralose when I was here, how did you know it was chloralose that killed the red kite?' There was a silence, which I eventually broke by saying, 'Let that be the last time.' It was indeed the last time and red kites have bred successfully on the boundary of that estate since that particular year, 2001. Pesticide abuse had been preventing the red kites' spread eastwards and that threat seems to have been removed.

There is always more than one way to skin a cat!

Chapter 27

The Brechin Freezer

A peculiar game of pass the parcel is played out with a suspect in a back green near Brechin, and it's clear that, in the prosecution game, the odds are stacked in favour of the defence.

I had a telephone call mid-way through one morning I was intending to spend in the office catching up with paperwork. Several police officers were searching a house on the outskirts of Brechin having received information that a firearm was likely to be found there. They had done their homework and established that no-one at that address was a firearm certificate holder. To search for a firearm or ammunition, police officers need to obtain a specially worded warrant authorising this type of search. Most searches carried out by police are in order to recover stolen property but in some cases, such as to recover firearms – as was the case here – to recover drugs or to carry out a search in relation to wildlife crimes, specially worded warrants are required.

The officers did not find any firearm but in the course of their search they encountered a freezer in the garden. The garden is an odd place to keep a freezer unless it is an old retired freezer used as some sort of store. This freezer was a store of sorts, though it was far from retired and in addition was connected to the mains. It was full of dead animals and birds, which posed several problems for the officers. Their first problem was that they had no idea what species the animals and birds were or whether or not the occupant was allowed to keep them, hence the telephone call to me. I set off right away to meet them to see what help I could be.

An hour or so later I was being shown the freezer in the garden. I couldn't believe that this freezer, out in the open during the month of February, was live and hadn't blown up! I looked in and saw that it was full to the top of dead beasties in poly bags. The top layer seemed mostly to be roe buck heads and I was more interested to see what lay buried underneath. The second problem arose in relation to the legality of the search. The search warrant covered the searching for and seizure of firearms and ammunition. The roe buck heads tended to corroborate the initial information that there was a rifle somewhere but the seizure of any of the freezer contents was most certainly not covered by the warrant.

There were two or three ways round this. We could apply for a further warrant to seize the items in the freezer, but at that point we still didn't know what was there and if whatever was there was legally held or otherwise. The freezer could still be fully searched as, even though unlikely, there was a possibility that a rifle was stashed underneath. I have certainly seen items, especially drugs, stashed in more unlikely places, for example inside light switches, electric fires, hollow doors and indeed inside fridges and freezers. The disadvantage of applying for a new warrant was the time that this would take – a report to the fiscal, a warrant typed out by the fiscal, then a meeting and discussion with a sheriff to have the warrant signed. Not exactly ten minutes work – more like half a day.

Next, we could simply seize any illegally kept carcasses and use case law to defend our actions, arguing that if we had not taken the items they would have been spirited away. This is always open to argument in court and the arguments are not automatically won by the prosecution. On balance this was kicked into touch. The last option was to explain to the suspect that the seizure of anything in the freezer was not covered by the warrant but that he could allow us to search the freezer for protected species if he wished, but that he was entitled to refuse. This was the best option and the one that we went for. The suspect agreed the request, signed the notebook of the senior police officer there to that effect, and the matter was resolved.

The search of the freezer was now over to me and I decided to ask the suspect for his help. 'You take the items out of the freezer one at a time and I'll decide whether you can hold them legitimately or whether you might be committing an offence. We'll make one pile of birds or animals that there is no problem with and another pile on which we will speak with you further.' This was agreed and the suspect began on the top layer of the freezer. Several roe buck heads emerged which the suspect said he was going to stuff and mount. There was no problem with these – though I did wonder whether they had been taken legally – and they went into his pile.

I wondered what they might have looked like once the suspect had got to work on them. I had seen his only effort at taxidermy, which was a buzzard. The buzzard had been a falconer's bird that he had obtained and kept for several years until it had died. In its mummified form it now looked nothing like the magnificent bird of prey it had once been, much more like an immature penguin in brown plumage. Strangely, the suspect was immensely proud of his first work, in the same manner as mothers always think their new-born baby is beautiful and nothing at all resembling a gargoyle. The beauty of babies improves with age – no such prospect for a taxidermy specimen.

The second layer of the freezer began to reveal its secrets. A short-eared owl and a barn owl were the first species in my pile, then a surprise – a canary. This had been a pet canary that had died and it was to be preserved for posterity, probably as something resembling a yellow duckling. I imagined it glued to a perch in a small cage, a silent yellow blob stuck at a jaunty angle with pride of place on a sideboard. The next specimen was no less surprising. It had been another pet, a hamster.

Several pheasants and ducks were produced, which added to the height of the householder's pile, then a fox cub, which again joined his legally acquired specimens. Clearly, many of the specimens had been in the freezer for some time as they were covered in ice, this in some cases making identification a bit more tricky. The suspect played on the opaqueness of the bags with the next specimen following the fox cub. 'This is another fox cub,' he said, about to throw it quickly on to his pile.

'No,' I said, that's not a fox cub.'

'It is,' he said, 'it's from the same litter as the other one.'

'No it's not,' I said.

'Honest,' was the reply, 'it's just thinner than the first one.'

'Wayne,' I said, I'm a wildlife crime officer. I shoot, fish and know a bit about the countryside and its inhabitants.'

'Sorry, you're right,' was the response, 'it's a pine marten.'

At the finish, I had a pile in front of me comprising a pine marten, red squirrel, wildcat, a badger's head, kestrel, short-eared owl, barn owl, buzzard, lapwing, three swallows, house martin, skylark, greenfinch, wren and song thrush. The suspect was asked if he could account for how he came by all of these. His answer was that he had found the pine marten dead under a tree and that all the rest had been road kills he had found at the roadside on his various travels.

While it is generally speaking an offence to be in possession of a protected bird or animal, the Wildlife and Countryside Act 1981 allows a defence if the person possessing the items *shows that the bird or animal had not been taken or killed at or from a place in Scotland otherwise than in contravention of the relevant provisions.* In plain language it means that a person can keep an otherwise protected animal or bird provided he can demonstrate that it had died naturally or had been killed accidentally. Some take the specimens to a vet for a cause of death but on most occasions, this can't be determined with accuracy without a post mortem examination, which of course could ruin the specimen for taxidermy. In most cases I am happy with a phone call about the circumstances of the find and note it in my diary.

It was possible that some of the birds or animals could indeed have been road kills but I was extremely doubtful about the three swallows and the house martin. I have seen most of the remainder of the species at some time or another lying on a grass verge or flattened on to the road surface but one person finding three swallows and a house martin was stretching credulity a tad too far. It can sometimes be difficult for a person to satisfy police that he has legitimate possession of protected birds and animals, even though the standard of proof is at civil proof level, in other words on balance of probabilities. In any event I had doubts aplenty and I took all of these creatures back to Perth with me for further enquiry.

Despite there being some onus on a suspect to prove his innocence, in other words a reverse burden of proof, I knew that in these days of human rights and fairness the procurator fiscal would not entertain a charge in relation to any of the animals or birds unless we could establish a cause of death. My first problem was with the wildcat. Was it a wildcat or was it a hybrid? The law protects pure bred wildcats but cats that are conceived as a result of a midnight union between a pure-bred wild tomcat and a domestic moggy or *vice versa* have no legal protection under the Wildlife and Countryside Act.

Digressing for a minute, it is extremely difficult to get a conviction for someone killing a wildcat. The police have first to prove that the cat was indeed a pure wildcat, and it was killed in the knowledge that it was a pure-bred wildcat (*intentionally* is the term in the Act) or without taking any basic precaution to determine if it could have been a wildcat or with complete disregard as to whether or not it was a pure-bred wildcat (*recklessly* is the term in the Act). Either of those concepts is fraught with difficulties in proof and it is not surprising that there has never been a case heard in court in Scotland on any aspect of crime committed against a wildcat.

My first telephone call was to Dr Andrew Kitchener, curator of mammals in the National Museum of Scotland, at Chambers Street, Edinburgh. Andrew agreed to see the wildcat the next day to determine if it had come from a pure bloodline. My next telephone call was to Professor Ranald Munro, veterinary forensic pathologist at the Royal (Dick) Vet School, Edinburgh. Ranald agreed to examine all of my subjects and wherever possible give me a cause of death. Lastly I put a call through to Dave Dick, RSPB Scotland, asking if he and his colleague, Keith Morton, could formally identify the bird species involved. I wanted no arguments in court on the species of birds involved and whether or not they were *wild birds* as defined in the Act. It is perfectly possible to cover all the difficult angles in an investigation and yet get caught out in court on something that is quite elementary.

All of us met in Edinburgh the following day and I left the wildcat with Andrew Kitchener, who thought at first sight it was a hybrid, but that he would have a better idea once it had thawed out. I was pleased that Dave Dick and Keith Morton concurred with my identification of the bird species and we left Ranald Munro to his extremely skilled and complex work in finding out how such small birds as a goldfinch and wren met their demise many months or even years after the event. Ranald is lucky in that he works with his wife,

Helen, also a veterinary pathologist, since the evidence of two pathologists is necessary bearing in mind the rule of corroboration of the main facts in any case in Scotland

The investigation of wildlife crime is little different from the investigation of any other sort of crime. The principles are the same in drawing the case to a conclusion that can result in charging a person and bringing him or her before the court, or in fact exonerating a person of any blame. In the murder of a human, two pathologists would be used to determine the cause of death, forensic odontology may be used to establish bite marks or other impressions made by teeth, forensic anthropology may be used to age and identify bones, and entomology may be used to establish the aging of insect larvae on a body. The only slight difference in wildlife crime is that in some cases the experts may be trained in veterinary medicine rather than human medicine.

I received the report from Andrew Kitchener within a few days. He had made a comparison of 'my' wildcat against a set of points that must be able to be ticked off to conclude that a cat is indeed a true wildcat. The cat I had seized was a hybrid, therefore unless I could prove that cruelty was involved in its capture or death and that the suspect had caused this cruelty, there was no case. This was a non-starter but at least I had saved the expense of having a full post-mortem examination of the cat.

I received Ranald and Helen's report about a month later. One or two of the specimens could be excluded from the case as the vets could not be conclusive about their cause of death. I was left with two swallows and a lapwing that appeared to have died through suffocation, a buzzard that appeared to have been poisoned though unfortunately the poison or pesticide used could not be determined, and a pine marten that had been shot twice with a .22 rifle. The injuries in all of these deaths were substantially different to those that would be expected from a collision with a vehicle on a road. The suspect therefore went to court on five charges relating to the possession of the four birds and the pine marten.

This case dragged on for almost a year, with the defence QC arguing that under Human Rights legislation, the police had no right in law to ask his client to account for his possession of the dead birds and animals in the alfresco freezer. The sheriff gave this argument much consideration and made a judgement in favour of the prosecution. The trial had been part-heard and evidence continued to be led at the second diet of the court, but even then the evidence was not concluded. At the third diet, the accused agreed to plead guilty to possession of a pine marten only, a plea which the procurator fiscal accepted. He was fined £500.

Even though I still consider the Scottish justice system as good as can be found anywhere, there are many aspects that annoy me. Hardly anyone ever pleads guilty when the case is called in court for the first time. This applies even to those who are caught in the act of committing the particular crime with which they are charged, even housebreakers caught inside premises. If we take this as an example, the evidence may be overwhelming but a case still has to be proved. If an accused is advised by his solicitor to plead not guilty, the solicitor may be looking for some chink in the strength of the prosecution case. When the trial draws near, the case may be adjourned because of some legitimate reason put forward by the defence or procurator fiscal. In each case it must be established beyond reasonable doubt that the accused is the person who committed the crime in question. The longer the case drags on, the more the memory of the witnesses fade and the more unlikely they are to recollect crucial facts, including the ability to identify the person who committed the crime. Because of the delays, the defence now has a strong advantage.

By the time the next trial diet comes around a crucial prosecution witness may not be able to attend the court for one reason or another. The trial is either adjourned at the request of the prosecution or the defence manages to get the procurator fiscal to agree a plea of guilty that only reflects a fraction of the circumstances that actually took place. This is yet another advantage to the defence. It always seems to the onlooker to be the case in trials that the defence call the shots and the procurator fiscal has to acquiesce.

If the case is continued and there is some other genuine but unfortunate reason the prosecution cannot proceed with the trial, the fiscal may be forced into abandoning the case altogether. An accused, found inside a house and charged with breaking into the house with intent to steal could be acquitted! I hope I am not being too cynical when I say that the defence agent will also have made a lot of money either from his client or from legal aid. Nevertheless – and I must stress this – the defence has done nothing illegal or improper.

Although I only cite this as a theoretical example, I cannot think of a single case where the prosecution has a clear advantage over the defence. Similarly I can think of very few cases in recent years when the accused has pled guilty at the first court appearance. In the cases I can think of, the advantage has been with the defence again. One particular wildlife case comes to mind where the sheriff was a visiting sheriff, spotted by the defence as being particularly lenient, much more so than the resident sheriff would have been, and a fine at the absolute bottom of the scale resulted. In other cases, the accused receives a reduced penalty for pleading guilty at a particularly early stage, though I must say I agree with this policy entirely. If this is an advantage to the accused by way of a reduced penalty why is an early plea not the norm? There are always committees looking to improve the criminal justice process and to devise a means of getting cases through courts in a way that breaks the never-ending logjam of trials. We are still waiting.

Chapter 28

The Art of Linking Crimes

It's demonstrated that crimes can be linked like two cut lengths of garden hose and that this is also an essential element in the investigation of wildlife crime.

By 2004 the abuse of pesticides to kill wildlife – at least in Tayside – was almost eliminated and we had left the red kite poisonings of 2000 and 2001 behind. Apart from a few estates that were never going to change unless the people involved with the poisoning were convicted and jailed, progress was being made. Yet two incidents took place in 2004 that perplexed me. On the scale of pesticide abuse they were near the top by way of baits recovered and victims poisoned, yet they were different from any others that I had dealt with. In policing, it is extremely useful to try to establish facts that will link separate crimes. As an example of linking crimes, I'll go back a few years to my days as a detective constable dealing with a series of housebreakings, termed burglaries in England and Wales.

Three houses in a small Perthshire town had been broken into. As the day shift detective officer starting at 8.00am, I attended to carry out a scenes of crime examination of the three houses involved. Coincidentally, a vehicle containing two career criminals from Dundee was stopped by the police as they made their way home from some nocturnal excursion. Since they happened to come from the direction of the town I was at that moment heading towards, I suspected that they may have been involved. The police officers searched the car but there was little of interest in the vehicle apart from a short length of garden hose that smelled of petrol and ten packets of vegetable seeds. They could not give an explanation of why they were making their way home at that time of the morning and I asked that the police officers detain them until I had made my examination of the three houses that had been broken into.

Several thousand pounds worth of items had been stolen, though of course none of this had been in the suspects' vehicle when the police in Dundee had stopped it. The uniformed police officers had noted full details of all of the stolen items but it was my job to link the crimes to the suspects in Dundee. What would make this easier would be if I could link the three crimes as having been committed by the same person or people. This was the type of investigation that I really enjoyed – half of the job had been done since there were suspects languishing in a cell at Police Headquarters. If they were the correct suspects I just needed the evidence to keep them there.

It was easy linking the first two housebreakings. The houses were next door to each other and both crimes had been committed between just after midnight and their discovery about 07.30 am. It would be highly unlikely for two groups of criminals to be out and about between these times and to happen to break into two neighbouring properties. I could link these houses with the third house, which was some distance away, as a torch stolen from house No 1 was found at house No 3. Now that I had the houses linked as being broken into by the same criminals, I needed to establish the identity of the criminals. My morning got better.

I was aware that a length of hosepipe was found in the Dundee criminals' car. At house No 2, a green garden hose connected to a tap in the garden had a two metre chunk cut out of it. When I checked the occupant's car, his petrol cap had been removed and was lying on the ground. It seemed as if the hose had been used for syphoning petrol from his tank. This was confirmed when he checked his fuel gauge; he had filled his tank the previous day and it was now less then half full. The man was a keen gardener so I asked if he was missing any packets of seeds. He said he had recently bought some and they were in his greenhouse. When he checked, the seeds were gone. He listed the seeds – all vegetable seeds – and I was able to confirm by telephone that the ten packets of seeds were the very same as had been recovered. The chance of our suspects having bought the same ten packets of seeds all from the same seed company was remote.

There were two further checks to be done. I had established that the length of hose in the suspect's car was indeed green, which was a good start, so I cut six inches off each of the 'new' ends of the garden hose, ensuring that the cut made by me on each of the two six inch lengths was clearly marked as *my* cut. I had also recovered a very small piece of black fibre at house No 3 where one of the persons had climbed in a broken window. I took the pieces of hosepipe and the fibres to the Identification Branch at Force Headquarters in Dundee.

Before long I had a physical fit of the hose recovered in the suspects' car with the pieces I had cut off. My two six inch pieces came from either end of the piece of hose in the car. I also had a comparison of the piece of black fibre I had recovered from the broken window with fibres taken as a control sample from a black donkey jacket worn by one of the suspects. I had linked the three crimes together, now I had linked the crimes to the two suspects. At the time, I never thought for a minute that in the future I would be dedicated to the investigation of wildlife crime and that wildlife crime was so much more difficult to solve than any other type of crime I had encountered.

Coming back to the pesticide abuse in 2004, the first incident related to a couple of dead rabbits that appeared to be poisoned baits found on a piece of land north-west of Aberfeldy. The rabbits were collected and I took them to the SASA in Edinburgh, where the presence of the pesticide carbofuran was confirmed in both rabbits. The rabbits had been gutted, showed the presence of dark blue granules inside the body cavity and were clearly poisoned baits. What was unusual in this case was that the land on which they were found had recently been bought by a consortium who wanted to use it for public benefit. They wanted to encourage the public to visit the land and walk their dogs, have picnics and generally enjoy this lovely part of Perthshire. There were signs at the roadside to convey this message. The rabbit baits had been found near to the roadside at the main point of entry to the land where one of these signs was displayed. Of all the places the baits could have been left, this was about the most likely place that they would be found. The owners of the land had no motive to kill anything on their newly-acquired land, in fact quite the opposite. They wanted a variety of wildlife for the visitors to see. Further, it was the new owners who had found and reported the rabbit baits. I was completely stumped with this case.

I gathered a small team together, including some of the owners of the land, and we had a search to see if any further evidence could be recovered. During this search we recovered a further two rabbit baits and two dead buzzards. One of the rabbits had been partially eaten by a fox but though we searched for some distance round the bait, we found no dead fox. I have no doubt that a fox had been killed by this bait, but it must have died somewhere we did not search. A later examination of the buzzards showed that they had been killed by eating bait contaminated by the pesticide carbofuran.

This looked like an ideal case to release the details publicly just in case a member of the public, on hearing the plea for assistance, had a snippet of information that could help. I put out a press release and spoke on Grampian TV news about the recovery of the rabbits. I hoped that someone, even anonymously, may have put us on the right track but there was no response apart from condemnation that someone would set out poisoned baits in such a place that would put adults, children, dogs and wildlife at such severe risk of ill health or death.

Ten days later, this time to the south east of Aberfeldy, this bizarre situation was replicated. A man walking his dog in a stubble field had to call his dog off half a rabbit in which it was showing a strong interest. The man, being a countryman, was alert to poisoned baits and did not want to risk his dog's life by allowing it to lick or pick up this piece of rabbit. His suspicions were confirmed when he saw a freshly dead buzzard lying near the rabbit. It was a Sunday but the man, being aware of my mobile telephone number, gave me a call. I attended right away and the man took me to the field and showed me the piece or rabbit and the buzzard. I could see nothing on the rabbit, which was well predated, but made an examination of the buzzard. When I opened the bird's beak I could see a small blue granule that looked suspiciously like carbofuran. At that point I was convinced that the rabbit had been poisoned bait and the buzzard an unfortunate victim.

The following morning, I took the rabbit and the buzzard to SASA and, even without the technical testing that would follow, they were able to confirm my suspicions. Dr Ken Hunter and Elizabeth Sharp of SASA, and indeed myself, had become so experienced in the abuse of particular pesticides that we could often identify the pesticide well in advance of the samples being run through the complex and costly machinery that was so accurate that it could identify the infinitely smallest amount of pesticide.

Two days after I had picked up the rabbit bait and the buzzard victim, I went back to the area with a police officer. The field where they had been found was a roadside field and as we drove alongside it we could see from our car on the A9 dual carriageway between Perth and Inverness, to our heart-stopping concern what appeared to be several dead buzzards in the two grass fields immediately before the stubble field where the first rabbit bait and buzzard had been found. Our fears were confirmed and in the grass fields we picked up a further two rabbit baits, a crow and five buzzards. I knew what the result would be but nevertheless I took this unfortunate collection to SASA. The results were as expected in each case.

This chapter started out as linking crimes, which I was considering here. At the first site we had poisoned baits set out on public land, near to the road, and in a position that it was inevitable that they would be discovered. The baits were gutted rabbits, laid out in as open a part of the land as they could possibly have been, and the pesticide was an extremely heavy and obvious lacing of carbofuran. The victims were irrelevant, as these baits are so indiscriminate that they could have killed anything at all, including humans. Further, it was obvious to us that no-one on the land where the baits and dead buzzard were found would have the remotest interest in killing any sort of predator or carrion-eater.

At the second site, the baits were visible to anyone driving along the A9. This was certainly not a place that someone would use to lay out baits to quietly and discreetly (and also illegally) dispose of some animal or bird that was causing concern. Like the first site, the baits or victims were certain to be discovered. Also, like the first site, the baits were gutted rabbits laced with the same pesticide, carbofuran, again in a dose that was much more than was required. On the second site, there was no-one who would have a motive either to set out baits or to kill buzzards, crows or foxes. The part-time gamekeeper had moved on some time before, and the estate had been taken over. The new gamekeeper was not yet in post. The tenant farmer had sheep that were lambing but they were not in that area. To me, the issue was not setting out poisoned baits to get rid of some species considered a pest or a threat, it was a wind-up of some sort. I even considered that I was a target of the despicable ploy, in which case I had a long-time suspect, but no evidence.

I knew very well that the two crimes were linked but this was a particularly difficult case to solve. I considered various options and decided that we should pay a visit to a person that had formerly been a gamekeeper at the second location – the one juxtaposition to the A9. He was not the person that I had a nagging suspicion could have been responsible but he may have had some information that would help the case. This was one of these situations where there were no grounds whatsoever to obtain a search warrant, nor was there any obvious link with the first location but at the very least I needed him eliminated from the investigation. In conjunction with our visit to him, I had arranged for other officers to have a quiet look round the estate on which he was currently working. In fairness, their search revealed nothing that pointed to him as a culprit.

We drove to his address but it was clear he was still in bed. His vehicle sat outside, as did another vehicle which I assumed belonged to his wife. Had he been a prime suspect, I would have had no hesitation in rapping on the door and arousing him from his extended slumber but I wanted this low-key. By 8.30 am. we could wait no longer and the two police officers with me knocked on his door while I waited in the police vehicle. There was no point at that time in overkill; two officers were sufficient and we did not want to panic whoever answered the door by being met by a gang. There was a response to the knock at the door, the two officers disappeared inside then came out shortly after with the householder.

I knew the man, who confirmed he was the owner of a four wheel drive vehicle sitting outside the house. He agreed to a search of the vehicle and garage beside the house, the garage being wide open in any case. We started with the 4WD, which had been left unlocked.

Our man stated that he had only had the vehicle for a couple of weeks and its condition reflected this. It was immaculate and almost empty apart from a spotlamp on the back seat. I started with a search of the front passenger side while the two officers with me began with a search of the front driver's side and the boot respectively. The first item of interest I spotted was a rifle clip filled with ammunition. It was a clear breach of the conditions of his firearm certificate to leave such a thing lying about in his vehicle, far less in an unlocked vehicle. Despite initiating the visit to this suspect, I still didn't think that he was the man we were looking for. If he had nothing to do with the setting out of the baited rabbit then I didn't want to make life too difficult for him. If there was evidence that he was the culprit then I would have no sympathy and he would have to bear the full brunt of whatever we would throw at him. Meantime I didn't want to overly complicate the issue with a firearms licensing breach that could cost him his firearm certificate and subsequently his job. I discreetly handed him the full clip and he, even more discreetly and with a distinct sigh of relief, pocketed it.

My colleague's next find was a completely different story. Under the driver's seat, Constable Sally Hughes, one of our wildlife crime officers, found a plastic container half full of a white powder. There was no labelling on the container and we both suspected the contents were the pesticide alpha-chloralose. The questioning was unusual. 'What is it you've got in here?' Sally asked. 'Alpha-chloralose,' was the honest reply. 'What do you use it for?' she asked. 'Just for rats round the house,' was the response. I explained that alpha-chloralose could only be obtained legally in a very dilute form and then only by an authorised pest controller. 'I didn't realise that,' he said. I asked how he used it for rats and he replied, 'I mix it with grain and put it down the hole.' I had seen evidence of rabbits round the house but none, so far, of rats. I asked him why it was in his vehicle. His response, which puzzled me, was, 'I just always have it, force of habit.' This was a completely illegal habit and I was not swayed by the answer in any case. Why would someone carry an item that he used 'round the house' in his new vehicle, while other items, such as traps and snares that he would use out and about daily, were lying on the ground beside his garage. I told him I was far from convinced by his answer. He tried again, 'I had it in my house for months and I heard about this (the poisoning enquiry) so I put it in my car to get rid of it, to bury it.' This contradicted his previous statement that 'he always had it' and also indicated his knowledge that it was illegal for him to have the substance at all.

Our man's day got worse. When we had a look in his garage, there was an almost full tin of Cymag, a white powder that could (at that time, but since banned) be used legally to gas rabbits and rats. Extremely dangerous substances such as this must by law be kept under lock and key at all times. Anyone opening this tin could have inhaled the fatal fumes given off by the powder once exposed to humidity and could have been killed.

He was charged with possessing alpha-chloralose for the purposes of committing an offence under the Wildlife and Countryside Act 1981, with storing it in an unlocked vehicle, and with storing Cymag in an unlocked garage. Although these were serious charges I could not help feeling a bit sorry for him. After having spoken to him, I was sure he had nothing to do with the even more serious crimes we were investigating and was, to a degree, a victim of circumstances.

Being a victim of circumstances cost him a fine of £1200 at Perth Sheriff Court. We were satisfied we had linked the two crimes under investigation but had only gone half-way compared to the case with the housebreakers who had the hosepipe and seeds. To this day we have not managed to establish who committed the crimes.

Chapter 29

Coursing the Hare

Like many 'country pursuits' traditional ties to hare coursing are hard to break despite changes in the law to help eradicate this savage practice.

Hare coursing has been around for many years, with evidence showing time and time again that many of those taking part were travellers. Indeed many of the travellers contend that they have a right to take rabbits and hares with dogs, with one in particular being adamant – and completely wrong – that the law allowed them to course hares provided they only took one.

Prior to 2002, when the hunting of mammals with dogs was banned under the Protection of Wild Mammals (Scotland) Act, coursing of hares could take place on land provided the permission of the owner of the land was given. In a very few cases permission was given but the police still received countless calls from farmers, gamekeeper, landowners or just simply folks passing through the countryside who witnessed hare coursing taking place. Farmers were in a tricky position since, if they allowed the coursing to continue and turned a blind eye, this would be recognised as a sign of weakness and the group involved would return again and again. If the farmer approached the hare coursers, they would apologise for being on the land and make one of the standard excuses that I earlier alluded to (their dogs needing to stretch their legs or needing the toilet). The men – women never seemed to be involved – would go back to their car and drive off. . . till the next time.

This was very much a short term and completely unsatisfactory solution. If the farmer told the men he was going to involve the police, he very often had threats made against him that if he did so he would find that his barn would mysteriously burn down or that all his gates would be opened and his cattle and sheep be allowed on to the road. To avoid these issues, a farmer would sometimes allow hare coursing once a month to appease the men, or worse still, would shoot all the hares in roadside fields so that coursing, with all its associated problems, was less likely to take place on his land.

In 2002 the situation improved considerably. Whereas under the Game (Scotland) Act 1832 a person can be fined for coursing, he can not be detained by the police for interview as the crime is not punishable by a jail term. Under the twenty first century legislation, a person convicted can receive up to six months imprisonment and there is a power available to the police not just to arrest those involved but to seize their dogs. Most of the people who were involved in coursing were well aware of the changes and lay low for a while to see how the situation would pan out against the one or two reckless enough to continue to course hares if they were unlucky enough to be caught.

In fact very little happened to these few people. In the first place, they are not easily caught as they are only in a field for five or ten minutes then away in their car or van to another location several miles away. If they happen to be seen, they may not be reported to the police. If they are reported to the police, the police are likely to take some time to respond as they could be twenty or more miles away. If the police are lucky enough to be close enough to locate the vehicle, it may have four occupants but only two had been seen in the field: how do they know which two? Do they have power to detain or arrest them? In any case if they have, how do two police officers in a police car get four men and four dogs back to the police station? Is the offence of hare coursing serious enough for all this bother? These are the issues – and indeed the logistics – that face police officers not used to dealing with hare coursing. The eventual outcome was that the men would most likely be warned, they would thank the officers and would assure them that this would not happen again. The police officers would drive off frustrated that they could not have done more. The hare coursers would be satisfied at the outcome and would be out again the next day at the same caper but in another area, so as not to push their luck too far. The farmer would be frustrated or furious and would be unlikely to contact the police again about hare coursing, and would tell neighbouring farmers that it was a waste of time calling the police in these circumstances.

The hare coursers began to gain in confidence. They were going in to fields, their dogs were chasing and catching hares and the police never appeared. It was just like the old days, in fact even better! They told their pals that no-one bothered about hare coursing in Tayside and their pals joined in as well.

This had to come to a head, and it did in the late Spring of 2004. I received a telephone call from a committee member of the Scottish Gamekeepers' Association, Bert Burnett, who told me that several of the gamekeepers in Angus were being pestered on an almost daily basis by people coursing hares. One gamekeeper had tackled the men and was about to be set upon but hit the biggest one on the chin with the butt of the shotgun that he was carrying when he encountered them. It must have been a good whack as he broke his gun, but he also broke the nerve of the group who were about to give him a beating. They jumped into their car and cleared out, and the keeper told me he was extremely relieved as he was miles from any sort of help. This was a situation where he could have had his shotgun and firearm certificate revoked but thankfully it was appreciated that the slight encouragement the men had received to depart the scene saved the keeper possibly being seriously assaulted. Nevertheless, hitting hare coursers with a gun, or even approaching hare coursers while carrying a gun, is not conducive to remaining a shotgun certificate holder. This incident was one of the last of the season, before the crops were too high and hares could not be seen, but I resolved to improve the situation when hare coursing resumed in the autumn.

During the summer, I prepared a briefing note that I circulated to all police officers who were likely to be dealing with hare coursing incidents. The briefing note laid out the three offences under the 2002 Act and the powers that the police had to deal with those offences. I also offered to be on hand to advise – even at the end of a phone – if the officer dealing with the incident still wasn't too sure of his or her ground. I could do little to ensure that they got to a location in time to catch the culprits but I could beef up their confidence to deal with the incident effectively and professionally once they did manage to get hold of hare coursers. I also wrote an article on hare coursing in the *Scottish Gamekeeper* magazine and did a press release for local newspapers, all with the purpose of encouraging the reporting of hare coursing incidents.

We got off to a good start in September 2004, when three men were caught with three dogs just outside Perth. The dogs had caught a hare by the time the police arrived. This was additional evidence and prevented the excuse that they were after rabbits, not considered to be mammals for the purposes of the Act. It was even better that one of the police officers attending happened to be one of the Divisional wildlife crime officers, Constable John Robb, who knew exactly what he was doing. The bonus in this case was that the men had two video cameras with them and were filming what they were doing. Terrific evidence!

I watched the film on one of the cameras, which ran for about three hours. It was non-stop hare coursing. It was a great insight into how these guys operate and of the proportion of the hares coursed that are caught. I could see that they just parked their car at the roadside once they had spotted a hare in a field and jumped the fence to begin the chase. Normally someone was left with the car – usually the person filming – and there was one amusing incident when the driver must have jumped out without setting the handbrake and the car started to run back down a hill. It would have been funny even without sound but with the sound it was hilarious. The cameraman had to remedy the situation. His language was choice and for a while, when the camera was swinging on a loop on his wrist, I was looking at an inverted world swaying like a pendulum. I could see the upside down car several yards in front of the camera as he chased after it. It came to a sudden stop and I secretly hoped it had banged into something extremely solid. That seemed likely as his tone changed from being panicky to being solemn and lugubrious. This also tended to indicate that he was the owner of the car. After a few minutes my world was righted and I could at last see what was happening in the field. The distraction had caused the ace cameraman to miss all of the action and the victors – or otherwise – were making their way back across the field to the car. I hope their luck in the field equalled that of the pal they had left in charge of the car.

The success rate of this group seemed to be about 50%. Some of the chases were short and the hare escaped into cover, where it was lost to the dogs. Greyhounds rely on hunting by sight, which is the opposite of gundogs that hunt by scent. On some of the chases, the hare and the dogs would disappear over a skyline, to the chagrin of all involved including the cameraman. The end result of these chases was unknown. What I found surprising was that as soon as a dog caught the hare, the camera was switched off. It was evident that they were not interested in the killing of the hare; simply that it had been caught.

All of the hares put a huge effort into escaping, jinking back and forth across the field and turning far more quickly than could the pursuing dogs. It seemed an unfair and unequal challenge when three dogs were set on a hare and the outcome seemed inevitable, yet very occasionally a hare would manage to outrun this pack and make good its escape. The escape in some cases may only have been temporary as I was once handed a dead hare by a gamekeeper who had found it in a field just after hare coursers had been in the adjoining field. The hare was in perfect condition with not a mark on it; an otherwise healthy hare had it not been dead! I had no way of confirming it but I am sure that hare died from the stress of being coursed by dogs over a long distance. I had the hare skinned and examined later by a veterinary pathologist who was of the same view.

This particular group, all of them travellers, were clearly training up the next generation of hare coursers as they often had kids with them on their exploits. The kids were at least as enthusiastic as their mentors, shouting encouragement to the dogs that were closing in on a hare to, 'Kill it. Kill it.' When the dogs did 'kill it' no-one went over to pick up the hare to take it with them either to make a hare stew or to feed the dogs. The hare was left wherever it had been dropped by the dogs, yet in court the plea to the sheriff is always, 'We were just out for a hare for the pot, Your Honour. We've a big family to feed.'

One of this group was caught the following month, again in Perthshire, this time coursing a hare with two dogs. The same person was caught coursing hares three further times in Angus, with a mixture of other friends or family in tow. It could be said that he did not have a good year, especially if he had been the cameraman the day the car came to life of its own accord. He and the others received a combination of fines and community service for these offences. As was to be expected, they shared out the convictions, some pleading guilty and the others entering a plea of not guilty that was accepted by the court, then reversing the pleas for the next case. That way no-one built up too many convictions and no-one was jailed. Justice was manipulated but I suppose the end result wasn't too bad. They just can't seem to give up coursing. Two years later, at the end of 2006, members of that group have a further two cases awaiting trial.

Between then and the following Spring we had eight hare coursing cases where we managed to charge at least one person. That wasn't a bad start but no-one had yet gone to prison and no dogs had been forfeited by the court. I was determined that we would do better.

Chapter 30

Signing with Dolphins

It's not all strong arm of the law tactics; sometimes a well-positioned information notice can help prevent the unnecessary disturbance of creatures in the wild.

It's a welcome change to get to a wildlife crime job on the coastline of Tayside and I'm always pleased to get a call from Elaine Roft of the British Divers Marine Life Rescue (BDMLR). Elaine and her colleagues in other parts of the UK monitor pinipeds and cetaceans round our coastline. I knew that cetaceans were whales, dolphins and porpoises but I had to ask Elaine to elaborate on pinipeds, which she told me were seals. As well as monitoring the populations, the BDMLR volunteer medics are trained in first aid that they can administer to any of these creatures in difficulties. Elaine lives for sea creatures and is a dedicated and enthusiastic volunteer. I have difficulties on some occasions convincing her that seals only have partial protection and can be controlled by shooting provided the person carrying out the shooting has a condition on his firearm certificate authorising him to do so. Elaine's law would be that no-one could harm seals. In any event this call concerned dolphins, not seals.

There are many dolphins off the east coast of Scotland, and the large pod that regularly travels between the coast of Fife and the Moray Firth is probably the most northerly pod of bottlenosed dolphins in the world. Two had taken up residence just off the coast of Ferryden, on the outskirts of Montrose, but there were reports from Elaine and others that they were being harassed by people in boats. For some reason, the dolphins had decided to spend most of their day in the close vicinity of a buoy anchored a few hundred yards from the lighthouse at Ferryden, and they passed a lot of their time jumping clean out of the water around the buoy, an activity termed 'breaching.' Dolphins are intelligent creatures and are happy to interact with humans, but the interaction must be on their terms. The reports alerted us to the disturbing situation that people were going out in boats to the buoy and sailing very close in on the dolphins, probably in the hope that they could get a really close view of the dolphins' activity and possibly also in the hope that the dolphins would bow-ride along in front of their boat.

Dolphins are fascinating mammals and all of these human reactions are understandable. Unfortunately some of them may be illegal. At the time of this incident, the law in relation to dolphins was that a person committed an offence if he or she intentionally disturbed them. What disturbs a dolphin is difficult to describe to a court. It was – and possibly still is – extremely difficult to obtain a conviction for intentional disturbance of a dolphin. These problems were appreciated by wildlife crime officers and my view is that it was better, and probably easier, to educate rather than to attempt to prosecute. I designed an advisory sign that was headed with the Tayside Police Crest along these lines:

> Bottlenosed dolphins are frequently seen in various parts of Scotland's coastline, including off the coast of Angus. They are exciting to watch but deserve to have their own space. Appreciate their beauty from a reasonable distance: do not feed them and do not harass them with boats or jet skis.
>
> Intentional or reckless disturbance or harassment of dolphins is an offence punishable by a fine of £5000 and/or up to six months imprisonment. Reports in Tayside of such incidents should be made to Tayside Police at 01382 223200 or to Alan Stewart, Tayside Police wildlife and environment officer.
>
> This area is being regularly monitored by Tayside Police wildlife crime officers.
>
> Your co-operation is much appreciated.

I made a number of these signs, simply by typing them in colour on the computer, printing them off and laminating them so that they would at least survive a few months. I then contacted Elaine and we decided on the most appropriate places to display the signs. One of the sites we decided on was beside the Scurdieness Lighthouse at Ferryden, the nearest land point to the buoy that had so much attraction to the dolphins. As we were putting the sign up, we were treated to the amazing sight of a pod of about thirty bottlenosed dolphins passing up the coast just on the seaward side of the 'resident' pair of dolphins, who swam out to greet their fellows, before returning again to their favoured haunt at the buoy. Shortly after that, the pair of dolphins headed at speed up into the estuary towards Montrose. Their radar had obviously detected a boat leaving the harbour and heading out to sea. They joined the boat in the estuary and appeared to have tremendous fun bow-riding on either side of the small and fast craft as it sped out to see. The skipper of the boat had committed no offence as the dolphins had deigned to join him and I'm sure all three of them enjoyed the interaction. The important factor was that the interaction was at the behest of the dolphins: dolphins joining up with humans, not humans joining up with dolphins. Even the two shore-based spectators enjoyed the spectacle.

It being early summer, the visit to Scurdieness was further enhanced by rafts of what at first sight appeared to be black and white ducks, but at closer quarters had many more colours. Drake eider ducks have a pinkish tinge on their breast and pale green on the back of their neck. They have an unusual shaped head, with a long sloping profile. It just seemed as if the drakes were lazily passing the time of day while the females incubated their clutches of eggs. The group was interspersed with an occasion female in drab brown – unexciting plumage but ideal for camouflage. In the case of these ducks the camouflage may not have been good enough and their eggs were probably taken by predators. The group of eiders drifted past barely 50 metres away, one occasionally making a crooning noise as if through its nasal entrances.

Slightly further out to sea were half a dozen smaller black and white birds, this time black guillemots, with their distinctive white wing patch. These are birds related to guillemots, razorbills and auks – birds that, like puffins, are not having the best of breeding seasons. Whether or not this is related to global warming and a consequent lack of sand eels I have no idea but the news of their almost total failure to breed on some cliff sites in Scotland is depressing.

Above the black guillemots a single grey and white fulmar glided along on wings that seemed absolutely rigid. Like many seabirds they are masters of gliding, often miles, without a perceptible flap of the wings. Where their flying prowess does not help them is in escaping from an old stone-built lime kiln a few miles down the coast at Boddin. Many fulmars enter the open top of the kiln in Spring looking for a nesting place but are unable to fly vertically out again and are trapped. The lucky ones are rescued either by concerned locals or by inspectors of the Scottish SPCA, though every year a few perish through starvation.

The dolphin signs appeared to work and there were no more complaints or concerns from locals about dolphins being disturbed. More recently, in early 2007, I used an adapted version of the dolphin sign at Broughty Ferry near Dundee as dolphins were being harassed by irresponsible people on jet skis. I was pleased to see that Dundee City Council also took this problem seriously and asked me for advice to produce their own posters to place on Council property near where the jet skis were launched.

Since the signs were a success I have replicated the principle to suit a variety of situations. For two successive years a similar sign has been successfully used to dissuade people using speedboats or fishing from disturbing a nesting pair of ospreys near the west end of Loch Tay. I make the signs and post them to one of the locals who keeps watch over the ospreys. He displays the signs where he thinks they will have most effect and the problems have been eliminated, to the delight of the pair of ospreys and their benefactor. In another instance, a golden eagle eyrie was receiving regular and unwanted attention from well-meaning but inexperienced bird watchers who failed to appreciate the capacity of a golden eagle's eyesight and walked in far too close to the nest site in the hope of getting a sighting of the eagle. The eagle spotted them long before the reverse was the case and left the nest. In cold weather the eggs or chicks could have chilled or in extremely hot weather chicks without a protective covering of feathers might have suffered from sunstroke. An appropriately worded sign in 2006 appeared to work and the pair successfully reared a single chick.

I don't put up these signs without consultation, as in some cases they could be counter-productive and advertise the location of a rare bird nesting site that otherwise would not have been known. The decision to use signs, the wording and the location of the signs is discussed with a variety of experts and stake-holders, not least the owner of the property on which the nest is situated. The concept of temporary advisory signs will be further utilised in 2007 to try to dissuade enthusiasts from venturing too close to several pairs of nesting marsh harriers in Perthshire. In 2006 one of the pairs was unable to get to the nest with food for the chicks because of bird-watchers situated half a mile away from the nest, but still too close for comfort for the nesting pair of birds. The consequence was the eventual death by starvation of the chicks. Had the over-enthusiastic bird-watchers known they were to blame they would have been ashamed of their ignorance and lack of respect for the privacy of some breeding birds. We don't want to be awash with signs in the countryside but appropriately worded signs, in the right place at the right time of year, have proved to be effective.

Chapter 31

The Myth of the Big Cat

Many people claimed to have seen one but it's hard to find any evidence to substantiate this most persistent and resilient of rural myths.

There are many sightings of big cats reported to the police. I have attended at several of the locations but in truth there is little that the police can do to either establish that the sighting was indeed a big cat or rebut the allegation as a false alarm with good intent. There is seldom anything to look at to make any sort of judgement as to the accuracy of the information or to be satisfied that the efficacy of any evidence leaves no doubt that the animal was a leopard, mountain lion, lynx or whatever exotic species had been imagined. I have never visited the location of a sighting where I have smelt anything that may indicate the presence of a big cat, or heard anything that resembled any sound made by a big cat, or even seen any mark that could without doubt have been made by a big cat.

Leaving aside smell, which has never entered the equation so far at any of the calls I have attended, the sound aspect was slightly more interesting. One family living in a rural location east of Perth were absolutely convinced that they heard the growl and scream of a big cat one winter's night, but did nothing to report the matter at the time. The sound seemed to have come from a field in front of the house and had been heard several times. As is sometimes the case the person who has the experience is sure that what he or she hears or sees is a big cat but is not convinced that the story will be believed.

A few nights later, in the pitch dark, one of the family was round the back of the house filling a bucket of coal for the fire. He heard a growling sound coming from the wood not many yards from where he was standing and was convinced at that time that the sound came from a big cat. He fled into the house, minus the bucket of coal, and was prepared to endure the cold rather than venture back for the coal. It was at this point that the police were contacted. There was little point of a police officer attending in the dark – unless a large furry creature with sharp teeth and sharp claws jumped out of the darkness and attached itself to him he would be no wiser at the end of his investigation of the scene than the householder whose teeth by this time would be chattering for two different reasons.

I attended in the morning and had a good search round, being directed but not accompanied by the householder, but there was not a shred of evidence that a big cat of any sort had visited the vicinity. One thing I didn't want was for the story of the phantom feline to hit the papers, but unfortunately it did. In my experience this triggers a string of sightings all over the place and there are suddenly more leopards, black panthers and lionesses (never lions) in Scotland – or even Tayside – than there are in the Masai Mara. This inevitably led to another two episodes that I'll come to shortly but before that there may be a satisfactory conclusion to this big cat that was heard but never seen.

This episode took place in 2003 but in 2005 there were a number of sightings of an eagle owl in exactly the same area. I've only heard the sound of eagle owls on television programmes but it seemed remarkably like what was being described. The owl was known to remain in the area for many months and who knows how long it may have been there beforehand. It was eventually caught and was confirmed as an eagle owl. This was about the same time as it was revealed that a pair of eagle owls had been breeding for several years in the north of England and there was considerable speculation that a number of eagle owls could be breeding unnoticed in other parts of the UK. It may be the answer, it may not.

Several days later a shooting agent, this time to the west of Perth, contacted me to say that he had been out shooting foxes at night with the aid of a spotlamp, a common and efficient practice, when he was convinced he had captured a huge black cat with a long tail in the beam of his light. He was so surprised that he didn't shoot it and it ran off up the field and out of sight. He telephoned me the next day to tell me about the incident and to say that he had found marks in the snow that seemed to be from a big cat.

I met him and we looked at the marks, which were indeed made by an extremely large animal. The animal had been running flat out and the full stretch of its stride was well over six feet. The marks were fairly clear in the snow, which was fresh and had not begun to melt, so I took some photographs and some plaster casts. Plaster casts are not easy in the snow as the snow has to be sprayed first to stop it melting when the plaster is poured into the print, then the plaster has to be allowed to harden before it can be lifted.

While the plaster was hardening I contemplated other prints in snow I had seen at past locations that had convinced the person who found them they were the prints of big cats. All had been in snow that had started to melt, which had caused the print to grow in size. One set of prints I was sure were those of an otter, yet looked almost as big as those of a lion. What convinced me that the prints were not made by a lion was the fact they were close together and had clearly been made by a comparatively small mammal. It is an interesting experiment to try the next time there is snow and there is a partial thaw. Examine your own footprints made in the snow the day before and they will have expanded in the thaw from your normal size shoe to one several sizes bigger.

When I was able to lift the plaster casts I could see evidence of a claw on each toe of the print. This had not been visible until they had been cast. Cats retract their claws when they are walking or running, dogs don't have this ability. Whatever the beast had been it had been canine and not feline.

Hard on the heels of this sighting and not too many miles away I attended a report of sheep worrying. Several sheep had been killed and the farmer had brought the carcasses in to the steading. He told me on the phone that they had been killed by a big cat and that he could see the claw marks of the cat clearly on the flank of the sheep. I went to the farm and had a look.

The sheep had all been killed the same way by gripping the throat of the animal. Before the *coup de grace* much of the wool had been ripped off in the struggle to bring the sheep down and there were indeed scratch marks on the flank of one of the unfortunate animals. I was of the view that the scratch marks were too shallow to have been a cat, which has very sharp claws, and not widely enough spaced for a big cat. It was my view that the animal had been a dog. I even elaborated the point that it had been a dog that had fairly sharp claws and probably spent much of its time indoors or at least on grass or another soft surface as the claws were not worn flat by hours of walking on concrete and were not quite sharp enough to penetrate the sheep's skin to any appreciable depth. The farmer disagreed. This was the work of a big cat.

Whatever had killed the sheep had started to eat one of them at the top of the back leg. I don't know too much of big cats from the African Plains but I would imagine their habits would be broadly similar to our feral and even domestic cats here, except on a larger dimension. When feral cats here eat the carcass of a rabbit or hare they start at the front end, invariably entering the body cavity through the ribs. There was no damage to the front end of the carcasses. This was my second point but I had not convinced the farmer. The killer of his sheep had been a big cat.

For the next couple of nights the local gamekeeper sat out with his rifle and awaited the return of the big cat. It did not materialise. What did materialise was yet another series of articles in the media of a big cat on the loose. I was asked for comment. I gave a comment that reflected my views – but this was played down as it was not conducive to a dramatic news story.

My views were vindicated less than two weeks later. An Alsatian was shot and killed while in the act of attacking sheep several fields away from our first farm. This was a dog that was normally either kept in the house or the confines of the garden but somehow had managed to escape. After that there were no more sheep-worrying incidents and no more reports of big cats in the area.

My last example of a big cat incident relates to a true story told to me by a retired colleague of mine, Inspector John Grierson, who until his retirement was the wildlife crime officer for Northern Constabulary. Before his appointment to that role he was in the traffic department and he and another officer were carrying out a night patrol in a rural part of Inverness-shire. As they drove along a dark road they saw a big black cat run across the road in the headlights. The cat was bigger than an Alsatian and had a long back tail which was stretched straight out behind it as it ran across the road. There was no doubt whatsoever that this was a big cat and it had been seen by two police officers. They turned the car at the first suitable point along the road to see if they could get a further look at the cat and drove back the way they had come. When they came to the same spot there was a black calf on the road that had managed to escape from a field and had panicked on seeing the approaching headlights. . .

I keep an open mind on the presence of big cats in our midst but I always wonder, with the number of farmers and gamekeepers patrolling their land at night with spotlamps and rifles on the lookout for foxes, why no-one has ever come in to a police station and said, 'You'll never believe what I shot last night. . .'

Chapter 32

The Law on Snares

Whether you agree with the practice or not, the legal use of snares is outlined in detail and breaches illustrated by case studies.

It's very common for people to think that snaring is illegal. There is no doubt that many people don't agree with snaring and indeed several organisations including the Scottish SPCA do not support the use of snares. Nevertheless, provided snaring is carried out properly, the practice remains a legal method of controlling some species considered to be pests. Thousands of foxes are caught annually by the use of snares. Tens of thousands of rabbits are also snared, as are a few brown hares and mountain hares. Apart from rodents, which are very seldom caught by the use of snares, there is no other wild mammal that may legally be snared. The police should have no moral judgement on snaring and should uphold the law as set out by the Scottish Parliament.

The principle of a snare is to catch and hold the target animal until the time that the snare is checked by the person who set it. It is not intended that snares kill mammals though this is quite often the outcome, as the rabbit or fox that is caught may get tangled round a tree or bush so that the snare tightens and it chokes to death. I have considerable experience in my younger days of snaring rabbits and I would say that one in every ten rabbits caught in snares was dead, mostly because the snare had got tangled round a back leg and the rabbit had choked in an effort to free itself. I have less experience of snaring foxes though I would imagine that the same proportion are found to be dead when the snare is given its daily or twice-daily check.

For snaring to be legal, the snare must not be self-locking, in other words the snare must 'give' slightly when the captured animal stops struggling, allowing it to breathe. It is an offence to possess, sell, or offer for sale a self-locking snare. In addition any snare used must be checked at least once in every period of 24 hours and anything caught in the snare must be taken out and either killed if it is the target animal, or released. These new provisions from the introduction of the Nature Conservation (Scotland) Act 2004 have made a considerable difference and did not come a moment too soon.

By-catch in snares is inevitable. There is no question that other mammals such as badgers, deer, pine martens and hedgehogs, and a variety of birds, especially pheasants, get caught in snares. Though this can never be completely eliminated, the incidence of by-catch can be minimised by experience and care. One case near Ballinluig in Perthshire in October 1999 demonstrated a complete absence of experience and care. A badger and a fox were found caught in snares about 100 metres apart, and were completely desiccated. When we traced the person who set the snares (a part-time gamekeeper whose lack of professionalism appears elsewhere in this book though I won't make the link) he admitted having set them in Spring but claimed that he had not had time to go back and check them. This was completely illegal and completely unprofessional. To make matters worse, he claimed that he seldom used snares for foxes and usually gassed them. Though he said that the snares were set for foxes he was aware of badgers in the area, which further demonstrated his reckless attitude.

My next encounter with a fox snare was on land to the south of Perth where I had done some rough shooting years before. The complaint this time was from a farmer whose collie had been caught in a fox snare set by the part-time gamekeeper employed by his brother. The owner of the collie had released his dog unharmed but had not seen the keeper near the area where the snares had been set for several weeks. He was convinced that he was not checking his snares daily, hence the telephone call to the police.

I attended at the farm the following morning with one of the Divisional wildlife crime officers, Constable Steve Band. We examined the snare, which we were satisfied was a free-running snare. We then went to look around the area where the snare had been found to see if we could find evidence that there were other snares set there and that they were not being checked in accordance with the law. This was prior to 2004, and the requirement was a daily check, which effectively meant that the snares could be checked just after midnight on day one, and just before midnight on day two, a period of almost forty eight hours. There was also no requirement to remove any victim from the snare, a failing in the law that infuriated me as it created a huge loophole of which miscreants could take advantage if they were switched on to the law.

Our search revealed a number of fox snares that had been knocked from their original position, probably by passing pheasants, hares or rabbits. By hitting against the snares, they had lowered them, making them less effective for foxes but probably even more effective against their fellow birds and lagomorphs as they had now dropped by a few inches from their original position. The proportion of accidentally knocked snares tended to indicate that they had not been checked for several days otherwise the operator would have re-set them.

Only one of the snares had a caught a fox – now dead, a further clue that the snares were not being checked regularly. I estimated that the fox had been dead for about a week. Its eyes were sunk into its head, its mouth was full of earth that had dried up, and even for the month of March, it had begun to smell a bit. I turned it over and saw that the grass under its body had gone yellow, having lost its chlorophyll. This confirmed my belief.

I photographed the fox before and after I turned it over, then we removed it from the snare, untangled the snare from the tree to which it was attached and took both as evidence that an offence had been committed. The fox was consigned to the freezer at Perth Police Station, sharing the large compartment with a roe deer, otter, several birds of prey, collared dove and a selection of hares, rabbits and pheasants, some of which were victims of poachers and the remainder, baits laced with a variety of pesticides.

I was unavailable the following day to interview the suspect with PC Steve Band, which meant he had to recruit a new colleague. He telephoned me after the interview to say that the suspect had claimed to have checked the snares on the same morning that the dog was caught, but just after its discovery. He also claimed to have been aware of the dead fox in the snare. It had been already dead when he found it and he had left it in the snare to encourage other foxes to visit the area, so that they might be caught in other snares set nearby. I knew this was lies. It was a standard excuse when people were caught out not checking their snares in accordance with the law. This excuse would be no use now that they are obliged to empty their snares at every inspection but the change in the law had come too late for this particular case. Frustration is an everyday occurrence in this job but thumbscrews are not an option for its relief!

Snaring is an emotive issue, but for whatever reason, the snaring of mountain hares seems to stir any onlooker into a fury. Part of the reason could be that mountain hares in their white winter coat with a chocolate coloured nose and ears, much like the Himalayan breed of domestic rabbit, are soft, furry and lovely looking creatures. As I have alluded to, the Scottish SPCA are keen to have the use of snares banned. I have no issue with their stance on snares. They are a charitable body, perfectly entitled to lobby for whatever change in the law they think will improve animal welfare. They are a pressure group in the same way as RSPB and the Scottish Gamekeepers' Society, who all want to change the law to what they think would be best. Scottish SPCA staff had looked at the Habitats Regulations, the Conservation (Natural Habitats etc) Regulations 1994 to give this legislation its full title, and had formed the view that the snaring of mountain hares is illegal. Looking at the wording of the Regulations, Section 41 states that *it is an offence to use for the purpose of taking or killing any animal included in Schedule 3,* which includes mountain hares, a variety of devices and methods, one of which is *traps which are non-selective according to their principle or their conditions of use.*

Legislation has always fascinated me. It needs to be looked at word by word and even then there are often differences of opinion as to the meaning. Much of Scots Law is based on judicial precedents, where the High Court of Justiciary has made some sort of decision on the application of the law to a particular situation. Even then, case law as defined and applied by one bench of judges may be changed in the light of changes in public acceptance and perceptions and, more recently, changes advanced by European law. Contrary to popular belief, the law is not written in tablets of stone and is – at least to some degree – fluid and adaptable.

On a much lower level, I have had to change my perception of a legal issue from time to time and the snaring of mountain hares was one such issue. I have absolutely no doubt, from considerable practical experience, that snares are *non selective according to their principle or their conditions of use.* A snare set for a mountain hare may well catch a pine marten, hedgehog, rabbit, pheasant, grouse, fox, roe deer or virtually any creature that comes along the track on which the snare has been set. Ninety-nine per cent of the catch may well be mountain hares but the risk of by-catch cannot possibly be eliminated. When I looked at the legislation I could not see a logical reason that mountain hares should not be snared, as after all they could legally be shot. Nevertheless the law has to be applied as it is written.

That is not yet the whole story, as the other part of the definition stated that mountain hares may not be *trapped.* Is a snare a trap? It catches the animal and prevents it from running off. It removes the animal's liberty. It effectively keeps or retains the animal where it has been caught until the operator of the snare comes along. The animal cannot escape or flee, therefore it is trapped. If it is trapped in these circumstances has it been caught in a trap or has it been snared? Or is one meaning the same as the other. My view was that a snare, in these circumstances, was a trap. Scottish Executive solicitors appeared to agree as, in order to legally snare mountain hares, a licence had to be sought and obtained from the Scottish Executive by way of derogation from the requirements of this part of the Regulations.

Putting all of this into practical terms I had several interesting experiences within a short period of time. After one extremely cold March weekend I had a telephone call from a hill walker who wanted to report having found some dead mountain hares in snares when he had been out walking the previous day. When he had gone home, he checked the internet and read that it is against the law to snare mountain hares. As sometimes happens in this technological age, he had taken several photos with his digital camera and had emailed them to me. I checked my email while he was on the telephone. There was no question that the animals were mountain hares, which even in death blended in with the snowy background, and there was no question that they were in snares. I obtained map references for where the walker had made this find and began to make plans to recover them as evidence.

I was not available the following day and arranged for two of the Divisional wildlife crime officers, PCs Graham Jack and Helen Learmonth, to follow up the enquiry. Since police officers have power to take other persons with them on to land when they are investigating a report of wildlife crime, I arranged for a Scottish SPCA officer, Jim Cormack, to go with them. Jim has a particular interest in the snaring of mountain hares and the experience that he has in this field would be of value to the investigation.

Before the day had done I received further calls from another two walkers who had been out on the same hill and had found the dead mountain hares in snares. Unlike the first caller, neither of them was aware that this was an offence but, like many people, they happened not to like to see animals being snared. Neither had taken photographs but I had more than sufficient evidence of what was taking place.

The following day I briefed Graham, Helen and Jim before they set off at 7 o'clock in the morning. In one way I was desperate to go with them as fieldwork beats attending a meeting hands down. On the other hand the weather had closed in and it was alternating between heavy rain and heavy sleet, blown along nicely by a strong wind. At the height they would be going to on the estate in west Perthshire, there is no question that the wind would be even stronger and it would be a blizzard. In that respect the thought of a meeting in a cosy room with coffee and scones seemed less of a second prize. (We have excellent wet weather gear for jobs such as this. I knew that it would be well tested but we had absolute faith in the combination of fleece, jacket and waterproof trousers keeping out all of the rain or snow and, equally importantly, a good deal of the wind.)

The trio returned in the afternoon. It had been a terrible day on the hill despite the best of clothing, but they had seen it through. The map reference meant that the snares were quite easily found but it was clear that someone had already made the daily check and emptied them of any contents. They photographed several of the snares and seized them as evidence, then had the good luck to run into the keeper returning on his quad bike with the carrier on the front full of dead mountain hares, one of which still had a snare round its neck. He admitted that the snares had been his but was not aware that he was breaking the law. The law was explained to him, photographs were taken of his cargo of hares, the one with the snare round its neck was taken as evidence and he was charged with contravening the Habitats Regulations.

This was the first case of its kind that we had dealt with. The day before the search to recover the snares I had checked with the Scottish Executive that no licence authorising the snaring of mountain hares had been issued to the estate concerned or to any of the game managers on the estate. I had also requested and received from Scottish Executive a blank copy of a licence. It seemed that we had a strong case.

A couple of weeks later I was giving a talk on wildlife crime issues to a training course for moorland gamekeepers run every second year at Invermark Estate in Glenesk in Angus. The organisers of this exceptionally good course are the Game Conservancy Trust (Scotland) and this was my third invitation to give a presentation. My objective in the presentation is to make the keepers as aware of the law as possible concerning their use of snares, the variety of traps they use, what predators and pests they can control and by which means. I spoke on mountain hares and of course stated that they cannot legally be snared as this would contravene the Habitats Regulations. I was challenged on this by Hugo Straker, the Game Conservancy Trust organiser of the course, but I assured him that the law was clear.

During the meal afterwards Hugo and I again discussed the mountain hare snaring issue. He made the point, as I made at the start of this section on snaring, that the law can sometimes be open to interpretation, and that a case had not yet been through the court to get the view of a sheriff. After a gentlemanly airing of our views, we agreed to differ.

No-one has a monopoly of knowledge of any part of the law. Hugo Straker has a very good grasp of wildlife law and I respect his views and interpretations, even if in one or two cases they are slightly different from mine. There was something niggling away at me about the taking of mountain hares by the use of snares. In almost all areas of the law I could see the logic in carrying out – or failing to carry out – a particular act that amounted to an offence. I could see no logic here. If mountain hares are endangered then I would have thought complete protection should be the legal solution, rather than allowing the taking by one method but not another. I really needed to resolve this problem.

Each area has an environmental fiscal, who is responsible for the decisions relating to the prosecution of all wildlife and environmental crime. I decided to contact the most senior of the fiscals, Tom Dysart, who is area procurator fiscal for Dumfries and Galloway and also chair of the Wildlife and Habitats Crime Prosecution Forum. Tom agreed to research the issue and get back to me. In the meantime, probably because of the doubts that Constable Graham Jack and I had, I was not surprised to see that the procurator fiscal was not proceeding with the mountain hare case. A further factor, I suspect, was because of the previously unblemished character of the gamekeeper accused.

If mountain hares are endangered then I would have thought complete protection should be the legal solution, not allowing the taking by one method but not another. I really needed to resolve this problem and asked experienced procurators fiscal and Scottish Executive people for their opinions.

There were contradictory interpretations of the legislation by legal experts. All agreed that snares were non-selective but differed on the issue of whether snares could not be considered to be traps. It was obvious that this was a very grey area of law and one in which, at least until the law is clarified, any suspect would have to get the benefit of the doubt. I hoped that the ongoing consultations in the closing months of 2006 on the Habitats regulations, and on snaring might clarify the position. Though I hate to be wrong, I don't think I have ever had too much difficulty in admitting my mistakes and I knew that one of my first apologies would have to be to Hugo Straker.

I had a flashback to my drug squad days and a time when we had a telephone call to say that drug dealing was taking place at a particular address in what is known in Dundee as a 'Multi', which for those who have led more sheltered lives is a block of high-rise flats. We obtained a search warrant and visited the flat. I was surprised that someone actually opened the door when I knocked. Normally drug dealers quiz the caller from behind a locked door before it is first opened slightly on a chain once the occupant has achieved a degree of satisfaction that those on the other side are neither police officers nor rivals who may want to steal his stash of drugs or his drugs money. Only once a full visual inspection of the caller has been made will the door be fully opened. The occupant's openness made us just that bit more cautious and we did not barge past him to gain entry.

I told the occupant of the information we had received and of the fact that we had a search warrant. He was angry that the police had come to his door suspecting him of being a drug dealer and was initially reluctant to allow us over the doorstep. Despite having the power of a warrant there are times when tact rather than force is called for and I could see that this was one of those times. I said to him that he may well have been 'set up' by someone he had fallen out with but if that was the case then we, as drug squad officers, had also been set up. I convinced him that now that we were at his door in any case we would have a quick look round the house and if we felt we were as much victims as he was, we would be out of his hair in a short time. He acquiesced and invited us in to his house to carry out a search.

Very little of a search was required to satisfy us that he was a victim of some nasty, sick acquaintance who, for whatever reason, wanted to create trouble for him. We had a 'nose' for drug dealers and our senses told us that he was not one of our customers. We completed the search in a very short time and as we were leaving I said to him, 'I'm really sorry for the hassle and inconvenience we've caused you. I'm happy that you have nothing to do with drug dealing.' The man visibly staggered back and I asked what was wrong. He told me that in all the time he had lived in Dundee he had never heard a police officer say that he was sorry. This really is a pity though in this litigious age I can understand the reluctance of police officers to admit that they are wrong and for them to apologise. In most cases an apology would diffuse a situation and prevent a complaint being made, but unfortunately, in certain circumstances and most definitely with one or two criminals I know, it would lead to the officer being sued.

Life's a bitch!

CHAPTER 33

Operation *Lepus*

The innovative use of revised bail conditions to fight hare coursing crime and a useful digression on the training of dogs.

Despite a good season for catching those involved in hare coursing from the Autumn of 2004 till the Spring of 2005 it did not stop it or even slow it down. It seemed a bit like catching drug dealers: as soon as one was caught another appeared out of the woodwork to take his or her place. From experience I knew that many of those involved in hare coursing were involved in other criminality such as drug dealing and as bogus workmen, charging the elderly a grossly inflated price for shamefully poor work. It annoyed me that they seemed to see little threat from law enforcement. They covered their tracks by seldom running a vehicle that was traceable to them, normally buying an older car that was still registered in the last owner's name, intended it to be sold on and replaced after two or three of their nefarious outings. They also made threats to farmers that if they were reported to the police they would come back and burn steadings or stacks of bales, threats that I have never known to be carried out.

Hare coursers were well aware that, unless they were unlucky, it would take the police some time – even if free from other calls – to arrive at the scene of the coursing. They also knew that many police officers were unfamiliar with this aspect of the law and of their powers on hare coursing, and they were as likely to receive a warning as to be charged. I was determined that this situation would change and that the police would offer a far more professional and effective service to the farmers and others who were being pestered by this criminal activity. The improved police response came in the form of Operation *Lepus*, this being the Latin generic name for hares and rabbits.

It began in August 2005 when I drafted a letter – signed by the Divisional Commanders in Eastern Division (Angus) and Western Division (Perth and Kinross) – to be delivered to as many farmers, landowners and gamekeepers as possible. This advised them that we had devised a strategy to deal with the coursing of hares, and hopefully would encourage them to report incidents promptly to give the police officers a chance to get to the scene before the coursers disappeared. Additionally, and maybe most importantly, the letter gave a resumé of the law and of the standard of evidence required to convict someone of hare coursing, and included contact telephone numbers. These letters were sent out simultaneously to a press release, which was covered well by the media and was an additional source of information to any farmer who didn't receive a letter.

Now that we had helped raise the farmers' game, we needed to ensure that we raised our own. I ensured that all police officers were aware of Operation *Lepus* and gave them a monthly update. I also prepared a briefing note for the Control Room that would be flagged up when there was an incident. It included a brief on police powers, a request to make me aware of the incident as it was ongoing, and suggestions for bail conditions to be requested by the court on hare coursers. Bail conditions can only be imposed if a person appears in court in custody, or on an undertaking to appear on a specified date after having been released from custody. A standard bail condition is that a person who appears before the court and is released on bail pending a trial is that he or she must not commit other offences while on bail. Many other conditions to suit a particular case may be requested of the court. In the case of hare coursers I wanted the bail conditions to be:

1. The accused persons, if resident in Tayside, must not travel more than a mile from their home address in the company of their dog or anyone else's dog;
2. The accused persons, if resident outside Tayside, must not enter Tayside in the company of their dog or anyone else's dog;
3. They must not sell or get rid of their dog;
4. If their dog dies, a vet's certificate to that effect must be produced to the court.

This was designed to curtail their illegal activities and also to allow a court to forfeit the dogs on conviction. I had already arranged with the Scottish SPCA that if dogs were forfeited, they would arrange for re-homing.

I could never claim that Operation *Lepus* ran smoothly, but it was most definitely an overall success. The first four persons charged with hare coursing were from Airdrie and were shell-shocked when they were arrested and kept in custody for court the next morning. Three hares were recovered, two in their vehicle and one in the field that they were in. It was a complicated case to be the first under Operation *Lepus*, as none of the witnesses could identify any of the accused, but could identify the clothing that they were wearing. They could also identify the dogs, which were slightly different sizes and a range of colours. I was desperate to keep the dogs till the case came up but I had already explored all possible avenues with Divisional Commanders and the procurator fiscal. Cost was prohibitive, plus there was an added risk of vets' bills if one or more dogs required veterinary treatment. Though keeping the dogs seemed a desirable solution it was a non-starter.

The four men were released with the bail conditions I had requested in relation to the dogs. The court actually went a stage further and made a bail condition that they must not enter Tayside except to visit their solicitor in the case. As residents of Airdrie, if they had wanted to visit someone in Aberdeen they really had a circuitous route to travel to get there without coming through Tayside.

This case had an unfortunate end in that after a trial lasting a whole day all four were found not guilty because of a breakdown in police procedure in relation to the identification of the clothing worn by the men. I was disappointed but I doubt that they will be back coursing in Tayside. In the ten months between the offence and the trial their lives had been made pretty awkward by the bail conditions. I do hope they passed the message on to other hare coursers from the west of Scotland.

Our next two hare coursers were also from the west, in this case Glasgow. They were arrested on a Saturday and kept till court on the Monday. As it happened the procurator fiscal thought that the evidence fell just a wee bit short, though on this occasion I didn't agree. The case was deserted but the older of the two accused had missed a Guy Fawkes night at which he was to play some starring role and would be Mr Unpopular on his eventual return home to his family two days late. I doubt they will be back so I think we had to treat the case as a success, especially if they told their tale of woe in their local Glasgow pubs. Though the power was available, keeping hare coursers in custody till the next court had not been the standard practice before Operation *Lepus*. It was a brand new risk that they had now to face.

Our next case provided a bit of variety: it took place at night. Coursing hares, and indeed deer, in the dark is unfortunately not uncommon. I was pleased when I came on duty at 7.00 o'clock one morning to find the night shift waiting to tell me about their capture of two men from Fife with three hares in their van and a fourth lying inside a field near the gate from which they had just emerged. I was even more pleased when I learned the two were those that we had run a special patrol trying to catch on the previous Sunday. They were now in custody due to appear in court and I was asked if I could help with the case.

I decided to go to the scene and took Constable Doug Ogilvie, a divisional wildlife crime officer, along with me. The field that we examined first of all was the wrong field but as it turned out the two men had also visited it. Their strategy, with the use of a spotlight and a battery pack strapped to the back of one of the accused, was to spot a hare in a field, walk up as close to it as possible then release the dogs. Unlike rabbits, hares act pretty stupidly in a beam of light. Rabbits are likely to scurry off to the safety of their burrows but hares will continue munching whatever the crop is in the field or at worst hop off a few yards. Taking hares at night with a spotlight and dogs must have a high degree of success.

In this field, which was a winter wheat crop, we could quite easily follow the tracks of the two men. They had entered the gate and turned left, then walked down the left hand side of the field. With a lamp they could quite easily spot a hare anywhere over the width of the field but it must have been empty. Their tracks went right down one edge of the field, with the tracks of two dogs off the leads visible fairly close by, sometimes to the left, sometimes to the right. A third dog must have been on a lead as its tracks were visible consistently close to the left of one of the men. Near the bottom of the field the tracks about-turned and came back up to the gate. They had drawn a blank in that field, obviously before the arrival of the police.

The next field along was also winter wheat and was the field that we should have been examining at the start. I was glad of our mistake as it gave us an insight into the tactics of the men as well as a bit of practice in tracking. The situation was completely different in this field. The two men had entered and had gone slightly left, probably having spotted a hare as soon as they went in the gate. The dog tracks were close to the men's tracks for the first forty or so yards but then disappeared. The soil was slightly more clay in this field and it was much more difficult to see the tracks. Luckily we were only a few hours after the event, which made all the difference.

A few yards further into the field we saw the tracks of two dogs at full stretch crossing the tracks of the two men from left to right. It looked like the hare had doubled back behind the men once the dogs were released. I have sometimes been able to see the hare's tracks when being chased but in a field with clay soil and six inches of winter wheat this was impossible. The dogs' tracks were a different story. They could be seen quite clearly, with the depth of the tracks and the spread of the claws revealing that they were running flat out.

We followed the chase round the field, sometimes following the two dogs' tracks and sometimes those of the men. The men were sometimes walking but mostly had been running. One also had a dog close to his left side that was obviously on a lead. At the extreme left hand side of the field we found a patch of flattened grain crop and a considerable amount of hare's fur. This was obviously the point of the kill. A hare has little chance of escape in these circumstances, being partially blinded by the light, while the dogs have the advantage of seeing the hare illuminated at all times. I photographed the relevant marks, including the point at which the hare was killed, and also drew a sketch map of the two fields we had searched. On our return I photographed the dogs, all greyhound types, kept at least in the meantime in the police kennels at Perth Police Station. This was the first time that I had been able to confirm that there had been three dogs. The third dog was a young dog, probably the one that had been kept on the lead and just out as an apprentice to gain experience for future coursing.

It was at this point that the Operation *Lepus* strategy went slightly awry. I had tried to telephone the environmental fiscal to make her aware of the case before the two men appeared at court. She was unfortunately having a day off but as the reporting police officer had asked in his report for the suggested bail conditions I was sure it would be OK. It wasn't OK, and the fiscal who presented the case did not appear to have asked for these special bail conditions – or if she did the sheriff hadn't acceded to the request. The two men pleaded not guilty and were released on the standard bail condition that they must not commit other offences while on bail. I was not best pleased.

Later in the morning I had the four hares examined by veterinary pathologists, who confirmed that the hares' injuries were consistent with having been killed by a dog or dogs. I have seen so many of these examinations now that I am happy to corroborate the vet. The injuries are fairly standard and a visual external examination of the hare nearly always shows some sort of loss of hair around a back leg or flank where the dog has either gripped or tripped the hare. Palpation of the rib area clearly shows broken ribs, this technique being shown to me when I used to train spaniels and labradors as gundogs. Most gundogs pick up a dead or injured game bird, rabbit or hare without causing further injury, but one or two dogs, described as being 'hard-mouthed', grip far too tightly and crush the ribs of the bird or animal. Hard-mouthed dogs seldom deliver a game bird alive to its owner and this trait, in gun dog trials, results in disqualification. It is one aspect in the training of gundogs that, once the dog has acquired it, is almost impossible to get rid of by any sort of training.

•

I digress here to touch on the training of dogs. As I write this at home there is a dog of about nine months that is kennelled outside at a house nearby and is barking almost continuously. It is a lovely dog but firstly it is bored, and secondly its owners have not the slightest notion about training a dog and think that shouting its name loudly is the solution. When I did a lot more shooting than I do now I kept up to five gundogs and at that time lived in Perth. Living amongst neighbours in a residential area it is unfair on everyone to have dogs that are incessant barkers. It is a behaviour that is so easy to stop. When my dogs were young and first arrived it was inevitable that they would bark. I would wait in the house with half a bucket of water behind the door until the young dog, in the run outside, started to bark. While it was still barking it received the contents of the bucket and immediately stopped barking and retired to its kennel. A cupful of water was all that was required on subsequent occasions and the barking ceased within a few days. There was nothing cruel about this; most gundogs in fact love jumping into water even on the coldest of days. A cup – or even a half bucket of water – over a dog does it not the slightest harm but hurts its feelings. It associates barking with its feelings being hurt and stops barking. Dogs need exercise and stimulation to prevent boredom and a combination of these factors with a wee drop water results in young dogs that can be left outside in a run without annoyance to neighbours. My neighbour's dog is still barking. Where's my bucket of water. . .

•

Getting back to our hare coursers who had been released without my preferred bail conditions, one of them, along with a new accomplice, was caught ten days later, this time in possession of one hare. Patrolling police officers from Kinross Section had seen a spotlight in a field and had made an excellent job of catching the two culprits, who claimed that one of their two dogs had escaped and had run off after a hare. It was a Saturday night and officers in the Section were committed with other incidents at the time. It made the task of arresting the two men difficult, as it would mean a police van to take their dogs to the kennels in Perth and another police officer to recover their vehicle and bring it to a police station. Such logistics are impossible on a busy Saturday night. The men were charged and released, though their spotlight, battery pack and hare were seized. We were beginning a good collection of spotlights and battery packs.

What was frustrating in this case was that the man involved in the first incident had not only breached the standard bail condition – that of committing another offence while on bail – but as a resident of Fife, he had entered Tayside with a dog. Of course the latter bail condition had either not been requested or granted at his first court appearance!

In due course the fiscal linked the two cases for trial on the same day. On the trial date one accused, who had only been involved in the first case, was already in prison for another offence and the case against him was deserted. The other accused who was involved only in the second offence, pled not guilty, a plea that was accepted. The third accused, involved in both offences and who had also breached the standard bail condition of committing a second offence while on bail for the first, pled guilty to all the charges. The sheriff took an extremely dim view, reminding the accused that he had been charged with hare coursing yet ten days later he was at it again. He was warned that jail was a likely outcome and sentence was deferred for reports.

A month later, the man who had pled guilty appeared for sentence. He received 200 hours community service, this being a direct alternative to imprisonment. With this conviction against him it would be almost certain that if he was caught and convicted again he would be going to jail. I also saw that he had been disqualified for two years and assumed that the disqualification related to the keeping of dogs. This would have been pretty unenforceable, since his wife, partner, kids or relatives could 'own' and keep his dog. Just to confirm, I made a bit more enquiry and learned, to my astonishment, he had been disqualified from *driving* for two years! This was the first time I had heard of a driving ban for anything other than a road traffic offence. I was stunned but delighted. That would put his gas at a peep!

I was unsure where the sheriff's power came from to disqualify the man and made further enquiries. No police officer that I spoke with had heard of this type of penalty before but it made complete sense. The man had used his vehicle in order to commit the crime, and in fact it was doubtful that he could have committed the crime without his vehicle. To have walked or cycled from his home in Fife to the place where he committed the crime would have taken the best part of the night with no time – or energy – left for coursing hares. Furthermore, the absence of a driving licence was going to be a realistic and effective curb on re-offending.

I made enquiry with the Crown Office and found that the answer was somewhat technical but the principle made absolute sense. I was referred to section 248A of the Criminal Procedure (Scotland) Act 1995, as inserted by section 15 of the Crime and Punishment (Scotland) Act 1997. I located the Act and read sub-section 248(1) first. It read:

> *Where a person is convicted of an offence (other than one triable only summarily) and the court which passes sentence is satisfied that a motor vehicle was used for the purposes of committing or facilitating the commission of that offence, the court may order him to be disqualified for such a period as the court thinks fit from holding or obtaining a licence to drive a motor vehicle granted under Part III of the Road Traffic Act 1988.*

This couldn't apply to the offence that had been committed in this case – hare coursing – as it cannot be heard under Solemn Procedure. In other words it cannot be heard in a Sheriff and Jury Court or a High Court, only in a summary court. The insertion in 1997 of section 248A extended the power under section 248(1) to sheriffs sitting in a summary court, so that they also could disqualify an offender from holding or obtaining a licence.

When this case was heard in September 2006 this new court disposal was being piloted only in Perth and Paisley Sheriff Courts. Scottish Executive Justice Department officials were in due course to consider evaluation reports and the next steps. The interesting outcome of this case was that our hare coursing incidents immediately faltered and by the end of September had almost stopped. In the combined months of October and November we had far fewer reports of hare coursing than in the month of September. The good news also travelled to the Scottish Executive Justice Department. I have a good working relationship with the staff there and, independently of any reports from sheriff clerks or sheriffs I submitted my own report on the positive effects of this single, ground-breaking, conviction.

Several other cases where coursers were caught at the time resulted in fairly substantial fines, but we broke new ground in other cases where those involved were not caught at the time. The Moorov doctrine was first used in cases of a sexual nature, where there normally was just the one witness – the victim. The principle of the Moorov doctrine is that where a person is charged with a series of similar offences which are closely related by character, circumstances and time, (not all three factors being essential) the evidence of one credible, but different, witness to each offence may afford mutual corroboration as each offence can be treated as an element in a single course of conduct. Through time the Moorov doctrine was applied to other offences that were not of a sexual nature and I could see no reason that it could not be applied to hare coursing. In many instances of coursing only one witness is available. If the suspects are not caught at the time then the importance of the case recedes as the officers involved become embroiled in other matters and the end result is that the case is not followed through. I had – or made – the time to change this situation.

In a case in the Spring of 2006 a man from Aberdeen was charged with six coursing offences, in most of which there was only a single witness. What made the Aberdeen man's case so different was that he had never left his vehicle. The vehicle, a red four wheeled drive, was registered to him, which was unusual and a good start. He was on photographic record and his photograph was picked out in two incidents by a single witness. In a third incident the person who saw him knew him, and in the other incidents he admitted having been there though not coursing. He wasn't coursing *per se*, but the Protection of Wild Mammals (Scotland) Act states that to hunt means to *search for or course.* Our interpretation of the law was that he was searching for hares, while those that were with him, whose identities were complete-åly unknown to us, were coursing. He was, art and part, coursing.

I had become used to unfortunate outcomes to cases and this one was little different. With wildlife crime cases the wildlife crime officer needs to ensure that he has a very good working relationship with the procurator fiscal. I had a good relationship with the procurators fiscal from two of the three Tayside offices but I was aware that there was about to be a new procurator fiscal at the third. I took my eye off the ball in a manner of speaking and the consequences were fatal to the case. Fiscals rarely get a chance to deal with wildlife cases so they get little chance to build up expertise. This is why it is so important that they know the wildlife crime officer and can make contact by telephone or email to get a bit more detail or explanation about a case if that is what they need. In this case, while the new fiscal was marking the papers, she was dealing with an offence that was brand new to her. This must be extremely difficult. In this instance the complexity of the case was compounded by six separate charges and the evidence of corroboration of the offences had been obtained in a manner that was legitimate but unusual or even unconventional in wildlife cases.

Once I had realised that the new procurator fiscal was *in situ* I made an appointment to see her. Once I knew her she was probably the most accommodating and easy-to-work-with fiscal I have encountered in forty years. I asked her about the hare coursing case, to be told that the case was closed. I have experienced this before when a case with insufficient evidence was put forward by the police but this can occasionally be remedied by re-submitting one with sufficient evidence provided this time to prove it. On this occasion there was no such possibility as the case had become time-barred. Unless a statute states differently or unless the case is in under Common Law, there is a statutory time limit of six months to get it to court. The six months was up. The case was down the tubes.

We discussed the case. I was a wee bit frustrated as PC John Robertson and I had put a huge amount of work into obtaining the evidence. The person involved was one of the most active hare coursers in the area and would probably have gone to jail. The farmers involved had been reticent, not only in making contact with the police but in giving statements. Attending court is an ordeal and a nuisance for anyone, not least a busy farmer. It is a long and boring day sitting in a witness room, and that is often the least unpleasant part of a witness's day at court! The farmers were also wary of the veiled threats from this accused and some of his associates in crime to cause damage to their farm buildings. Coercing the necessary evidence from them had not been easy.

Looking at the case from the fiscal's point of view, she was the new kid on the block and wasn't aware of my availability at that stage to make comment or give further advice on the case. The case had also been very late in being submitted. The accused had been hard to track down for interview by Grampian Police wildlife crime officers on our behalf. Annual leave delayed the investigation further, as did several subsequent offences that we considered had been committed by the same accused and we wanted to report all at the same time. This meant further interviews by Grampian Police so that the whole investigation could be submitted as a composite case, binding several cases that if looked at in isolation would be weak or insufficient into one fairly strong case (in my view). While there was still enough time to beat the time bar when she received the case I could appreciate the fiscal's problem. An unusual and complicated case, almost time-barred, no previous wildlife crime experience and no one to advise. Case marked no proceedings. End of story.

There is absolutely no question that fiscals are overworked and in many cases can't do justice to cases but that is not their fault: it is the fault of the system. My delay in contacting the new fiscal was simply to allow her time to settle in. It was a miscalculation, and the death of the case was an unfortunate combination of circumstances. On the positive side there was no injured victim or stolen property.

The new fiscal admitted to being a townie but I could see that she was enthusiastic in gaining experience in prosecuting crime of a more rural nature, cases concomitant to her new post. We discussed a further pending wildlife case where I expected it to be fought all the way because of the money behind the accused. She was not daunted in the least and told me she was looking forward to the challenge. Like me, she had a determination to show that money does not put someone above the law. There is no doubt at all that money can help, in that the best of lawyers can be obtained, but we were determined we would give it our best shot.

Chapter 34

Raptor Study Group

Hard lessons in the difficulties and pitfalls of partnership working in this project surveying the breeding habits of raptors on highland estates.

Most wildlife crime officers try to work with all relevant organisations. This is sensible and may sound fairly easy, but in fact it is one of the most complex and stressful aspects of my job. Many of the organisations from which I seek cooperation have their own agenda and in some cases are almost at opposite ends of the spectrum. There are heated arguments aired regularly between game managers and RSPB; Raptor Study Groups and pigeon fanciers; and the League against Cruel Sports and foxhunting enthusiasts to name but a few. Groups can be categorised as follows:

1. Those that actively support field sports and such activities as pigeon racing;
2. Groups that would want to see all or most field sports banned;
3. Those with no ill will against field sports but lobby for moderate changes.

To try to work effectively with all of these groups is at best a challenge and at worst a nightmare. I don't necessarily agree with everything that *any* of these organisations do. Most put into practice many policies that are beneficial to wildlife or to our environment but if I tell them there is an aspect with which I don't agree then I am seen to be taking sides with the 'enemy'. Many times the bickering, the pessimism and negative views, the criticism of one organisation by another just gets me down and I think, 'Bugger it. I'm not in this job for the money, I should just get out of it and spend my time with my family, garden and dogs.' It's strange but it's the very fact I don't do this for the money that keeps me going. If I have a bad day I sleep on it and rise to the challenge the next morning even more determined to do my part to improve the situation. Though my primary job is the prevention and detection of crimes against wildlife, one of the routes towards achieving that objective is to try to get disparate groups to try to reach some kind of compromise on the aspects with which they disagree. In 2000, as good a year as any for a turning point and for new ideas, I had some success.

In some parts of Tayside particular species of birds of prey were clearly having a lack of breeding success. This could be down to a number of reasons not necessarily related to criminal acts. Increased access to the countryside by people with more leisure time meant that there was the potential for disturbance of breeding birds, albeit unintentional or even un-noticed. Some birds, such as golden eagles and marsh harriers, are very susceptible to disturbance. It takes very little to make them desert their nest, or if they are kept off their nest in extreme cold or extreme heat this may have a fatal consequence for eggs or chicks. Egg collectors still posed a risk, as did illegal trapping, shooting or poisoning. Predators were a real threat to ground nesting birds such as hen harrier, merlin and sometimes peregrine, though this risk should always have been reduced on well keepered ground. Lack of available prey can thwart successful breeding, with the best example being the humble vole. In good vole years there is an abundance of young short-eared owls and hen harriers in particular, and in poor years, with few voles, a dramatic reduction in the number of these birds. Lastly, the vagaries of the weather: late snow or wet Springs create a particular problem and often result in widespread failures. Without a magic wand, some of these factors were completely beyond my control. But I would have a damn good try at altering the effects of the others.

I decided to try to get estate staff to take on the responsibility to look after birds of prey, the best people to help with this being the keepers. Gamekeepers know every inch of their ground, the very same way as a police officer knows his or her beat. A gamekeeper is on the estate a good part of the day and night: a police officer patrols his beat by day and by night. Both are aware of the main places of interest on their respective beats. A police officer has knowledge of premises vulnerable to crime, addresses of career criminals, knowledge of people that are on the go in the early morning such as posties or milkmen, or late at night such as gamekeepers, key road junctions for road checks and the like. With the gamekeeper it may be the knowledge of traditional nesting sites of birds of prey, fox dens, pockets of rare mammals of birds, favourite places for deer to be found depending on the prevailing wind, natural regeneration of native trees or the presence of rare plants such as orchids. I wanted to harness this knowledge to reduce wildlife crime. Even if the keeper had been up to things he ought not, then my motto is that I'm not interested in what happened yesterday, I want improvements for today and tomorrow. I hoped that the gamekeepers, with the blessing and co-operation of the landowner, would be 'police officers' on their own patch, and help the police reduce wildlife crime.

Estate staff and raptor study group people were not, in most cases, exactly the best of friends. The people who studied birds of prey, receiving a mileage allowance from Scottish Natural Heritage in return for collecting data on breeding birds of prey, pretty much distrusted keepers. In one respect I didn't blame them as gamekeepers had been bumping off birds of prey for years, if not centuries. Where I took issue with the raptor study group folks was that some of them did not acknowledge that the situation was changing; that far fewer gamekeepers were risking being caught and ending up in court. I suspect their point was that raptor persecution (a term of which I'm not overfond) had slowed but had not stopped. Practices of successive generations cannot change overnight.

I had also been trying for some years to encourage raptor workers to liaise with the keepers, a practice that I was sure would benefit everyone. Firstly the keepers would know where the raptor study folks were going to be on the estate and could direct them away from a particular location where their presence may make a vixen move her cubs to another den before they could be dealt with. Secondly they could tell the raptor workers what birds of prey were at what particular nest site or area, since they spent just about their every waking hour on the estate and missed very little that was of interest.

Some of the raptor workers disagreed with this kind of accountability and were of the view that they could sneak onto the estate, locate and watch birds of prey at their nest, and that the keeper would neither be aware of their visit nor the presence of the particular birds of prey. I think not! This cloak and dagger stuff should be left to MI5. In any event I wanted Tayside Raptor Group onboard this project, with the proviso that they liaised with the estates involved when monitoring birds of prey.

I discussed the embryonic project with Patrick Stirling-Aird, a lawyer who is also secretary of the Scottish Raptor Study Groups and a member of both Tayside and Central Scotland Raptor Study Groups. He was enthusiastic and had little problem with advance notice of visits to estates as his own liaison and dialogue with estates was good. The next step was to recruit landowners in contiguous estates so that we could have a large tract of uplands forming the project area.

Since I knew most landowners in the west of Tayside from my days of being inspector in the Crieff Section, and that Patrick monitored golden eagle and peregrine in the same area, this was where Operation Countrywatch had to be located. Three landowners agreed to come on board and we were under way. Though the prevention of wildlife crime was one of the objectives, of equal standing – at least to me – was an improvement in dialogue, understanding each other's difficulties and capitalising on points of common interest or agreement between the Tayside Raptor Study Group and the estates.

The areas of common interest and agreement were important. The estate owner, the keepers and the raptor workers all loved the uplands, with its solitude, heather, white grass, clean air and its wildlife. As a profession who manage the uplands, gamekeepers had no qualms about legitimate management of predators. They effectively manage the predators that can legally be controlled, such as foxes, stoats, weasels, rats and crows. Despite this management the numbers of these species remained fairly constant. Some keepers dearly wish that they could extend their management to protected species, such as pine martens, badgers and of course some birds of prey. Were this to be permitted by law some may do a very good job but some might, in colloquial terminology, 'tear the arse out of it.' I have many times suggested to gamekeepers that as a first step to increased likelihood or even possibility of derogation to allow control of any species that are meantime protected, and certainly as a major step up the ladder of public acceptance and recognition, they should change their role title to wildlife managers. Some agree and some are vehemently opposed to such a change.

I don't think that the aspirations of raptor groups are much different, except that they would have no truck with the killing – or culling – of birds of prey or of a 'quota system' where only a given number of birds of prey of a particular species would be allowed to breed successfully on a particular estate.

Everyone involved in Operation Countrywatch recognised the common ground and began to build on it. By the end of the first year working relationships were less strained though it would still take a while to build complete trust. Best of all, nesting birds of prey were noticeably more successful, and peregrine nests that had seen many years of failure fledged chicks. The reasons for this improvement may have indicated a change in policy but I did not delve too deeply, I was just pleased with the results.

More estates joined in, multiplying the success rate and increasing dialogue and trust. One disappointment was the abandoning of a long-time nest site on one of the estates by a pair of golden eagles. It was, unfortunately, on a crag that was by-passed regularly by hillwalkers and its seemed that the daily disturbance was just too much for the eagles. They moved out and their place was taken by a pair of peregrines, birds that are a bit more tolerant of humans near their chosen nest site. Coincidentally I was notified of a new nest by a nearby landowner and taken later in the year to see it by his gamekeeper. I was sworn to secrecy and had no problem in keeping my word. The new site was well looked after and that satisfied me. It looked a fairly easy climb for egg collectors but had the advantage in being at a site that was not known to them.

In 2003, partly because of the generally decreasing golden eagle population in Tayside and the reasons for this being mainly out of my remit (in other words probably unrelated to criminal activity), we decided to include more conservation organisations in the Operation.

Scottish Natural Heritage (SNH), the statutory government advisers on matters pertaining to wildlife and habitat, and RSPB Scotland joined the group. The group then had a slight change of name, reflecting the increased partners, to Operation Countrywatch Partnership. Tayside Police and SNH were joint chairs of the group, which by this time had increased by several more estates. Members were asked to sign up to a three-year agreement and the partnership flourished. One issue raised regularly was the culling of buzzards but, though some sympathised with the argument, the law states that buzzards are protected and it was not the remit of the partnership to lobby for changes in the law. I was pleased that such issues were raised as 'one side' of the partnership could see and appreciate the problems of the 'other side'.

During the three years of the partnership, the main birds studied were golden eagle, peregrine, hen harrier, merlin and black grouse. A field worker was employed by RSPB and worked alongside members of the raptor study group and gamekeepers to survey breeding attempts. The results were positive, even though golden eagles were still struggling. The rest of the species either seemed to hold their own or even showed a slight increase. Black grouse, in particular, did very well on the estates. I was overjoyed at this as I love to listen in the early Spring mornings to the lovely bubbling, cooing sound that the males collectively make when they are lekking. They strut around on the portion of ground they have gained for themselves on the lek site, their lyre-shaped tail held high showing its white underside, and the large red wattle above their eye acting as a warning of danger to their fellow males if they step over the invisible territorial boundary. They are puffed up to half their size again, wings held low towards the ground in an attempt to assert their dominance over the others so that that they will attract most females. Normally the strongest male is at the centre of the lek and the younger or weaker ones towards the outer perimeters. Operation Countrywatch Partnership was having good results, but there was one particular problem that arose, and it caused me to make yet another apology.

Though there was a paid field worker to monitor some of the breeding birds of prey, some were still being monitored by members of the Raptor Study Group. On one particular estate hen harriers were being monitored by the field worker but unknown to her were also being monitored – at least to some degree – by a member of the Raptor Study Group. A hundred different people could monitor a nesting hen harrier without causing it any problem provided they did not visit the nest or indeed go too close to the nest. Hen harriers are not unduly disturbed by distant human activity and (as I have often done) an observer can sit in the heather quarter of a mile from the nest and the male will still come in with food. The female will come off the nest, the male will pass the food in mid air and the female will land close to the nest to have a feed before returning to the nest and to incubating the eggs or sharing what is left of the prey with her young if the eggs happen to have hatched. Problems only arise when people visit the nest or go too close.

On this particular estate the Operation Countrywatch Partnership field worker had located a nest after watching a food pass from a distant vantage point, but did not think that it was safe to visit the nest as the full clutch may not yet have been laid. If the clutch had indeed been laid, the field worker was of the view that the bird may not yet have fully settled and a visit to the nest may cause it to desert. She decided to wait and observe over the next few days then visit the nest when she was satisfied that it would be safe to do so.

The following day the field worker heard that a Raptor Group worker had been on the same estate later in the same day and had also seen a food pass – the main method of identifying the location of a nest. The Raptor Group worker appeared to have been less cautious, had visited the nest, and was able to state that it contained five eggs. Understandably this had annoyed the field worker, who reported the matter to me. I hoped that no harm had been done and the field worker told me that she intended to monitor the site of the nest closely.

During one of the years I had been monitoring hen harriers as part of a schools project I asked my wife, Jan, if she wanted to come out with me one day to watch a nest. She sounded quite keen and asked what was involved. I told her that it was simply a case of finding a vantage point far enough from the nest that the birds wouldn't be disturbed, settling down in the heather, and watching. So far so good;

this still sounded OK and she still sounded interested. There was almost an agreement to go but there was a caveat, 'You know I would get bored if I have to sit too long, what period of time do you mean?' 'Probably about four hours,' was my answer. I was about to add that there are always interesting things to see apart from hen harriers but never had the chance. Jan, like many folks, expected action within the first fifteen minutes and four hours was out of the question. The idea was vetoed and I was left to my own company.

After two days the field worker reported that there had been no sign of a food pass and she intended checking the nest the following day. I agreed that this would be the best course of action. The field worker was licensed to disturb nesting hen harriers, a Schedule 1 bird that by law is protected from disturbance while nesting. Even with licensed people disturbance should be kept to an absolute minimum. As we both feared would be the case, the nest had been deserted and the eggs were chilled.

This was a tricky situation as there was no proof that the visit of the Raptor Group worker caused the desertion. Even if the visit had been the factor that caused the bird not to return to the nest, the Raptor Group worker was licensed. She had not committed an offence though had not carried out best practice. I thought about it long and hard but decided to leave the situation as it was and take no further action. After a few days, however, I did make enquiries with Scottish Natural Heritage as to the licensing position and discovered to my horror that the Raptor Group worker had not applied for a licence to disturb nesting hen harriers that year and should therefore not have gone anywhere near a harrier's nest. I considered the available evidence and decided that it was still something that we couldn't prove.

A couple of months went by and I became aware of rumblings from the Scottish Gamekeepers' Association (SGA), a group with which I had always had a good working relationship. By coincidence I had a meeting with some of the SGA committee on matters that were of mutual interest and the visit to the harrier's nest was raised. The representatives from the SGA were disappointed that the police had not investigated the desertion of the harrier's nest, their view being that if a keeper had disturbed the harrier then the keeper would have been interviewed and probably charged. They reckoned that we were not working from a level playing field and that we had shown favour towards the Raptor Study Group. I shouldered the blame for the absence of an investigation and assured them that I would see to it that it was investigated forthwith.

I wanted to remain impartial and passed the investigation to one of the Divisional wildlife crime officers, Constable John Robb. John interviewed the few witnesses that there were, the main ones being the field worker and the person to whom the Raptor Group worker had allegedly informed about her visit to the nest. The raptor worker was interviewed under caution and admitted having visited the harrier's nest in the late afternoon or early evening of the day that the nest had been discovered by the field worker.

At the conclusion of the investigation the following was established as fact:

- A hen harrier had nested on the estate in question;
- A hen harrier is listed on Schedule 1 of the Wildlife and Countryside Act 1981;
- It is an offence to intentionally (nowadays this includes recklessly) disturb a nesting Schedule 1 bird without a licence from Scottish Natural Heritage;
- The suspect had no such licence;
- The suspect had visited the nest to examine the nest contents;
- When the suspect visited the nest it had contained five eggs;
- The suspect contacted another Raptor Study Group member to tell her of finding the nesting harrier and of the nest containing a clutch of five eggs;
- Neither the female nor the male harrier was seen on either of the two days following the visit to the nest by the suspect, despite observations by the field worker;
- When the field worker eventually visited the nest the eggs were still there and were cold.

The case was reported to the procurator fiscal who, rightly in my view, marked the case 'no proceedings'. The offence we were trying to prove was one of intentional disturbance to a Schedule 1 bird without having a licence to do so. Scots law needs the principal elements of a case corroborated and we just could not do that. We knew from the admission of the suspect that she had visited the nest but we could not prove that the consequence of the visit was to flush the bird from the nest, thereby disturbing it. That evidence was only from her admission and could not be corroborated. Further, we could not prove that the visit had caused the bird to desert. It may well have done, especially in the early stages of incubation, but that could not be proved beyond reasonable doubt. Who was to say that the bird had not collided with a power line or had died from some other accident or natural cause. A case must be proved beyond reasonable doubt. An element of doubt still remained.

The conclusion was unsatisfactory and the Scottish Gamekeepers' Association members were still not convinced. I could understand their doubts but I'm not sure even yet if I ever managed to allay their suspicions about everyone being treated equally. I'm glad that we did eventually investigate the incident and submit a report to the procurator fiscal. The fiscal had taken the same view as I did and my conscience was clear.

CHAPTER 35

Cases of Cruelty

Cases of animal cruelty are all too common, with Yorkshire terriers and hedgehogs being among the victims.

For some reason cruelty offences seem more commonly associated with city rather than rural areas or even smaller towns and villages. Though many of the incidences of cruelty are not towards wild animals I nevertheless monitor anything that has to do with animals, since it is an aspect of policing with which most officers are not too familiar. This is hardly surprising as there is such a vast amount of legislation of which police officers must at least have a working knowledge. Many pieces of legislation or parts of Common Law are used by officers almost on a daily basis, and through familiarity they deal with these crimes or offences with ease. There are other statutes in which the police receive considerable training, even though they may not deal with breaches of the statute very often. I suppose the best examples are laws pertaining to betting, gaming and lotteries, licensing laws and many of the traffic laws. The preponderance of investigations – in Scotland at any rate – take place under Common Law, which certainly simplify matters as there are considerable, standard, powers to deal with suspects. Cruelty offences, however, are under statute, the now almost completely revoked legislation – the Protection of Animals (Scotland) Act 1912 – brought into more modern times with the passing by the Scottish parliament in October 2006 of the Animal Health and Welfare (Scotland) Act 2006.

There seem to be three categories of people that are involved in cruelty; those that are drunk, those that appear just to be wicked, and lastly young people. It amazes me how many calls come in to the police control room to the effect that someone is being cruel to a dog. Reports of dogs on leads being kicked or beaten by the person in charge of them are unfortunately all too common, the most recent being a report in late 2006 of a man in Dundee badly kicking his Yorkshire terrier. The man had disappeared by the time the police arrived at the scene but the officers were checking the camera trained on the users of a cash machine at a nearby bank to see if they could get his image. The amount of CCTV cameras in our midst is a concern to some, but they are a real boon to police officers investigating a whole range of crimes and offences from murder and terrorism to theft, vandalism and rowdyism to cruelty.

In a Perth cruelty incident in late 2005, police officers were investigating a common law crime (from memory I think it was a robbery) and discovered that a cruelty incident had also taken place. The accused person had set his two dogs on a cat, which ended up with them savaging the cat and killing it. As if to cover his tracks in setting the dogs on the cat, he pretended to onlookers that the dogs had escaped and that their fatal pursuit of the moggy was not of his doing. He grabbed the dogs by their collars, lifting them off the ground, and carried the struggling dogs into the house in that manner. By the time he had reached the house one of the unfortunate dogs had suffocated.

The man was arrested and appeared before the court from custody. As is often the case his eventual plea was to the common law crime and the procurator fiscal accepted a not guilty plea to the cruelty incidents. It is not unusual for a person not to want to be stigmatised as being cruel and willingly plead guilty to a charge with a greater penalty available to the court than that available for the cruelty offence. Though this helps to get the case through the court without a trial and the time associated with such proceedings, the unfortunate result of accepting a not guilty plea is that the person cannot be banned from keeping animals.

In a 2006 Dundee case, three youths picked an argument with a young man walking a dog, again a Yorkshire terrier. The argument became heated and resulted in the three youths kicking the wee terrier about the street. The terrier sustained near fatal injuries. With good veterinary treatment the dog pulled through but despite an extensive police investigation the three thugs were never traced. As the owner of two Yorkshire terriers myself I monitored this case and offered any assistance that was required. I would have given anything to trace these three cowards and can only imagine what it was like for the owner of the dog to witness such wanton cruelty to his pet.

Cruel acts cannot be assumed and must be proved. One example is a report I had in the Autumn of 2006 of a cat in Dundee having been poisoned. The owner of the cat was offering a reward for information that led to the conviction of the person who poisoned the cat. I was asked by our media relations people to give comment to the press on this incident but could find no trace of the incident having been reported to the police. It turned out that it had indeed been reported the day before I was asked for comment, but that the report had not been put on the computerised recording system. These things happen but of course it meant that I did not have prior knowledge of the incident, nor did I know the cat owner who had made the complaint.

The press were good enough to make contact with the cat owner and asked her to phone me, which she did the following day. It was a Saturday and I was working in my vegetable garden. Coincidentally I was cursing cats for digging in the newly-turned soil and wondered what I could do to prevent this happening the following Spring when I was sowing seeds. The cat owner explained that she had let her cat out at six in the morning and less than an hour later was told by a neighbour that it was lying dead in a pathway next to her garden, having been poisoned.

The cat owner was adamant that the cat had been poisoned. I could not blame her for her views as several cats had died mysteriously in that Dundee housing scheme and someone with a predilection for gardening and with a store of a particular liquid to ensure a car is kept mobile during cold winter days was being blamed. I am reticent in naming the commodity as it is frequently used in urban cat killing and I don't want to add to the reports of suspicious feline fatalities that we already have. I assured her that, even with a reward, we could not convict someone of killing her cat without (1) establishing how the cat had met its end, and (2) that the means of its death was illegal.

I asked if the cat was available for examination by a veterinary pathologist and was pleased to hear that it was buried in the garden rather than having been incinerated.

My colleague from SEERAD, Willie Milne, is well practised at exhuming dogs and cats. I decided to let him share this dubious privilege with a Divisional wildlife crime officer, Constable Helen Learmonth. The cat was exhumed and examined by a veterinary pathologist at the Scottish Agricultural College vet lab in Perth. The verbal report from the vet was that it was unlikely to have been poisoned as the post mortem findings were more consistent with being a road traffic victim, or, at worst, having received a very hard kick. At the start of the investigation, all of the indications were that the cat had been poisoned. By carrying out basic police work, poisoning had been eliminated and the chance of the cat dying from a criminal act was diminished considerably.

An examination by the same veterinary pathologist had saved a hunt for a maniacal cat killer in Pitlochry some months earlier. A cat had been found hanging by a rope from a tree and the press had reported that some cruel beast was on the loose in north Perthshire who appeared to get a kick out of killing cats by strangulation. The article was published before the veterinary post mortem showed that the cat had been dead before being strung up from the tree. Stringing a dead cat from a tree is maybe a pretty sick act but whoever carried this out had neither been cruel to the cat nor had broken the law.

In another incident a horse found dead in a field near Comrie in Perthshire was suspected of having been shot with a high powered rifle as what was thought to be an exit wound of a bullet was found on the belly of the horse. Rather than start an immediate search for a lunatic with a rifle I asked Professor Ranald Munro, a veterinary forensic pathologist at the Royal (Dick) Vet School, part of Edinburgh University, if he would attend at the field and carry out a post mortem examination of the horse. My thoughts at the time were that it would confirm or otherwise the suspected cause of death and might recover the bullet for ballistics examination. The post mortem result was a surprise but saved many hours of unnecessary police investigation. The horse – which was an excitable animal and prone to try to mount cattle in the same field, had fallen on top of a sharp object, probably a fencepost – possibly during one of its attempts to produce a horse/cow hybrid – and had been fatally stabbed.

Firing at animals and birds with a variety of weapons is unfortunately a regular occurrence, invariably carried out by youths. Having obtained a weapon – usually an air gun – they feel that they must test it out on something that is living so that they can observe the reaction to being struck by a pellet. Normally neighbours' cats or wildfowl on a pond are the targets. I have now x-rayed several swans, courtesy of Dundee Airport in allowing me the use of the x-ray facility normally reserved for passengers' luggage. The highest number of air gun pellets I have found in a single bird is seven. A swan is a big bird and is difficult to kill with a totally unsuitable weapon such as an air gun. From the position of the pellets in the body it is likely that the swan was still alive even after being hit several times and possibly died much later as a result of the injuries. In another case a duck was found with a bolt through its body. Scottish SPCA was contacted and took the duck away for veterinary treatment. Luckily the bolt missed the duck's vital organs and it survived. Despite a press release the culprit was never found.

Hedgehogs are one of the most common victims of cruelty, probably because they are so easily caught. In fact it was because of cruelty to hedgehogs in particular that the Wild Mammals Protection Act 1996 was enacted. Prior to this Act there was no legislation that covered cruelty to wild mammals unless they happened to be in captivity. The catalyst in the change in thinking resulted from an incident where boys were kicking hedgehogs about as if they were footballs. Hitherto this had not been an offence but in 1996 it was recognised that this behaviour was totally unacceptable. I'm just amazed it took until 1996.

I became aware of two hedgehog incidents around the same time in 2005, one in Dundee, the other in Perth. In each case the hedgehogs had been speared by teenagers – in the Perth case fairly senior teenagers. In Perth the people involved had been arrested over the weekend and charged with other crimes and were due to appear in court from custody on the Monday morning. I read the report and immediately looked at the list of items taken as productions in the case, hoping to see a dead hedgehog listed. No hedgehog. The hedgehog had not been taken as production. Normally I would have expected a note on my desk – or better still a call at home – to contact the arresting officer and organise to have the dead hedgehog examined. There is an easy defence in stating that the accused admitted spearing a hedgehog but that it was one that he had found dead. How can we prove otherwise if the police officer had not taken possession of the body of the hedgehog? It would be a fairly easy task for a veterinary pathologist to state that the hedgehog had been alive when it was speared and it was the instrument entering its body that had eventually caused its death. The Dundee case was little different. No hedgehog = no forensic evidence of cruelty = no case. Failing to take possession of the hedgehog's body was frustrating but I reminded myself that police officers cannot be expected to be specialists in all aspects of the wide variety of law with which they are expected to deal.

In a more recent case a Dundee primary school requested a talk to a particular class on wildlife crime as a means to educating the pupils and preventing crime committed against animals and birds. The reason for the request followed the discovery that two of the pupils had set a live hedgehog on fire. Sgt Andy Carroll, our Dundee wildlife crime officer, was delighted to agree: if it helped in any way to improve the kids' respect for animals, and consequently their fellow man, it was well worth while.

In Scotland, the procurator fiscal prosecutes on behalf of the public, as does the Crown Prosecution Service in England and Wales, and makes a decision based on a number of factors as to whether or not a case reported by the police should go to court. The main factors are: is there sufficient evidence to proceed and, if so, is the prosecution of the case in the public interest? A court then decides whether or not there is sufficient evidence for a finding of guilt against the person accused of the crime. In some more complex cases the police and the procurator fiscal might discuss the evidence before the procurator fiscal comes to a decision but that decision is the responsibility of the procurator fiscal. Police officers may have private thoughts if a case that they think is strong enough does not proceed to court or if, having gone to court, the verdict or the sentence is not what they would have expected. Thoughts or private discussions are as far as this dissent should go since the police officer, even having investigated and reported a case, might not always be privy to how the evidence is presented in court. I make this explanation in advance of the next case, which had a verdict slightly different to that which I had expected.

In May 2005, a number of witnesses saw a brood of young oystercatchers on a building site in Dundee. This is by no means uncommon, as piles of gravel or rubble on many urban building sites in Springtime tend to attract oystercatchers. The birds see these as a replica of their preferred nesting sites of gravely beaches or newly cultivated fields with an abundance of small stones. An oystercatcher lays its three eggs in an indentation it scrapes on the ground and lines with small pebbles. This may seem a rough and ready nest but in effect the eggs are extremely well camouflaged in this sort of terrain. Most ground-nesting birds tend to rely on camouflage for their eggs. A large number are lost in any case to gulls and crows, but many more would be lost without the advantage of camouflage. A person walking past an oystercatcher's nest would be hard pressed to spot the eggs unless that person was actively looking for the nest.

The eggs and chicks of ground-nesting birds in urban situations are at huge risk therefore from foxes and cats as well as avian predators. They are also at risk from being flattened accidentally by ongoing building work. What they do not need is deliberate interference from workers on the site.

In fairness to the majority of construction workers once they either become aware or are made aware of the presence of ground-nesting birds, respect their space and do their best to allow them to hatch their eggs and rear their chicks in safety. There are many times now that I have drawn the attention of nesting oystercatchers to a site foreman, tactfully explained the law and receiving the most sincere assurances that the nest will be left undisturbed. In the main the promises are kept and the birds eventually fledge a number of young.

In one incident on a building site, one of the labourers was seen by witnesses dropping a half breeze block on top of young oystercatchers. According to the witnesses the man had killed two oystercatchers though only one was subsequently recovered by the police officer who attended and carried out the initial investigation. The man was charged with killing a wild bird, under the Wildlife and Countryside Act 1981 rather than a cruelty charge under the Protection of Animals (Scotland) Act 1912. I liaised with the reporting officer and took the dead oystercatcher to Professor Ranald Munro for a veterinary examination. The conclusion was that the bird had sustained extensive injuries on one side that would be consistent with having a heavy object dropped on it. What I was also seeking from Ranald was evidence that the bird was absolutely healthy, with no broken leg or suchlike, before the labourer dropped a lump of concrete on top of it. Unfortunately because of the damage to the bird it was impossible for Ranald to come to this conclusion.

A date was set for trial but at the last minute the defence asked for an adjournment so that an examination could be carried out on the bird by a veterinary pathologist acting on behalf of the defence. I learned about this from the procurator fiscal and decided to get the bird ready at the top of the freezer awaiting the visit from another veterinary pathologist, probably from Glasgow University. The freezer I use is a large chest freezer which is situated in a building at Perth Police Station that also houses the generator that drives a number of heating and other electrical systems in the complex. The generator is deafening and bursts into life when you are least expecting it. I hate going in to that building. If it is silent I try to sneak in, get what I am looking for and leave quickly before the damn thing comes to life. Inevitably I have my head buried in the freezer and I jump out of my skin when the infernal racket starts up. The generator seems to have an ambition never to let me in to the building without exploding into its thunderous laughter just when I think I have, for once, sneaked in without it noticing.

The ordeal with the generator paled into insignificance when I couldn't find the dead oystercatcher in the freezer. I had everything couped out on the floor; otter, wildcat, buzzards, hares, peregrines, barn owl, rabbits, pheasants and many more beasties. No oystercatcher. I had got rid of several dead animals and birds a few weeks before from cases that had been through the courts. I remembered one of the birds was a collared dove that had been shot by a teenager. I seldom remember my specs when I go to the freezer so can't read the labels tied to the bags. In these circumstances I rely on my memory of cases together with the size of the carcass in the polythene bag. Had I got rid of a collared dove or had I got rid of a bird of about the same size, a young oystercatcher? The generator roared in my ear again but I was now oblivious. I double-checked everything as I put them back in the freezer. Still no oystercatcher.

Failing to be able to produce the oystercatcher for examination by the defence would be the end of the case. I decided to say nothing in the meantime. There was certainly no point in letting the fiscal know at this stage as he would be obliged to desert the case. Time enough to let him know if and when I was approached by the defence for the examination they were seeking. I had seen a similar sort of defence ploy before: playing for time with no real intention of having any follow up.

As time went on with no contact from the defence I became a bit more confident. There was even the advantage that the accused might be obliged to plead guilty otherwise his defence would have to explain why he had asked for an adjournment and did nothing about an independent examination of the bird. Days and weeks passed and two weeks from the trial I was sure that no examination would be called for at that late stage. I intended to let the fiscal know a couple of days before the trial that I had lost the oystercatcher as I reckoned by that time he, also, would be sure of a guilty plea. By chance I met Professor Ranald Munro at an evening event in Edinburgh and we spoke of the forthcoming trial. I confided in Ranald that I had somehow managed to throw out the main production in the case, the dead bird. 'No you haven't, Alan, I've got it in my freezer at the Royal (Dick) Vet School. I was going to bring it on the day of the trial as I always do with productions.' I was flabbergasted. And relieved. I had no recollection of leaving the bird with Ranald and would have put money on having taken it back to Perth with me. I was glad I had held my nerve and kept my head down.

On the day of the trial all the witnesses turned up at Dundee

Sheriff Court. The accused pleaded guilty and his solicitor convinced the sheriff that he had killed the bird out of a misplaced sense of mercy, believing that the bird was unwell. He was convicted but admonished, in other words there was no penalty levied against him. Though I am seldom annoyed at a sheriff's decision – after all that is his role and I have already played my investigative part – I was a bit surprised that he had believed the defence line in this case. What made me furious was the fact that all the witnesses in the case had turned up for court, almost a year from the date of the incident, and it had taken all that time for the accused to decide that he was guilty. Eight witnesses were inconvenienced and had waited two hours in stuffy witness rooms. In the circumstances I would far rather the case had gone to trial and all the facts been allowed to come out. I suspect that the outcome of the case would have been substantially different.

•

One of the most regular animal-related complaints to the police is that of dogs either attacking humans or attacking pets, most often other dogs. As a dog owner it infuriates me when I see a person walking a dog that is not under control. I am of the firm view that no dog should be walked on a road unless it is on a lead. There is a real risk that even the best trained dog might suddenly run across a road to greet another dog, even another human that it recognises, and is struck by a vehicle. It is also a pet hate of mine to see a large dog, such as an alsatian, dobermann or rottweiler either off the lead in a public place or, equally as bad, on a lead but in the 'control' of a young person that it could easily pull off his or her feet if it felt the need to do so. Small dogs may be yappy wee mites but they do not have the potential to kill or injure as do large dogs. The outcome is unfortunately often a kid or a smaller dog being savaged, and all totally needlessly.

The law in relation to dangerous dogs – in fact the law in relation to all dog offences – is either archaic or, in the case of the Dangerous Dogs Act 1991, a botched and rushed reaction to the threat from pit bull terriers and other potentially dangerous dogs such as the Japanese toza, the *dogo Argentino* and the *fila Braziliero*. The legislation that deals with dogs out of control and attacking people or other animals is the Dogs Act 1871. That is 1871, not 1971. When a person is charged under this Act no penalty can be imposed by the court. A person cannot be fined £200 for being in possession of a dog that attacks someone; the person can only be ordered by the court to keep the dog under proper control. Failure to do so may lead to the court ordering that the dog be destroyed. In fairness, when an owner is ordered to keep a dog under control that is in most cases what happens. Nevertheless if a penalty were to be available, and this fact widely known, it could make dog owners more responsible. Attacks on humans or other animals by dogs demonstrate a failing on the part of the owner, not the dog.

In a variation on this type of incident a man regularly walked his Alsatian, off the lead, through woodlands on the outskirts of Crieff in Perthshire. The dog, according to a local gamekeeper, ranged about through the wood, causing him to have words with the dog owner. The dog owner stated that the dog liked chasing things. This is completely unacceptable. Even before the Land Reform Act there was little to prevent access to the countryside in Scotland but the Land Reform Act sought to encourage *responsible* access. A code of conduct was drawn up that allowed access with dogs *under control*. This does not mean that all dogs have to be on a lead but it does mean that they must be able to be controlled, in other words have a degree of training that makes them respond to particular commands and to remain within a reasonable distance of the person walking them. On the same Crieff estate, on an autumn day in 2001, I watched a large black dog one day on the other side of the loch from where I was, chasing a blackfaced ewe. The dog was at least five hundred yards from its handler, who was shouting at the dog for all he was worth. The dog paid no attention and was intent on its own mission. It maybe lacked the stamina of the ewe and eventually gave up but the ewe finished up at the lochside and I was surprised that it did not take to the water. In January 2007, at exactly the same spot, a woman was charged after her two dogs chased two sheep into the loch, where they drowned, and killed another that failed to make it to the lochside. This is totally unacceptable.

In the case of the Alsatian, the gamekeeper was driving through one of the woods in the summer of 2006 when he encountered the Alsatian tearing at a young roe buck that was upside down in a ditch. The buck was squealing in distress while the dog savagely ate at its hindquarters. Had the gamekeeper been carrying his shotgun I'm sure that (wrongly in law but probably morally defensible) he would have shot the dog. As it was the dog ran off when the keeper got out of his vehicle, leaving the keeper no option but to cut the throat of the deer to put it out of its misery.

Shortly after the incident I saw and photographed the deer. It was in a terrible mess, with a large part of its haunch torn open and rips on its sides where the dog had tried to bring it down. I went to the wood with the keeper and we could see exactly what had happened by reading the signs. The deer had been chased down a steep hill right towards a deer fence. It had run straight in to the deer fence, causing a large dent in the netting and accounting for the extensive damage to its antlers – at that time in velvet and particularly sensitive. The deer had turned right and had tried to get through the deer fence again, this time being caught by the dog. The evidence was the dent in the fence and the large tufts of hair on the ground. The deer was unfortunately committed then to run down a track with a deer fence on either side. There was no escape and it was clear from the tufts of hair that the dog was mauling it all the way down the track. At the bottom of the track it turned left, still between two deer fences, and it was a further two hundred metres down this track that the keeper eventually found it being worried by the Alsatian.

A few days later, along with one of the divisional wildlife crime officers, Constable Dave Elliot, I visited the owner of the dog to charge him with this offence under the Dogs Act 1871. We asked to see the dog and, within the house, it turned out to be one of the friendliest Alsatians I have encountered. In a completely different context, loose in a wood with a fleeing animal, it was a savage killer. Had it encountered a child at any stage of its pursuit I wonder what might have happened. This incident reinforced my view that, when outwith their home environment, as well as being *under control,* dogs must be *controllable.*

Chapter 36

The Case of Oeuf and Poodle

Egg thieves cease or adapt their criminal behaviour in response to the success of Operation Easter but some just cannot resist the temptation.

By 2003 Operation Easter had bagged many of the UK's egg thieves. The risk of being caught and sent to prison was real and had them exactly where we wanted them. We never for moment thought that all egg collectors would give up. That was tantamount to imagining that when legislation relating to the carrying of knives in public places was tightened up, everyone who had by habit carried a knife would leave it in the kitchen drawer. The more timid give up; those that are less timid – which maybe equates to the more stupid – adapt or continue to offend. In the case of egg collectors this meant that the really stupid continued as before and ran the associated risks. Some adapted and went abroad to collect eggs, to countries where the police are less vigilant in bringing egg thieves to book, and some substituted the taking of eggs from nests for the taking of photographs of eggs in nests.

We were aware of many nest finders already. These were birding enthusiasts who sought out nests and photographed the eggs *in situ*. There is nothing wrong with this, and certainly nothing illegal about this practice, provided the rarer and more vulnerable birds included in Schedule 1 of the Wildlife and Countryside Act 1981 were not included in their list. Intelligence, often gleaned from egg collectors who had been caught, showed that some former egg collectors became nest finders. This was an improvement on their previous 'hobby' and perfectly acceptable if they kept their attentions away from the protected Schedule 1 birds. Forty years of policing had made me slightly sceptical but I was pleased that intelligence showed that some egg collectors seemed to be following the straight and narrow path. The converse was true of one or two others; they were still so obsessed with rare birds that they were clearly continuing to visit nests, with or without a camera.

A particular golden eagle eyrie in north Perthshire was especially pestered by nest finders' attentions. In fairness to those involved there was never a suspicion that they were there to take the eggs of the majestic bird but their actions were equally illegal and potentially as damaging to the breeding success of the birds. In 2003 a number of men from central England visited the nest in early June. We will call the leader of this group Mr Oeuf, French for egg but a word close enough to oaf. In this case the eggs had hatched so I was satisfied that there was no intent to have taken the eggs. Evidence unfolded that they had picnicked under the nest, in full knowledge of the presence of the nest and of the parent eagles soaring above. They had also videoed the nest – and their picnic – erstwhile describing what was happening above for future beneficiaries of their irresponsible adventure. Even folks from the non-birding world would have the wit to eschew this activity, knowing that the adult birds were distressed.

Two of those involved, one being Mr Oeuf, had come to the attention of Operation Easter in June 2003 when they were seen acting suspiciously on the Wilden Marshes bird reserve near Kidderminster. They were in the midst of a colony of nesting little terns and the witness thought that they were taking the birds' eggs. This backed up other intelligence that even before 2003 had brought these men to the attention of the police in connection with nesting birds. As a result of this surreptitious activity, police wildlife crime officers, assisted by RSPB investigations staff, searched the houses of the men involved and recovered a number of photographs and video tapes. This evidence implicated the two – plus a further two men – in the Tayside golden eagle nest disturbance. It also involved them in the disturbance of a nesting white-tailed eagle on Mull, and particularly irresponsible disturbance of a dotterel, another Schedule 1 bird, in Perthshire. During this escapade Mr Oaf – sorry Oeuf – and the others had filmed themselves at the nest in the rain over a period of forty minutes. This may well have been enough to chill the eggs and prevent them hatching.

The other two men were traced and all pleaded guilty and were sentenced at Redditch Magistrates Court. Sentence was deferred on Mr Oeuf and friend while the other two men involved were fined £1000 with £750 costs and £2000 with £750 costs respectively. When the case was recalled for the sentencing of Mr Oeuf and friend a month or so later, each was fined £1000 plus £1000 costs, and also sentenced to six week's imprisonment, to be suspended for two years. It was a good result.

Just prior to the men appearing at Redditch Magistrates Court I received intelligence that Mr Oeuf and others were intending to visit north Perthshire again in 2004 on a further bird watching holiday. I circulated this to all police forces in Scotland and arranged a special lookout by Tayside Police officers for the vehicles they used. We had particular concerns since the intelligence was to the effect that they were to be staying in rented accommodation a few miles from the eagles' eyrie they had so wantonly disturbed by their 2003 picnic. The informant indicated that the men were adamant it was their right to look at birds and that they intended them no harm. They intended to apply the law the way that suited them.

There had been no sign of any of their vehicles by the Friday of that week and on the Friday I took a run round the area as I knew many of the places they were likely to visit. I was in luck and found one of their cars parked at the roadside, albeit about five or six miles as the crow flies from the golden eagle nesting site. I watched the car for an hour but since no-one appeared I requested the local officers to keep tabs on it whenever they could during the rest of the afternoon. This was one of the far-flung outposts of Perthshire and I doubted the car would receive much attention because of the distance the officers would have to travel.

I discovered the following day that the car had still not moved by 4.30 pm that day. There was another bit of interesting news: the previous day the car had been seen by the local police officers and it had been stopped for a check. Though nothing was found the officers were able to confirm that the occupants of the car were Mr Oeuf and friend, two of the men involved in the golden eagle disturbance the previous year. I made contact with the local gamekeeper and learned from him that he had spoken to five people with English accents in the middle of the week and had met two of them again on the day I saw their car parked at the roadside. From the description given by the keeper one of the two men fitted the description of Mr Oeuf, the registered keeper of the car. Later investigation revealed that the second person was previously unknown to us and was from Staffordshire. I'll call him Mr Poodle. I know that it should be Mr Terrier from Staffordshire but he was not a strong enough character for a terrier so Mr Poodle it is. Mr Oeuf and Mr Poodle had been particularly interested in a tree-nesting merlin – a Schedule 1 bird – on the estate and had mentioned to the keeper that they had seen eggs in the nest. This meant that they had either climbed to the nest or had been close enough to see into it. In either case this action almost certainly disturbed the nesting merlins. This was an offence and certainly an irresponsible action for any experienced birdwatcher to have undertaken.

To complete the investigation I submitted a report to the procurator fiscal requesting warrants to search the houses of the only two out of the five people who had been identified – Oeuf and Poodle. Constable Sally Hughes, one of the divisional wildlife crime officers, went before the sheriff to clarify any points not included in the warrant application. The sheriff was satisfied with the evidence we had presented to him and he granted both warrants. Once these warrants had also been signed by a magistrate from the area in England in which the suspects resided this gave the police officers the equivalent powers of search that they would have had in Scotland. This meant that in effect the searches, and any subsequent action following on from the searches, were being carried out in England but under Scottish law. As in any search warrant granted under the Wildlife and Countryside Act 1981 the police could take other nominated persons with them on the search to offer advice. The warrants therefore authorised Constable Sally Hughes and any other officer of Tayside Police, along with officers of West Midlands Police and Staffordshire Police plus investigations staff from the Royal Society for the

Protection of Birds. At each of the two addresses a Tayside police officer, a police officer from the force in which the suspect's address was situated and an RSPB investigations officer would attend.

It was suspected that Oeuf and Poodle, as they did in their previous visits to Schedule 1 birds, would have taken photographs. The purpose of the search was to uncover anything that would point to their guilt, and photographs or video footage would be ideal. As with egg thieves, any recovery of marked maps and diaries could be equally incriminating. The officers did not have a lot of luck in the search, and although one or two items were seized, there was almost nothing recovered by way of damning physical evidence or even evidence that might be helpful to the prosecution case. Exceptions were a diary that Mr Oeuf had tried to hide in the bathroom of the house and a diary with obliterated entries found at Mr Poodle's house. Oeuf's diary had dates of his visit to Perthshire and abbreviations for the merlin activity he observed (which he later disputed in court) though Poodle's diary did not lend much support. Everything mainly depended on the interviews under caution if either of the men was to be charged.

With any complex interview there has to be an element of planning. It is absolutely true that failing to plan equates to planning to fail. In an interview it is always good to set the scene, to try to establish who was present at the time of the offence and if possible to find out who was doing what. In any charge the various elements have to be proved beyond reasonable doubt so questions need to be built in to the interview to try to establish these facts. In this case we had to establish that the birds were merlin, that they were Schedule 1 birds; that the suspects did not have a licence issued by Scottish Natural Heritage to allow them for any purpose to disturb the birds while nesting, that indeed they did disturb the birds, and that they did so intentionally. The questions were designed to elicit these details.

There was an admission by both Oeuf and Poodle that they had been at the merlin nest site and that the two parent birds had been flying around close to the nest while the men were there This was a good start as this tended to show disturbance of the nesting birds. Nesting birds try to keep as low a profile as possible so as not to draw attention to their nest. Where they digress from this conduct is when the nest is threatened and they try to mob the intruder in a display of aggression or, in the case of more timid birds, fly around in a panic. There was also an admission by the men that they had been bird watchers for many years and that they were aware that Schedule 1 birds, while nesting, could not legally be disturbed without a licence. I think this admission was very important and I'm not sure if its full import was either made clear to the court, or if it was, if the evidential value of this statement was realised. Neither man admitted in interview to seeing eggs in the merlin nest though they did admit to climbing up the side of the hill to get a better view of the nest. The distance they were from the tree nest at different times was established and, from the prosecution point of view, seemed to be within the proximity at which the parent bird or birds would be disturbed.

Mr Poodle then came out with a bombshell: twice during the week they were in north Perthshire they had visited the golden eagle tree nest which led to the earlier conviction of one of them.

Naturally the officers needed more details of this admission as it was obvious that the nesting golden eagles may also have been disturbed. On the first visit the nest tree had been approached to within about 150 metres. This was far too close and the duties of the eagle on guard either at or near the nest would have been interrupted and it would have left while the men were still more than a quarter of a mile away. Note the word *interrupted.*

I was acquainted with this nest and had in fact visited it along with eagle experts about the same time of year in 2006, a year in which it was suspected that egg collectors from Merseyside had taken the clutch of eggs. With its vision many times better than that of a human, the eagle spotted us and left the nest when we were at least a quarter of a mile away. This of course was a good sign as it indicated that the nest was okay. Indeed it was and we could see a single chick on the nest from probably the exact spot that the suspect was describing in his interview.

Mr Poodle told the officers that on the second visit the two had approached the nest from the right hand side rather than the left hand side and had gone further up the hill to get a good view of the eagle. On this occasion he said that one eagle was soaring in the sky and the other was on the nest trying to shelter the two chicks from the rain. This was very interesting from my point of view as I didn't think that an eagle would remain on a nest while it could see humans in the vicinity. Dave Dick, senior investigations officer of RSPB Scotland, a golden eagle expert, told me that in adverse weather conditions the eagle would be torn between leaving the nest to get away from and to keep watch on the people in the vicinity, and remaining to keep the chicks dry and warm in the rain. To me the eagle would be disturbed by this dilemma and the action of our suspects was irresponsible. It really does not take an expert in rare birds to realise that a bird is disturbed when it is flushed from its nest or kept off its nest. Almost everyone will have seen this in their garden when they have accidentally disturbed a nesting blackbird, robin or some other common garden bird from its nest. The parent chatters annoyance at the person who has disturbed it and very often keeps this up until it can return to its nest again. A common garden bird when put off its nest is just as disturbed as rare birds like golden eagles and merlin; it is just that it is not against the law to disturb them while they are nesting. Common sense dictates that the *intrusion* of these visits close to a nest must cause all of these birds *worry or concern*. Again note these terms.

When, under caution, the two visits to the golden eagle nest were put to Mr Oeuf he by and large agreed with Poodle's version. What was interesting of the two suspects in a perverse sort of way was that they were adamant they were not disturbing the birds. I don't doubt at all that their intention was not to harm the birds but they had demonstrated irresponsible and reckless behaviour, especially on the inclement day they visited the eagle. It was not even as if the birds could differentiate between the two suspects and egg thieves or from someone who was intent on harming them.

By the end of the interviews it was clear that Mr Oeuf had played much more of a 'leading' role, while Mr Poodle was more of a 'follower'. It was therefore decided to charge the 'leader' and to use the 'follower' as a witness. The evidence against Mr Oeuf consisted of his admissions under caution plus the evidence of his erstwhile colleague. He was charged with intentional disturbance of a nesting merlin and two charges of intentional disturbance of a nesting golden eagle.

The offences took place in June of 2004, just prior to the provisions of the Nature Conservation (Scotland) Act 2004 becoming law in October of that year. One of the main changes in law was that, had the offence been committed after the enacting of the new legislation, the offence would have been intention *or reckless* disturbance. To prove an act has been committed intentionally is extremely difficult but that was the wording of the law at that time and that was the difficulty that faced us. I would have had confidence in our accused being convicted of *reckless* disturbance but that wasn't yet an option.

The trial took place in the late summer of 2006. Two days of prosecution evidence were heard by the court and at the conclusion the defence put forward a submission that there was no case to answer. I had given evidence and was in court at this point. My thoughts were that the sheriff had listened intently to the complicated and unusual case. It may even have been a welcome change for him from the humdrum breaches of the peace and petty thefts to which he would have been much more used to listening. He wanted some time to reconsider the evidence before coming to a conclusion on the defence submission. Two days in October were set aside for the defence evidence but the sheriff stated that he would have made his mind up long before that time and if he agreed with the defence solicitor that there was no case to answer neither the accused nor his defence witnesses need make the return journey to Perth.

We have had many difficulties in the past with the term 'intentionally' and I doubted that the case would survive to the next stage. The sheriff had no case law to work from and I was sure that he would concur with the defence. Equally I thought that, if the sheriff happened to repel the defence motion, we would gain a conviction. I had the advantage of knowing the background and the previous conviction of the accused. In the UK justice system the sheriff can not have this benefit. The law states that previous findings of guilt must not be made known to a sheriff and that the sheriff must treat all accused as first offenders, using the evidence that is presented during the trial to make judgement. The theory is sound but I'm not clear how this works in practice when regular offenders appear in front of the same sheriff time and time again, often being sentenced for a crime one week and appearing as a 'first offender' in another crime the following week. Nevertheless, with few exceptions, the justice meted out by sheriffs is balanced, considered and fair.

A few weeks later I learned from the procurator fiscal that the sheriff had repelled the defence motion of 'no case to answer' and we were in business again. I attended court just in time to hear the last half hour of the two-day defence evidence and was not convinced at all by their 'expert', in fact I thought he was one of the worst 'experts' to whom I had listened. The summing up by the procurator fiscal and the defence, and the verdict by the sheriff was adjourned till a later date as there was insufficient court time left that day to conclude the case.

The summing up took place on 15 November 2006. The summing up from the procurator fiscal lasted an hour and the summing up from the defence was not much less. I can't recall having heard such a lengthy summing up in a summary trial, though addresses of this length are by no means unusual in Sheriff and Jury or High Court trials. Each address to the sheriff encapsulated the main evidence from the witnesses, picking out the valid points so far as they might benefit their particular side of the case. The fiscal ensured that he showed from each witness's evidence how the actions of the accused affected and disturbed the birds – either the golden eagles or the merlins. He also tried to demonstrate that the disturbance was intentional, which in essence was the crux of the case. None of us had any doubt that this single word, intentional, would make or break this case.

The other major difficulty in this trial was the evidence of Mr Poodle, who had been interviewed under caution by the Scottish police officers during the part of the investigation that took them to the Midlands of England. His evidence was the main corroboration of the actions with which Mr Oeuf was charged. He had been much more vague and elusive in giving his evidence in court than he had been when interviewed by the police in 2004. The fiscal made comment on this and put forward the view to the court that some of the time he had been lying. I wasn't sure if this was a good move. Mr Poodle was our star witness and I worried a bit about the fiscal trying to discredit parts of his evidence. I had to trust the fiscal's judgement as I had not been in court to hear the evidence since at that time I still had to give my own evidence and was languishing in one of the stuffy – but thankfully now smoke-free – witness rooms. The fiscal rubbished the evidence of the defence expert, Peter Robinson, formerly of RSPB Investigations though he worked much more on the administrative than practical side, and whose experience of golden eagles in particular was minimal. He also urged the court to accept the evidence of the expert for the prosecution, Dave Dick, RSPB Scotland senior investigations officer based in Edinburgh whose practical experience of golden eagles would be as good as that of anyone in Scotland.

The defence lawyer put forward some good arguments against conviction, again going over the evidence of the various witnesses and putting forward points of view that were in opposition to those of the fiscal. I thought he may have capitalised on the fact that the fiscal referred to the main prosecution witness, Mr Poodle, as a liar, though he did not. My thoughts were that if the fiscal was accusing him of lying while giving evidence, could he not justifiably be accused of lying about the very damning admissions he gave to the police during the 2004 interview, admissions which were led as evidence in court – as they were entitled to be – by the interviewing police officers.

The defence also made much of the interpretation of the term 'intentional.' At times he did not deny that the conduct of Mr Oeuf may have been reckless, but recklessness was not a concept that could be considered in this trial as it was not incorporated into the legislation until 1 October 2004, four months after the date to which the charges related. The defence also made reference to a similar set of charges in a trial in England where most of the charges resulted in a Not Guilty verdict. The magistrate in the trial had difficulty with the terms 'intentionally' and 'disturbance', though he appeared reticent in making helpful definitions that may have assisted other cases. The defence solicitor omitted the fact that there had been a guilty verdict on one of the charges but I was not bothered as the sheriff had a copy of the case and by this time would have been much more familiar with it than I was.

The defence also read out the dictionary definition of the verb 'disturb'; I thought it would do his case no good.

To intrude on. There was no doubt there was intrusion on the birds since the prying eyes of the accused and the star witness were at most within 100 metres of the nests.

Interrupt. When the accused had been in the vicinity of the merlin nest the male and female merlin were flying around the nest. They had been interrupted from their hunting for food and the incubation of the chicks.

To worry or cause concern. These terms applied to the merlin, and almost certainly to the golden eagle trying to shelter its chick in the rain while human onlookers were present. The golden eagle, with more than a century of persecution, must see all humans as posing a danger: it cannot differentiate between someone who may want to shoot it or someone who may just want to look at it. Though the defence had brought out these definitions I'm sure that the sheriff had at some stage of the trial consulted his dictionary and had come to the same conclusion without the assistance of the defence.

The sheriff adjourned the court for fifteen minutes so that he could gather his thoughts together. I was sitting beside Dave Dick in court and discussed the various aspects of the evidence with him. Neither of us was convinced there would be a guilty verdict.

The sheriff re-entered the court and we all rose in deference. In his address he described the differences between the first charge, that of intentional disturbance of nesting merlins, and charges 2 and 3 those of intentional disturbance of nesting golden eagles. The merlins had suffered the more serious disturbance but he agreed that in all three instances – all three charges – the birds had been disturbed. So far so good. The sheriff next pontificated on the term 'intentional'. He stated that he had no doubt that Mr Oeuf had not intended any harm to come to the birds, and indeed the birds seemed to have fledged chicks successfully that year, though that fact was incidental and had no bearing on the charge. His view was that for the disturbance to have been intentional it had to be demonstrated that the accused had knowledge before he went to the nest sites that the outcome of his visit would be the disturbance of the birds. He had not been satisfied by the evidence that Mr Oeuf was aware of what the outcome would be and had decided to find the accused Not Proven on each of the three charges.

For those who are not used to criminal investigations and court procedure it may seem that this was a disappointing result. Though I would much rather have had a finding of guilty – even to one of the charges – I was nevertheless pleased with the verdict. I felt that a Not Proven verdict had vindicated the effort we as the police, and indeed the procurator fiscal, had put in to this case. Though Not Proven as a verdict is not a conviction, neither is it a clear cut exoneration of the offence charged. It is a unique Scottish verdict that leaves an element of doubt hanging over the actions of the accused. I was also pleased that after delivering the verdict the sheriff advised the defence agent that if the law at the time of the investigation was as it is now, with the option of *reckless* disturbance, the verdict may have been substantially different and that he should advise Mr Oeuf accordingly.

The case has clarified in my mind, and in that of Dave Dick, what constitutes 'disturbance' to a nesting schedule 1 bird. Undoubtedly this will assist in further enquiries of this kind. Police wildlife crime officers have battled with the problems of the almost impossible proof of an 'intentional' act since 1982. These difficult times are behind us, a fact partly due to the work of Dave Dick and I who as members of the PAW Legislative Working Group researched, debated and provided practical and common sense grounds for many changes in wildlife law. I look forward to the next disturbance case when the public interest is more evenly balanced in relation to the interests of a person accused.

•

An easier bird-related case to prove was one of offering of birds' eggs for sale. Many people still have old egg collections and it is not an offence to hang on to them or even give them away provided the eggs were taken before 1954, the date that the Protection of Birds Act came into force. It is an offence to sell an egg collection or to offer it for sale. This fact was clearly known to a man who phoned me one Monday morning.

The man had been at a car boot sale the previous day and had seen a smallish egg collection being offered for sale at one of the stalls. 'There's about thirty eggs in a box,' he said 'and a £30 price tag beside it.' I told him I would get someone to have a look the following Sunday and began to ask directions to the stall. It was obvious within seconds that I was talking to a man who wanted a deputy sheriff's badge to adorn his lapel. 'I can meet the officers and take them to the stall' was his suggestion. I hate car boot sales and had only been once at this one. It was huge and half an hour of it was enough for me: I left without making a purchase. Finding any particular stall would have been a piece of detective work in itself: it would have been like finding the centre point of a maze. I could see two easy options for finding the stall with the bargain pack of birds' eggs; if it had a blue flashing light and siren so that the officers could home in, or if Deputy Dawg took them to it. I opted for the latter and arranged a rendezvous point for the following Sunday.

Six days later our guide was as good as his word. He met the incognito officers, one of them Divisional wildlife crime officer Constable Davie Elliot, and took them to the stall. The eggs were still on display, a mediocre mix of fairly common wild birds' eggs but no sign of the vendor. As the officers studied the eggshells the stall owner appeared as if from nowhere. 'If you're interested they're only thirty quid,' he explained, 'it's a real bargain.' The officers identified themselves while Deputy Dawg merged into the crowd and continued his search for bargains or for an item on sale that could gain him a higher grade of deputy sheriff's badge. The eggs were seized and the stall owner was charged with offering wild birds' eggs for sale.

When I heard about the case the following day I thought it was a very straightforward case. I was not surprised that a not guilty plea was entered as everyone nowadays seems to plead not guilty. I *was* surprised when the case went to trial and wondered what defence the stall owner could have. The trial went ahead, with the accused defending himself – often quite a good strategy as there is always considerable help from the sheriff. In this particular case the accused was maintaining that the eggs were taken before 1982, the year the Wildlife and Countryside Act 1981 became enforceable. Though some of the eggs looked slightly newer than the rest, none of the prosecution witnesses was in a position to say categorically that they must have been taken post 1982. It mattered not a jot in any case: the offence was in offering the eggs for sale. Whether the eggs had been taken in the year 2000, 1900 or even 1800 the offence was the same.

I felt a bit sorry for the stall holder. As all of us gave our evidence his line of defence was the same, 'These are very old eggs, taken well before 1982.' None of us contested the point: it was a point which was irrelevant. He had either taken no legal advice before the case or the advice he had received was worse than useless. At the end of the trial the sheriff fined him £250. I was surprised at the level of the fine for offering 30 pretty run-of-the-mill eggs for sale but my job is to investigate wildlife crime, not to sentence those who are found guilty. Had he pleaded guilty at the outset, the fine would most likely have been a maximum of £200 as a reduction in penalty must be given by the court for a guilty plea. Having said that the potential fine could have been £5000 per egg, a total of £150,000!

CHAPTER 37

Some Short Cases

Not all reported cases involve protracted investigation as in the case of the suspected destruction of a red squirrel habitat and prisoners suspected of deer poaching.

Many of the wildlife cases we investigate take anything from a few days to several months from the point at which we are notified of the incident to the time that we have gained sufficient evidence to put a case to the fiscal. Many more incidents are dealt with within an hour or at most a couple of days. There are a variety of outcomes. In some cases there is evidence enough either to submit a report to the procurator fiscal or to warn the person responsible. In others a crime has clearly been committed but no evidence can be found to identify the culprit. In one or two cases it is suspected that a crime has been committed but there is no evidence to substantiate a crime. Here are several short examples that fall in to one or other of these categories and take comparatively little time to deal with

I had an unusual telephone call from an open prison one day. Deer poachers had been active in the area around the prison, except that they were deer poachers with a difference: they were inmates of the prison. Prisoners sometimes get items that we take for granted outside prison walls but might be considered to be luxuries to the inmates. On this occasion they had a barbeque to help pass the time. I can imagine that a barbeque would certainly pass the time. I have had several experiences with barbeques and more time seems to be spent on trying to get the damn things alight and thence to the correct temperature before anything remotely culinary can take place. I always seem to have plenty smoke and a distinct lack of heat. My contact at the jail told me that the entrepreneurial convicts may have wanted to choose their own food to cook and had hit on the idea of fresh venison. A roe deer had already been caught in a snare and there were several other snares awaiting an equally mouth-watering victim.

I attended at the jail, which happened to be the first open prison I had visited. I was surprised at the freedom the prisoners seemed to have to wander around almost at will but I was advised – though not necessarily convinced – that on the scale of convicted baddies they were somewhere near the bottom rung of the ladder.

My contact at the jail took me into a young plantation near to the prison where he showed me several snares. They had been fashioned out of wire that was utilised for different farming jobs that the prisoners carried out and I was quite impressed with the design. Whoever had made them had made a small ring at one end so that the snare would tighten quickly around the neck of any beast that happened along and put its head through the noose. I was less impressed by where they had been set and the height at which they were placed off the ground. They were slightly more likely to catch a hare than a roe deer, but even a hare can be barbequed. Whatever my criticism of their technique they had already caught a roe deer so they must have been doing something right.

I took possession of about half a dozen snares, handling them carefully to avoid cross-contamination as I intended to submit them for DNA testing. The prison had a suspect and if I could get his DNA from the snares then the case was solved. I was not hopeful though as there had been heavy rain for a good few days prior to my collecting the snares and this was likely to have washed off any DNA. Nevertheless it was worth a try.

I submitted the snares for DNA testing along with the details of the suspect. Since the case was so unusual I don't think I have ever been more desperate to get a DNA hit but it was not to be. No DNA was available on the snares and this time the prisoner had escaped detection for his crime. I have kicked myself ever since this incident for not asking what the suspect was in jail for. It would have been ironic had it been for deer poaching!

•

In a case near Kinross in the year 2000 we learned of a trap in the form of a small cage set in a wood. The information available was that the cage belonged to a man who kept racing pigeons and had been trying to reduce the sparrowhawk population that, no doubt, were in turn reducing his racing pigeon stock. There is no doubt that sparrowhawks – at least the larger female – will take pigeons, and I have seen our resident sparrowhawks regularly take collared doves in my garden.

We visited the trap but it was not in the 'set' position and therefore unable to catch any sort of bird. One of the Divisional wildlife crime officers, Detective Sergeant Neil Macdonald, visited the trap periodically during his night shift but there was no change; the trap remained unset. There *was* a slight change one night: the trap had been moved into our suspect's garden adjacent to the wood and had been hidden under a cover.

Had this taken place now, the suspect would have been charged with possession of an item that he could have used to commit a crime against the Wildlife and Countryside Act 1981, but even in 2000 we were not so switched on and still in a steep learning curve. In effect the suspect had a visit from Detective Sergeant Macdonald. He received a warning for the possession of the trap and he relinquished ownership to the police. He said that he was giving up keeping racing pigeons in any case as he was losing too many to birds of prey.

The trap was well designed, probably because our suspect was a joiner. There was a bottom compartment in which a pigeon would be placed as a decoy to lure a bird of prey into the top compartment. The lid of the top compartment was held open by a T-shaped piece of wood, with the crossbar of the T designed to present a landing perch for the victim. When a bird landed on this perch the whole T-shaped piece of wood fell into the trap along with the bird and the top-mounted door fell down, preventing any escape.

The unusual aspect of this trap was that it was not a spring trap, which would have required government approval. It simply – and cleverly – operated by gravity. The trap fell outwith the definition of a Larsen trap but could have been termed a 'cage trap' since that is not defined. Had a dead rabbit or pigeon, or some eggs been placed in the bottom compartment of the trap it may well have lured in a crow or a magpie, an activity that would not have been illegal. The separate bottom compartment was the giveaway; it was designed to hold live bait such as a pigeon or sparrow which in turn would have lured in a bird of prey and in effect made the trap illegal.

The interpretation of legislation has always fascinated me, and none moreso that wildlife legislation. There is very little wildlife crime case law, where a sheriff's interpretation of the law has been given consideration by one or more High Court judges. There *are* one or two reported cases outlining why a sheriff has come to a particular decision in a case, though a sheriff in another court with a similar case may well come to different conclusion. Despite these vagaries, I am still firmly of the view that in Scotland we have a fair and competent justice system leaving little room for a miscarriage.

To exemplify the fairness and the consultation in relation to prosecutions in Scotland I have just had a telephone call from the procurator fiscal in relation to a case submitted. The case related to the possession by a career criminal of a young buzzard. The buzzard was about twelve weeks old and by its screeching for food was obviously imprinted on its human 'parent'. The excuse for the possession of the bird was that he had found it on the ground, possibly having, he claimed, fallen out of the nest. My view at the time was that this was unlikely, though for the purposes of the court it was always a slight possibility. It was much more likely that a person had climbed up and removed the chick from the nest before its eyes opened. The chick was in fairly poor condition, not having been fed on a proper diet of meat, fur, bones and feathers, but simply fed dog or cat food. Because of the poor diet its bones – especially leg bones – were not well formed and the bird was not suitable for release to the wild.

We had charged the person with possessing a wild bird, contrary to the Wildlife and Countryside Act 1981. There is a defence available if a person had a bird that has been rescued with the intention of returning the bird to the wild once it is fit to do so. In this case the person with the bird had made no effort to seek advice on how to look after it, and because of this the bird's condition had deteriorated.

There are different ways to look at this. Had the person, as I suspect, taken the bird from a nest he was solely responsible for its poor state of health. Had the bird been on the ground, he had ignored the standard advice given by the police and the SSPCA – to leave young birds where they are. Having said this, a young buzzard at an age when its eyes are still not open, and on the ground, would definitely have perished or been taken by a predator. The only evidence we had of how the accused person had come to possess the bird was by his own admission. Forty-plus years of policing has made me question almost everything I'm told, but the accused had to get the benefit of any doubts that I had. This was the point that the procurator fiscal was making: that it may not be in the interest of the public to prosecute. I did not disagree. We, as Tayside Police, had carried out our part of the chain of investigation. Sergeant Andy Carroll, one of the Divisional wildlife crime officers, had investigated the incident and submitted a report to the procurator fiscal. It was the fiscal's job to decide what action to take with the evidence presented to him and he was of the view that a warning letter would be the best disposal of the case. I was pleased that he had shared his thoughts with me.

•

One incident that caused me great frustration for a number of reasons was the felling of a number of mature conifers to make way for a housing development. With complaints about development I am always wary that the police are being manipulated to influence the cessation of work, as a particular development may not suit either an individual or a number of people. In this case that may or may not have been the case but the person who telephoned me stated that there were a number of red squirrels resident in the condemned woodland and was adamant that there were red squirrel dreys in some of the trees.

The law in relation to red squirrels, as a Schedule 5 animal, is that its place of shelter – a drey – *must not intentionally or recklessly be damaged or destroyed and that it must not intentionally or recklessly be disturbed while it is occupying a structure or place that it uses for that purpose.* To establish that there is at least one active red squirrel drey in any particular woodland is a job for experts, and not a fact about which I could give evidence in court. Normally I would ask Scottish Natural

Heritage or someone from a red squirrel group to establish this for me but it cannot be done in an instant. Further, as it is primary evidence and crucial to a conviction, it requires to be corroborated, hence two experts are required. Unlike pine cones, a favourite food of the red squirrel, experts don't grow on trees. In the meantime trees were being felled and I had no means of knowing whether or not the tree fellers or developers had any idea of the presence of red squirrels. An offence is only committed if the act is carried out intentionally or recklessly, not in ignorance.

In this instance I established details of the developer and his agent from the local council, and made contact by telephone. The developers knew of the presence of red squirrels and assured me they were aware of the law in relation to the felling of a tree that has a red squirrel drey. They sounded competent and were co-operative. They assured me that this was not to be a clean fell, as many of the mature trees were being left to make the housing development more attractive.

I monitored the situation and when the work was completed there were indeed several conifers left standing and no evidence of any being taken down that held a red squirrel drey. The law appeared to have been complied with but I suspect that the red squirrel population would still have been displaced. Red squirrels are much more secretive and much more arboreal than greys. They prefer to move from tree to tree via the branches rather than come on to the ground and with the scattering of trees left I doubted that would suit them.

Should I have considered the whole piece of woodland as *'a place a red squirrel uses for shelter or protection?'* I thought not, but was I entitled to use my own interpretation of the law or should I have reported the case for the consideration of the procurator fiscal. To have done this would have meant stopping all the development work and would be an extremely serious decision to have taken. Where cases are more clear-cut this has been done in the past but I was of the view that this was not the road to go down in this instance. A lesson I learned from this and other similar incidents since is that we must put more pressure on developers to produce an environmental impact assessment before any planning permission is granted and I am working closely with local authorities to try to ensure that this is done.

•

The subject of trees brings me on to the final incident which involved a body hanging from a tree. A friend of mine, Bert Burnett, who is a gamekeeper in Glen Prosen in Angus, was being pestered by buzzards at his pheasant release pens. Young buzzards in particular can be a nuisance to gamekeepers as they try out their skills at killing birds. Young pheasants contained in release pens are an ideal target and though the young buzzards can kill one or two, the biggest damage is probably caused by the birds being panicked into a corner of the pen where a number of them can be smothered by their terrified brethren. Though Bert makes no secret of the fact that he does not like buzzards any action he might take to minimise their impact on game birds is within the law.

Bert was surprised one day to see two police officers on the estate walking towards one of the woods. He though to himself, 'What do they want here.' To elicit the answer he hot-footed it down to the wood to meet the officers. The answer to the question was that someone had reported that a man had hung himself from a tree in the wood and that the officers were responding to that call. The 'man' was a scarecrow that Bert had hung in his pheasant pen to discourage attacks on his pheasant poults by birds of prey. He had painstakingly made the dummy from light wire that he had formed roughly into a human shape and clothed in light and brightly coloured attire. He then hung it from a thin, springy branch of a tree where even on the slightest puff of breeze the dummy would move and simulate a human. His efforts had been too precise and had panicked a walker into calling the police. Despite seeing for themselves that the 'suicidal man' was a scarecrow – or scarebuzzard to be more exact – the police insisted in taking the dummy away with them. I can't understand why but it added to Bert's indignation, and eventually amusement, that they did so.

It was doubtful that a post mortem examination was required to establish that the man was a dummy and it was eventually returned to Bert by the police officers once they were absolutely satisfied that there was no need to report the matter as a suicide to the procurator fiscal. Having already initiated an embarrassing situation they compounded it by telling Bert that, at the time they took the 'man' away, a person had been reported as missing and was wearing similar clothing!

Chapter 38

Mushrooms and Migration

The great migration that occasioned the G8 summit in 2005 provides the backdrop to a case involving sand martins and dramas are played out on a local and an international stage.

Every year I look forward to the arrival of the first migratory birds. In the Autumn, normally between 15 and 22 September, the calls of the first skeins of grey geese passing over is a precursor to witnessing the trees and hedgerows that are filled with fruit and berries gradually sharing their bounty with birds, fieldmice, badgers and even hedgehogs, then losing their crop of leaves that will in turn convert into compost to ensure the nutrients are fed back into the plants themselves. Everything in nature is cyclical.

In October 2006 I marvelled at the huge crop of berries and of mushrooms when out for a long walk in the country with my dogs, Marci and Meg, and my granddaughter, Hannah. I am no expert in mushroom identification and am no more adventurous than collecting only two or three well known varieties. We passed a huge crop of chanterelles, some shaggy ink caps and some puffballs, all of which are edible, and I wished that I had a bag with me to collect some for a fry-up later in the day. I suggested that Hannah's woolly hat would be a perfect receptacle but her reluctance at the thought of having wee woodland beasties nestling in her hat and thence her hair put paid to that idea. There were mushrooms of every size and colour. I never fail to be amazed that the ones with the red parasols – ones I would always avoid as in some cases their red warning colour means that they are poisonous – always seem to have been nibbled by small woodland creatures, either mice or rabbits. I looked carefully at a lone fly agaric mushroom, the deadly poisonous one with a red parasol flecked with white. It was a welcoming splash of colour against the monotonous dull brown of the leaf litter encircling it; the archetypal mushroom of children's books and normally a perch or shelter for gnomes with pointed hats. There was no sign of it having been attacked or even tentatively tasted by the tenants of the wood. How on earth do they know which are poisonous and which are not?

To me, the Autumn bird migration has a better variety than that of Spring. As well as geese there are countless different waterfowl visiting us from the Russia and the Baltic States, fieldfares and redwing from Scandinavia, and in colder months the lovely waxwing and brambling. When I walk in the hills near where I stay there are always packs of snow buntings as well, confident birds with humans and real cold weather birds that I suspect we might eventually lose to global warming.

In Springtime the wintering birds are replaced by birds from Africa; the osprey, swallow, house martin, swift and of course the earliest of all the migrants to visit us, the sand martin. These brown and white martins arrive in March and are birds that have always fascinated me. As a boy I can remember very small colonies of sand martins nesting on any sandy bank of the River Earn in Perthshire wherever there had been a bit of slippage of the riverbank over the winter time. A steep sandy bank is ideal for them in which to dig their elliptical metre-long nest burrows and rear usually two but maybe even three broods of chicks. I often sat on the river bank and watched the human and natural fishers: men with fishing rods, grey herons with long legs and dagger bills, and the exquisitely coloured and miniature kingfisher, normally just a flash of orange and turquoise as it flashed either up or down the river. There were always a few pairs of sand martins darting back and forth low over the river catching flies. Behind me, when I turned slowly round I could see a huge rabbit warren on the slopes of the grass field with dozens of young grey-brown coloured rabbits basking in the sun, and just occasionally, one or two that were either black, a sandy-orange colour or grey-brown with a pure white chest area just like the domestic Dutch rabbits. Most people seem to think these unusually coloured rabbits are descendants of domestic rabbits that have been released to the wild but my view is the opposite: that domestic rabbits are descended from these colour mutations.

Before I get carried away and start to write about rabbits, of which I have a lifetime of experience both wild and domestic, I intended this chapter to be about sand martins. Over the years I saw many sand martin colonies, large and small, normally transient populations that depended on the habitat that was available for nesting that particular year. One population that was a bit more stable nested in a large sand quarry beside a narrow country road close to the world-famous Gleneagles Hotel at Auchterarder. Driving along the road, anyone with even minimal observation skills could see clouds of sand martins over the quarry, reminiscent of an angry swarm of bees that had been disturbed. I watched this sand martin colony off and on for a number of years, unaware that it would form the subject of a wildlife crime investigation.

In July 2005 Gleneagles Hotel hosted the G8 Summit. Policing this event was by far the largest commitment that Tayside Police had ever encountered. We have numerous major events in Tayside, including T in the Park at Balado at Kinross, where one would imagine, in policing terms, that the potential for violence with 50,000 youngsters and lots of alcohol would eclipse a hundredfold anything that could remotely be related to the meeting of a few heads of states of world-wide countries. Wrong. The T in the Park enthusiasts are like lambs compared with the some of the committed anti-G8 protestors; activists that were drawn from all over the world.

The policing of the Summit involved police officers from all over the UK. Such was the draw on personnel that even the Tayside Police wildlife and environment officer was ensnared! Because I had previous experience working with media I was asked if I would work in the Force Media Services office in the two months prior to the Summit, then act as the Media Relations Officer at Gleneagles Hotel during the Summit itself. I was reluctant but acquiesced provided that I could maintain my wildlife crime role, and be paid overtime for doing so, overtime being something that I had never hitherto (or since) claimed. This was agreed and my working week increased dramatically.

It was a decision I never regretted. I still managed to keep tabs on wildlife crime issues and farm out a larger proportion of enquiries than normal to Divisional wildlife crime officers. It was also valuable experience working in Media Services and dealing on a day-to-day basis with the media on a whole range of issues, from spates of vandalism and fatal accidents to crimes of the most serious nature and I made many good media contacts during these two months.

I had dealt regularly, in my former life as a police officer, with local media. National media, especially reporters from tabloid newspapers, were on another scale. The persistence of one reporter in particular at trying to get me to reveal information that I was party to but could not share with him on a fatal accident drew on all I had learned in interpersonal skills. Despite repeated telephone calls he got nothing more than the detail given in the fairly bland press release given to all the media earlier. I saw his article in the paper the following day and he had stuck to what I had told him. It was little more than a couple of paragraphs. No embellishments, no speculation and nothing more than any other newspaper published. To his credit he phoned me the next day and thanked me for my co-operation.

On the days of the Summit itself I was at the tented village specially built for the media at Gleneagles Hotel. There were literally thousands of media representatives from all parts of the globe and the facilities laid on for them by way of food, news and broadcasting facilities were second to none. Part of the facilities was a large dome organised by VisitScotland advertising Scotland – particularly Perthshire – to the world. Thousands of pounds worth of free gifts were given to the media (I managed to get a stress ball and a pen!) and I'm sure that it was money well spent on advertising Scotland as a place to visit.

There were two highlights of my Gleneagles visit. Those that were policing the area inside the hotel grounds were mainly recruits from the Metropolitan Police, having had their training course shortened by a week to facilitate this week of invaluable practical experience. Considering they were newly trained these recruits showed great professionalism in their duties and were amazed at the policing of the rural environment in which they found themselves compared with what they were used to. They appeared to relish the fresh air and the backdrop of hills and many told me that they would take a holiday in Scotland before too long. On the second day of the G8, when the bombers carried out their terrible carnage on the transport system in London, the frustration in these young recruits was palpable, and they were just desperate to get back to London and assist their colleagues in dealing with this human disaster. I could understand this with seasoned officers but with men and women with just a few week's service under their belt the dedication and call to duty that was already engrained in them was remarkable.

The second highlight focussed on a completely new concept for UK police in dealing with demonstrators. The whole of Gleneagles Hotel grounds had been protected by a double ring of metal fencing, many miles long, with police patrolling both inside and out. I could see a huge group of protestors on the outskirts of Auchterarder, separated from the security fence by a field of growing barley about 300 metres in width. In dribs and drabs this group began to run through the barley field towards the fence. The dribs and drabs grew larger and a veritable army of protestors was suddenly flattening the farmer's crop to get to the fence.

I was two hundred metres on the inside of the fence and had a grandstand view. I could see police officers, including a number of officers on horseback, converging on the part of the fence towards which the protestors were heading. There was a stand-off for a short time but the police officers were well outnumbered and a number of protestors broke through the cordon and reached the fence. They then began to rock the fence backwards and forwards and eventually managed to breach the first half of its double security.

About this time I heard a Chinook helicopter approaching. The helicopter got closer and closer until I could see it approaching the crowd of antagonistic protestors. As it flew over them it seemed to dip lower and at that point the noise and vibration must have been frightening. It landed in the field between where I was and where the protestors were and almost immediately dropped its tail door. To my surprise forty or so police officers in riot gear ran down the tail gate directly towards the protestors. This exercise was repeated a few minutes later and the protestors fled. It was an amazing exercise to witness and its effect was almost instant in changing the intent of protestors from fight to flight. The responsibility for public and delegate safety at the G8 Summit was squarely on the police but a wee bit help from the military did no harm at all. I spoke to one or two media representatives after the event who told me they were among the crowd of protestors when the Chinook buzzed over their heads. They had heard several protestors stating that it was time to retreat, and this view was reinforced when the helicopters disgorged their load of riot-clad police officers.

Yet again, I have digressed. I intended to tell a story about sand martins and have finished up at the G8 Summit with a military style police operation that has not the remotest connection with sand martins and the low policing priority of wildlife crime. Or has it?

The G8 Summit took place on 6 to 8 July 2005. Coincidental to the drama of the G8 at Gleneagles and its associated colony of reporters, another drama was beginning to unfold at the sand martin colony juxtaposed to the hotel. The main part of the sand martin colony was in a large block of sand almost in the centre of the quarry which jutted out of the ground like a giant tooth in an undulating orange gum bereft of any other teeth. According to nature photographers and ornithologists from whom I later noted statements, this colony normally housed somewhere between 400 and 900 pairs of sand martins. It probably was one of the biggest colonies in Tayside. The vertical sand faces were pock-marked with small oval holes and from mid March till late August the area had avian hustle and bustle equivalent to human activity in any of the UK's largest cities.

Those who monitored the colony had some concerns in late June and early July as they saw a bulldozer gradually flattening the quarry. They had no idea why the area was being levelled but as the bulldozer seemed to be working round the sand martin colony they assumed that it was to be left and would be safe.

I had several telephone calls regarding the workings of the bulldozer from concerned locals but as I had more than enough to keep me occupied at that time I asked police officers from Auchterarder if they would take a look in the passing and let me know if there had been any major change in the sand quarry. Their report confirmed the information I already had received; that the sand quarry was being flattened but the main colony still seemed to be OK.

On 13 August I had a frantic call from a bird enthusiast to say that the whole sand quarry had been levelled and that all the sand martins had been killed. I went right away to the sand quarry, more accurately as I found out when I arrived, the ex-quarry. The former sand quarry now resembled a desert, and a major breeding location for sand martins was no more.

Though I have a good working knowledge of natural history I am not experienced enough in the ecology and breeding dates of sand martins to have known for sure that nesting would still be have been under way in the middle of August, and had certainly not enough experience of the subject to satisfy a court. I know that sand martins are the first migratory species from Africa to arrive here and to breed. I knew also that they were the first to leave but was not sure of the dates. It meant that a lot of evidence had to be gathered to build a case, if indeed a crime had been committed.

I liaised with Constable John Robb, one of the Divisional wildlife crime officers, and he and I visited the quarry site to take a series of photographs. If an offence had taken place I wanted to show how the quarry looked now and if possible how it looked while it housed an active, vibrant sand martin colony. The evidence gathering was going to be a long process and I took on this responsibility since it was doubtful if John would have been allocated the time to do so. If I established a crime had been committed I intended to pass the case back to John at that point to deal with any suspect and to report the matter to the procurator fiscal.

The first statement I noted demonstrated that there would still be young in some of the nests at the time the pinnacle of sand was flattened. The witness was a nature photographer and he was able to tell me that he watched the feeding activity of the parents at some nest holes towards the end of the third week in July. He was also able to say that the quarry had been completely levelled sometime between 9 and 12 August.

The next witness I traced was also a nature photographer, who painted much the same picture from his visit at the very end of July.

Both he and the first photographer were able to supply photographs of the birds still occupying nest holes during their visits. The second photographer was of the opinion that one or two of the nests may still have contained either eggs or very small chicks, since when a parent bird flew into the nest hole it did not reappear. In the experience of the photographer these birds were incubating eggs or spending some time heating up young chicks that had cooled somewhat during the absence of the parent on a foraging expedition. In addition, the second photographer had spoken to the bulldozer operator. The bulldozer driver had asked the witness when the birds would leave the nests. He was told that it would be at least the end of August, maybe the middle of September. His response was that this was a nuisance as the job had to be finished as soon as possible. I was almost sure that a crime had been committed but needed to speak if possible with someone else who had visited the quarry in August.

My next call was at the house of the head gamekeeper for the estate. Gamekeepers, like police officers, are alert to what is happening round about them. In addition, most of them have a good working knowledge of birds and animals as this forms a considerable part of their job. He was able to narrow down the date that the pinnacle of sand was flattened, and was also able to state that the only person he ever saw driving the bulldozer was the owner of the sand quarry. This now gave me a suspect. The gamekeeper was also aware that sand martins often remained in the area into September, which again indicated that at least some were likely still to have been breeding at the time the pinnacle had been levelled. In turn this tended to confirm the fact that an offence had been committed.

Though the two photographers and the gamekeeper gave me some specific dates on which sand martins were using the nest holes, I now needed some expert evidence on the breeding and migratory habits of sand martins. This I obtained from RSPB, who also suggested a further source of information; a man who made a study of a variety of water insects and birds in the area of the sand quarry. I made contact and discovered that this witness had kept nesting records of the sand martin colony for a number of years and it was he who said that numbers could reach 900 pairs in a good year. He was able to tell me that in 2005 there were 300 pairs nesting, a comparatively low number, but that on his last visit on 4 August there would be up to twenty pairs still nesting. The interesting fact from the last two witnesses was that their advice, similar to that of the photographers, would be that potentially sand martins could nest right through August and that to be *absolutely* safe, their nests should not be interfered with until the end of September.

The case was building but there can never be too much evidence so I kept digging. I found a woman, who happened to be a countryside ranger, who had recent photographs of the sand quarry and the huge cluster of sand martin nest holes. They had been taken in 2004 and gave a view of the virgin site for the court's information. I now had my 'before' and 'after' photographs and even some photos of chicks at the mouth of nest holes taken by the two photographers immediately before the flattening of the colony.

During my investigation I had become aware that the lease granted by the local authority to remove sand expired at the end of 2005, which gave me the reason – or part of the reason – for the bulldozing work. I made contact with the local authority planning office and gleaned two interesting pieces of information. Firstly the owner of the sand quarry had to restore it to what it had been before the quarrying began. This had to be done by the end of 2005 so there was no need for the active sand martin nests to have been a 'nuisance' or for the job to be completed 'as soon as possible'. There had to be something more that caused the work to be rushed at the last minute.

I found the probable cause in an application to develop part of the site for housing. The planning permission had been refused but there had been an appeal by the applicant. A review of this appeal included a site visit, which was scheduled for 20 September. It seems likely that the applicant could have been of the view that if the site was flattened, grass seed sown and a reasonable sward of grass showing, this may give a favourable impression and the planning permission might be more likely to be granted. To go ahead and complete the levelling of the quarry on 12 August gave an ideal time frame for this landscaping to take place. To have left the flattening of the last remaining original feature of the quarry even until early September would have precluded this option.

In due course the suspect was seen by Constable John Robb and charged with the destruction of an unspecified number of sand martin nests while they were in use. He admitted being the person who operated the bulldozer but stated that he had spoken to a countryside ranger who had told him it was now safe to flatten the pinnacle of sand with the nest burrows. John traced the countryside ranger – a different one from the woman who supplied me with the photographs. Her evidence was that she had advised him that the nests should *not* be interfered with from the beginning of March till the end of September.

Nearer the time of the trial, John Robb was notified by the procurator fiscal of two defence witnesses. The procedure with defence witnesses is that when they are made known to the procurator fiscal, the police visit them and note a statement so that the fiscal has some knowledge of the evidence they are going to provide at the trial. It is exactly the same with prosecution witnesses; the defence are made aware of what they are likely to say in court. John had gone on holiday and arranged for the statements to be noted and sent to me for onward transmission to the fiscal. When I saw the defence statements, one caused me very little concern but the other was obviously taken from a person who had a good knowledge of nesting sand martins and was disputing some of what the Crown witnesses were saying. To ensure that we still had the best possible case, I made enquiries to see if we had another sand martin expert who could contest what was being said by this defence witness. You can never have too much evidence.

After some telephone calls to people who were in the know about these matters, I traced a man that was widely recognised as the UK expert on sand martins. This gentleman had even constructed an artificial sand martin colony in his garden that was used every year by a small number of nesting pairs. Finding Mr Sand Martin was a real bonus and I learnt a huge amount from him. He was able to send me a historical table showing the percentage of pairs still with broods in the nest burrow on particular dates. He had recorded annual percentages and mean percentages. From this I was able to gauge the percentage of sand martins likely to still have a brood at our site on the date it was flattened. Of the 300 breeding pairs in 2005, on 12 August it was likely that twenty five pairs still had dependent young in the nest burrow. Another important fact from Mr Sand Martin was that for a while after they fledge, young sand martins depend on the safety of their nest burrow at night. Equally relevant for the prosecution case, the expert stated that sand martins migrating south sometimes depend at night on burrows of their relatives to seek safety, before moving on further south within a day or so. This gave a new importance to the burrows. Looking at the wording of the charge, *to intentionally or recklessly take, damage, destroy or otherwise interfere with nests of wild birds while they are in use or being built,* this revelation gave the charge a whole new meaning. The nests, which included the burrows, were not only *in use* when occupied by birds with eggs or dependent chicks, but by chicks that had recently fledged and by birds on passage south in the first stages of their migration to North Africa.

Mr Sand Martin told me that in a good summer sand martins breed over a longer period, many of them trying to squeeze in an extra brood. Conversely, in a very wet year, breeding is reduced and the birds may well start their migration south considerably earlier. 2005 was a long dry summer and I obtained a statement from a local weather expert to prove this fact to the court. I learned something else from the local weatherman: the fact that his son was a police officer in Tayside and that I had taught him about poaching and wildlife crime law in a training session a few years earlier.

I am conscious that cases do not always run smoothly and there can be glitches or even fatal errors in procedure resulting from an oversight by the police or from the procurator fiscal. I don't say this as a criticism but simply as a fact. When resources are stretched, as they are both in policing and prosecution circles, mistakes occur. I am in the relatively lucky position that I now have a narrow field of responsibility: a luxury that allows me to monitor wildlife cases more closely than normal run-of-the-mill cases. I had been in touch with Mr Sand Martin about ten days before the trial and was surprised when he told me that he had never received a witness citation. I made contact with the fiscal and told her that a person I considered a very important witness in this case had not been cited to attend the trail. This can happen when new witnesses are added in some weeks or even months after the original case has been submitted. It is something I can easily monitor with thirty or so cases being submitted annually but much more difficult for the procurator fiscal, with tens of thousands of cases passing through their hands from the police alone, not including the many other agencies such as SEPA and Trading Standards that also report direct to the fiscal. This problem was therefore averted.

Two days had been allocated for the trial and the night before the start I had spoken to the procurator fiscal depute who was taking the case. She was preparing all the case papers and taking them home that night before the trial but I felt heart sorry for her. To do this case justice I knew that as well as being a procurator fiscal she would also need to be an ornithologist. Like police, fiscals have a wide variety of crimes to deal with. However because of the relatively low number of fiscals – even though there are designated environmental fiscals – they do not have the luxury of being able to spend the volume of time that even part-time police wildlife crime officers can in specialising in any area of law that is particularly complex.

I spoke with the fiscal on the morning of the trial. She admitted to being nervous but more than willing to give it her best shot. Along with the other witnesses I waited in the witness room, and after a relatively short time the fiscal came in and said that the defence had offered a deal, which would result in a guilty plea from the accused in destroying twenty five sand martin nests. The expert for the defence knew of Mr Sand Martin's knowledge and reputation and just did not want to stand against him in court. The guilty plea sounded fine so far but there always has to be a catch. The catch was that if the guilty plea was accepted by the procurator fiscal it was conditional that there would be no mention in court of a building application for the former sand quarry.

There is nothing improper in either the making or the accepting of such a deal. I considered the options. We had a guilty plea to the destruction of twenty five active nests. In principle this was good and reflected exactly what the evidence suggested had happened. The downside of the offer was that the sheriff would not now know the reason why there was a particular rush to make the sand quarry presentable and attractive, plus the obvious monetary advantage to the accused if the planning permission was approved. John Robb and I knew that the sentence would be much less than it probably should have been but on the other hand with a fiscal who knew little about nesting sand martins – and I say this in the nicest possible sense – the trial *could* have resulted in a not guilty or not proven verdict and two days would have been wasted. The maxim 'a bird in the hand is worth two in the bush' was never so appropriate and we agreed that the fiscal should accept the defence offer.

The fiscal then asked me if I would sit with her at the table in front of the court to ensure that she could accurately present the prosecution summary to the sheriff and that she could answer any questions that he posed. I had no hesitation in agreeing.

The fiscal gave a very good account of the circumstance of the case and there were only one or two points that I had to clarify for her. There was one interesting point when the sheriff asked her what the penalty for the particular offence was. She deferred to me and I said that the penalty was defined under Section 77 of the Criminal Justice (Scotland) Act 2003 and that it was six months imprisonment and/or a fine of £5000. . . She cut me off and repeated my definition of the penalties to the sheriff. At this point the defence solicitor – a man that I have crossed swords with on many occasions in the past in trials and have a great respect for as a defence lawyer – leaned across to me. He asked if the penalties were really as severe as those that had just been narrated by the fiscal, to which I replied, 'Much worse. I never had a chance to finish my explanation to the fiscal but the fine in fact is £5000 *for each offence*.' He had just tendered a plea of guilty on behalf of his client to the destruction of twenty five active sand martin nests. Leaving imprisonment out of the equation the maximum fine in this particular case was £125,000.

The sheriff deliberated for some time. He was not convinced that the act was intentional but may have incurred a degree of recklessness in that the accused never sought proper advice and went ahead and flattened the sand quarry only after, as his defence claimed, he had checked all the nest holes to ensure there were no chicks in them. His defence had also stated that many sand martins were now nesting in another part of the quarry area, which was in fact a steep sand face caused by water erosion. We had checked this and there was indeed a very small number that had taken advantage of this site that was created by nature and which in no way could be attributed to the accused as benefactor. The final decision of the sheriff was that the offence had been at the lower end of the scale and as such he would fine the accused £400.

There is no question that a fine of £400 was representative of the lower end of the scale, but in fairness a sheriff can only sentence on the information that is put before the court. Had the case gone to trial and all the evidence had been available to the sheriff the outcome would no doubt have been substantially different. But of course with an extremely complex case and a procurator fiscal that, through no fault of hers, was not an ornithologist there was always the chance that we could have lost the case.

Should I not be incandescent with rage at this apparently paltry penalty? We agreed after discussing the options with the fiscal that the defence offer should be accepted and we expected a comparatively low fine so it was not a surprise. The answer lies in having a whole legal system, from investigation, through prosecution to sentencing where there is more awareness and knowledge of wildlife law and better trained participants to deal with it at all levels. In November 2006 a consultation document, entitled *Strengthening and Steamlining: The way forward for the enforcement of environmental law in Scotland,* was launched by the Scottish Executive. Part of the document invites discussion on the formation of specialist environmental courts. After much preamble and information in the document the last part reads: *We have reached the conclusion that the case for a specialist environmental court is not made because...* and lists a number of reasons. It then poses the question for the consultee: Do you agree that the case for an environmental court for Scotland is not made out? This seems a negative manner in which to consult and I suspect the outcome of this part of the consultation will be equally negative. Pity!

CHAPTER 39

Moss and Plunder

The first investigation of its kind in Tayside into the theft of moss and a useful interpretation of the legality or otherwise of bramble-picking.

The investigation of crime committed against animals forms the preponderance of my work, whether the animals are badgers, golden eagles or freshwater pearl mussels. Plants seem to be the poor relations, much to the frustration of the plant experts and enthusiasts I work with from Scottish Natural Heritage, Plantlife and Kew Gardens. There are some absolutely beautiful plants but the fact that they appear inanimate often kicks them into touch and there is no question that they don't get the same attention as furry or feathered wildlife. I was quite pleased, therefore, to get a report that concerned crime committed against plants. It was not the picking of rare orchids, or the digging up of wild snowdrops without the landowner's permission, or even the selling of wild bluebells: it was the taking of sphagnum moss on a commercial scale. I knew of a similar case in Strathclyde, where a garage full of sphagnum moss was found prior to Christmas. On this occasion the amount of moss taken was less but it was the first investigation of its kind in Tayside.

I heard of this case the day after it took place, a date in late November 2005. The two men involved in the taking of the moss, who were travelling folk, had been charged with *theft* of the moss. The circumstances were that they had been witnessed filling bin liners of moss by the gamekeeper of a Perthshire estate. The keeper recognised them as the same men he had caught doing the same thing the previous year and had asked them not to come back as they had not had permission. He had been backed up in this decision by the landowner.

When I learned of the incident, I thought that a charge under the Wildlife and Countryside Act 1981 would be more appropriate and I consulted with the environmental fiscal, who agreed with me. I next contacted the police officer who had dealt with the incident and said that we would proceed with the case under the Wildlife and Countryside Act rather than as Common Law theft. I needed a sample of moss to establish the variety, and to see if we were dealing with one of the rarer mosses listed under Schedule 8 of the Act, or simply with one or more of the more common species.

I learned that the men had filled eight black bin liners of moss, which, when they were caught, had been tipped out in to the wood at the area in which it had been gathered. I went to the wood and photographed the pile of moss for court purposes, and took a sample – a chunk about a foot square – so that I could have the species identified. It is in the field of contacts for all matters remotely relating to wildlife that a wildlife crime officer comes into his or her own. Wildlife crime conferences are not all about buffets, meals and drinks in the bar. These benefits are very pleasant and sociable by-products but the real value is in networking: getting to know who to contact in order to efficiently and professionally progress a whole spectrum of wildlife crime issues. In this particular case I made contact with the Royal Botanic Garden in Edinburgh and arranged for my moss sample to be identified the following day.

My visit to Edinburgh was fascinating. David Long, BSc, PhD, head of cryptogamic botany, is a world expert in mosses. I gave him details of the incident and explained what I was requiring. He took the chunk of sphagnum moss from the bag and studied it. Without hesitation he picked out a single moss plant and said, 'This is *Hylocomium splendens*, more commonly known as gluttering wood moss. About three quarters of the sample is made up of this species.' He then delicately picked out another single plant. 'This is *Pleuorozium schreberi*, which is the red-stemmed feather moss. There is also,' he said, picking out another plant, '*Scleropodium purum*, which is neat feather moss, and *Rhytidiadelphus squarrosis*, which is springy turf moss.' By this time David had laid the four plants side by side on a piece of white paper. I studied them and could discern very little difference. How he could just pluck them individually from the large chunk of moss that I thought was all the same species I have no idea. To the layman the whole lot looked the same. This is why the police need experts in a whole range of fields, not just in wildlife but in DNA, ballistics, forensic pathology and a whole lot more.

David Long wasn't finished. He had made these identifications from his vast experience of moss, but he still wanted to test his judgement against a range of dried moss samples in the collection held by the Botanic Garden. He proceeded to bring out folders full of dried samples in professionally prepared laminated pouches. He checked each of his four samples and it was only when he showed me the corresponding species in the laminated pouches that he was satisfied he had made the correct identification. I felt honoured to have watched an expert at work.

In a case like this it is important to place some sort of value on the commodity that is at the heart of the case. I was surprised at the value put on the 100 kilos of moss by a garden centre. I would have thought the value to be somewhere around £80, but the garden centre only valued the moss, if sold to them, at £10. We had no way of knowing if the moss would be sold to a garden centre or whether it might have been made up into wreaths or baskets for the Christmas market by the two accused men. If this had been the case the value would have been considerably in excess of £10 or even £80.

In a case where there could be a range of values, an accused person always has to get the benefit of the doubt, and the official value was put at £10. I knew then that the case would not get to court and in the circumstances it was dealt with by a fiscal's fine. Procurators fiscal, as well as taking cases to court, can deal with some of the less serious cases ether by a warning or by a fiscal's fine, which means that the accused person pays a penalty which does not result in a conviction. This, to me, is a very sensible option. It helps to keep the courts from being cluttered with trials involving low level crime and, if the person involved has no convictions recorded against him, that situation remains. I had no complaint about the outcome and I felt that I gained considerable experience during the whole investigation. Commercial collection of moss is quite commonplace and if a future moss case happens to involve a much larger quantity then we have served our investigative apprenticeship.

Many different wild crops are harvested in the countryside and there must be a sensible balance struck. No-one will complain if a person out for a pleasant walk in the countryside gathers some mushrooms or other wild crop for personal use, but a problem may arise if the crop is harvested commercially and no permission has been sought from the owner of the land. I did a live telephone interview with Euan MacIlwraith on BBC Scotland *Out of Doors* one Saturday morning on the subject of this commercial harvesting. We discussed a number of potential 'crops', including mushrooms, moss and brambles. The point that I was making was that gathering any of these fruits of the forest in moderation does no harm, and in fact should be encouraged so as to get folks out in to the fresh air and eating food that is not contaminated by pesticides. If a person wants to develop a money-making venture out of gathering wild crops, there will be no problem provided permission is obtained first. Plundering the land without permission is a breach of the Code of Conduct in relation to land access, and might well constitute a crime if a complaint is made by the landowner.

It was pure coincidence that two days after the radio programme, I received a telephone call from an estate making a complaint of staff believed to have come from a nearby hotel out gathering mushrooms. The scale of the operation described seemed to determine it as a commercial enterprise and the estate factor had asked the people involved not to come back. He was most annoyed when they returned a few days later, taking no heed of his request, and again began to harvest mushrooms. On this occasion the estate asked that we warn the mushroom gatherers, which we did. Had they approached the estate and asked permission to harvest mushrooms, which I assumed were for use in the hotel, permission would doubtless have been granted.

In my contribution to the radio programme I wanted to be sure that genuine small-scale bramble and mushroom pickers were not put off by thinking they were committing a crime, and assured ladies of the WRI that there would not be a police officer hiding behind a bush waiting to pounce on them when they gathered their brambles to make the delicious jam that all WRI members seem to produce.

It crossed my mind at the time that over the last forty years I have hidden behind bushes and in a variety of other places waiting to pounce on someone who was involved in some crime or other. One such ambush comes readily to mind; it was an attempt to catch youths that had begun a stoning campaign against police vehicles. Like every town or city, Perth had its rougher areas and in one of the more run down streets, when any police vehicle passed along in the early hours of the morning youths started to hurl stones and half bricks at it. They then ran round the corner into the next street and disappeared into one or other of the three tenement closes. This stoning had occurred twice on our night shift and we were getting a bit fed up with it.

I was a sergeant at the time and I told the car crew for that area that I would quietly go through the back gardens and wait in one of the closes so that I could grab at least one of the culprits as they ran through in the darkness. I use the term 'garden' here in its loosest possible sense to include scrub, long unkempt grass, broken fencing, all manner of rubbish and the booby traps left by the myriad of mongrels on the housing estate to stick to the feet of the unwary nocturnal visitor. The officers in the car were to give me time to get into position then drive along the street.

I had been out the back of the houses in the area sufficiently often in daylight that I was confident I could navigate in the darkness. I made my way to the middle close of the three and stood in the darkness, waiting. The street outside was well lit and I was standing back a few feet into the close so that I could hear what was happening outside. I intended to move back a few feet further once I heard the thunder of hooves so that I was behind a right-angled bend in the close leading to one of the ground floor doors and my hand could come unseen out of the darkness and snatch one of the retreating rogues whose antagonism towards the police had gone just a bit too far.

When dealing with young people who for a number of reasons rebel against any type of authority, there is a line in the sand over which they generally know not to cross. Police officers put up with –

either good naturedly or with gritted teeth – name calling, a range of cat-calls, whistling and hissing. Mental pressure we largely ignore, or bear in mind for another day. Physical assault needs a prompt and effective response.

The officers told me by radio that they had started to drive up the street, then minutes later that stones were being thrown at the car as they came near the end of the street. The group of about six or seven yobs was now hot-footing it in my direction. I heard them coming and was about to step back further into the close when I heard shouting coming out of the darkness from the school playing fields at the top of a steep grass banking on the other side of the road, and at a height considerably above the level of the road. Obviously some of the youths' pals, for whatever nefarious purpose, were in the school grounds and had spotted me in the close. One was shouting at the top of his voice to warn his chums, 'There's a pig in the close. There's a pig in the close. Watch out, there's a pig in the close!' I could hear him clearly but for whatever reason the runners heading towards me either didn't hear him, chose to ignore him, or maybe, with their entrepreneurial hats on, thought that it was a *real* pig in the close that they could make into a pet or, more likely and practically, convert into bacon butties. Whatever their thoughts were they came hurtling through the close and I managed to catch not one but two and held on to the struggling bodies until my colleagues came to my assistance. The two being arrested put an end to the stone throwing and I've had many a laugh recounting the story of the 'pig in the close'.

Epilogue

A fair chunk of my job entails attending meetings and conferences. I attended the annual Police and Customs Wildlife Crime Conference in September 2006, which was held at Northampton University. This was one of the few conferences I have attended where I had no presentation to deliver, and I was looking forward to sitting quietly in the audience, listening to the presentations and throwing in the occasional question or comment if I felt the need. The delegates at these conferences are made up of wildlife crime officers, a handful of senior police officers, and members of statutory and non-government organisations that are involved in some aspect of wildlife crime investigation. Like all good conferences, much of the value to the delegates comes from networking with others. It is organised by Defra and is chaired by Richard Brunstrom, chief constable of North Wales Police.

In the afternoon of the first day we had come to the part when the Worldwide Fund for Nature Wildlife Enforcer of the Year award was just about to be announced. Richard said that before he disclosed the winner he had another important announcement to make and asked me to come to the front of the conference theatre and join him. I did so, wondering what he was talking about. He then announced that in 2006 there was a new, one-off award from WWF and that it was to me. I was to receive a Lifetime Achievement Award.

I was dumbstruck. The award – as always with awards from WWF – includes the presentation of a cuddly panda, which is their logo. My response on being presented with the award and the panda was that I already had two dogs at home, two guinea pigs and now I would have two pandas. Should I start to build an ark? Richard detailed part of my career, making a special and complimentary mention of the work I had carried out on Operation Easter and the positive results that this national operation had achieved in detecting and deterring egg thieves. I considered it a great honour to receive this award, particularly when there is nothing particularly difficult about the work that I do. I admit that it gets 100% of my attention, something that my family – especially my long-suffering wife, Jan – gently (or not so gently) remind me of from time to time.

As I write at the beginning of 2007 I still look forward to getting into work in the mornings and it is seldom that I arrive in the office much after 7 o'clock. Similarly, I am seldom away from work before 4 o'clock and I make or deal with phone calls at home including at weekends. When I hear others complaining of the tedium of their jobs I consider myself extremely lucky and I am very reluctant to give up the job that I am doing for the many reasons set out in this book. My office colleague, Callum Beaton, is in exactly the same position. Like me, he retired after reaching the rank of inspector and now works as a firearms enquiry officer. We each have a huge amount of experience and personal contact built up over forty years. In my view it is sensible that a number of retired police officers are re-employed in a role in which their previous training and experience is invaluable. We each do a job that releases a police officer to concentrate on general police work, and we each in our specialist roles provide support and advice to well over 1000 serving officers in Tayside.

So was this award a hint that I should retire: that I had achieved sufficient in the world of wildlife crime? Should I hang my binoculars up, put my slippers on and take things easy? Should I concentrate more on my garden on globally warmed summer days and clean the kitchen windows or search for the starting handle for the vacuum cleaner during wet winter weather? Not on your bloody life. As you will have realised having read this far there are one or two hotspots of wildlife crime in Tayside not yet satisfactorily addressed. So I have some unfinished business that I hope to report on the next time I put pen to paper.

In this connection, I am often asked if wildlife crime is on the increase. While my working day is never quiet I am satisfied that the incidence of wildlife crime is actually falling. In Tayside and in some other police forces we have been alerting the public to wildlife crime issues through talks, leaflets and the media. This new-found knowledge of a sizeable chunk of the public no doubt results in increased reporting of wildlife crime, as happens when any type of crime is highlighted, but I think figures have peaked and the line on the graph will now begin to fall. It is fair to say that in policing crime patterns change, and one welcome change, at least in Tayside, is the tendency for there to be less wildlife crime associated with game management. There are some who are not convinced and theirs and my differing views will be worthy of discussion in the future. I am not stating for a minute that the situation is perfect but there are seldom surprises; the estates on which poisoning and illegal trapping of birds of prey take place are well known to us but we must bide our time. Criminals – and indeed they are criminals – slip up and at some stage their run of luck will end.

I have a note on my desk from an officer needing advice about a hare coursing case. I had hoped this morning to investigate the release of a pair of beavers in Perthshire but I have also just had a disturbing phone call that needs immediate action: within the last half hour a buzzard has been caught in a trap on the estate with the worst poisoning record in Scotland . . .

Index

R

S